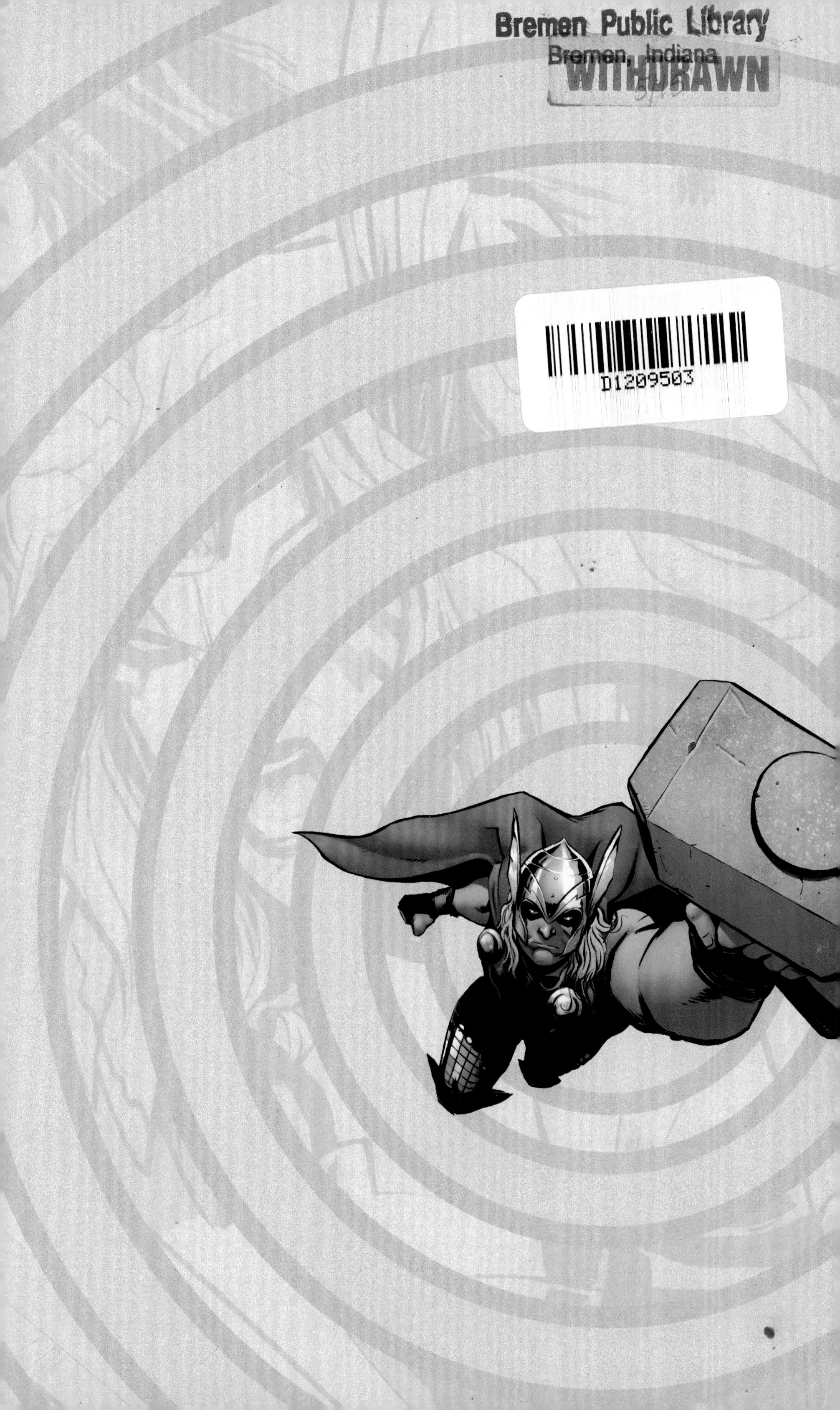

ORIGINAL SIN

Collection Editor: **Jennifer Grünwald**
Assistant Editor: **Sarah Brunstad**
Associate Managing Editor: **Alex Starbuck**
Editor, Special Projects: **Mark D. Beazley**
Senior Editor, Special Projects: **Jeff Youngquist**
SVP Print, Sales & Marketing: **David Gabriel**
Book Design: **Jeff Powell**

Editor in Chief: **Axel Alonso**
Chief Creative Officer: **Joe Quesada**
Publisher: **Dan Buckley**
Executive Producer: **Alan Fine**

ORIGINAL SIN: THOR & LOKI — THE TENTH REALM. Contains material originally published in magazine form as ORIGINAL SIN #5.1-5.5. First printing 2014. ISBN# 978-0-7851-9169-8. Published by MA
WORLDWIDE, INC., a subsidiary of MARVEL ENTERTAINMENT, LLC. OFFICE OF PUBLICATION: 135 West 50th Street, New York, NY 10020. Copyright © 2014 Marvel Characters, Inc. All rights reserved. All characters fea
in this issue and the distinctive names and likenesses thereof, and all related indicia are trademarks of Marvel Characters, Inc. No similarity between any of the names, characters, persons, and/or institutions ir
magazine with those of any living or dead person or institution is intended, and any such similarity which may exist is purely coincidental. **Printed in Canada.** ALAN FINE, EVP - Office of the President, Marvel Worlde
Inc. and EVP & CMO Marvel Characters B.V.; DAN BUCKLEY, Publisher & President - Print, Animation & Digital Divisions; JOE QUESADA, Chief Creative Officer; TOM BREVOORT, SVP of Publishing; DAVID BOGART, S
Operations & Procurement, Publishing; C.B. CEBULSKI, SVP of Creator & Content Development; DAVID GABRIEL, SVP Print, Sales & Marketing; JIM O'KEEFE, VP of Operations & Logistics; DAN CARR, Executive Dir
of Publishing Technology; SUSAN CRESPI, Editorial Operations Manager; ALEX MORALES, Publishing Operations Manager; STAN LEE, Chairman Emeritus. For information regarding advertising in Marvel Comics
Marvel.com, please contact Niza Disla, Director of Marvel Partnerships, at ndisla@marvel.com. For Marvel subscription inquiries, please call 800-217-9158. **Manufactured between 9/19/2014 and 10/27/201**
SOLISCO PRINTERS, SCOTT, QC, CANADA.

10 9 8 7 6 5 4 3 2 1

THOR & LOKI:
THE TENTH REALM

STORY	SCRIPT
JASON AARON & **AL EWING**	**AL EWING**

ISSUES #1-3
ARTISTS: **LEE GARBETT** & **SIMONE BIANCHI**
COLORISTS: **NOLAN WOODARD,**
ADRIANO DALL'ALPI, SIMONE BIANCHI
& **SIMONE PERUZZI**

ISSUE #4
PENCILERS: **SIMONE BIANCHI** & **LEE GARBETT**
INKERS: **SIMONE BIANCHI,**
RICCARDO PIERUCCINI & **LEE GARBETT**
COLORISTS: **ADRIANO DALL'ALPI**
& **NOLAN WOODARD**

ISSUE #5
PENCILERS: **SIMONE BIANCHI, LEE GARBETT, SZYMON KUDRANSKI** & **MARCO CHECCHETTO**
ADDITIONAL INKS: **RICCARDO PIERUCCINI**
COLORISTS: **ADRIANO DALL'ALPI, NOLAN WOODARD** & **PAUL MOUNTS**

COVER ART
DALE KEOWN & **JASON KEITH** (#1), **DALE KEOWN** & **IVE SVORCINA** (#2) AND **SIMONE BIANCHI** (#3-5)

LETTERER	ASSISTANT EDITOR	EDITOR
VC'S JOE SABINO	**JON MOISAN**	**WIL MOSS**

ANGELA CO-CREATED BY TODD MCFARLANE & NEIL GAIMAN

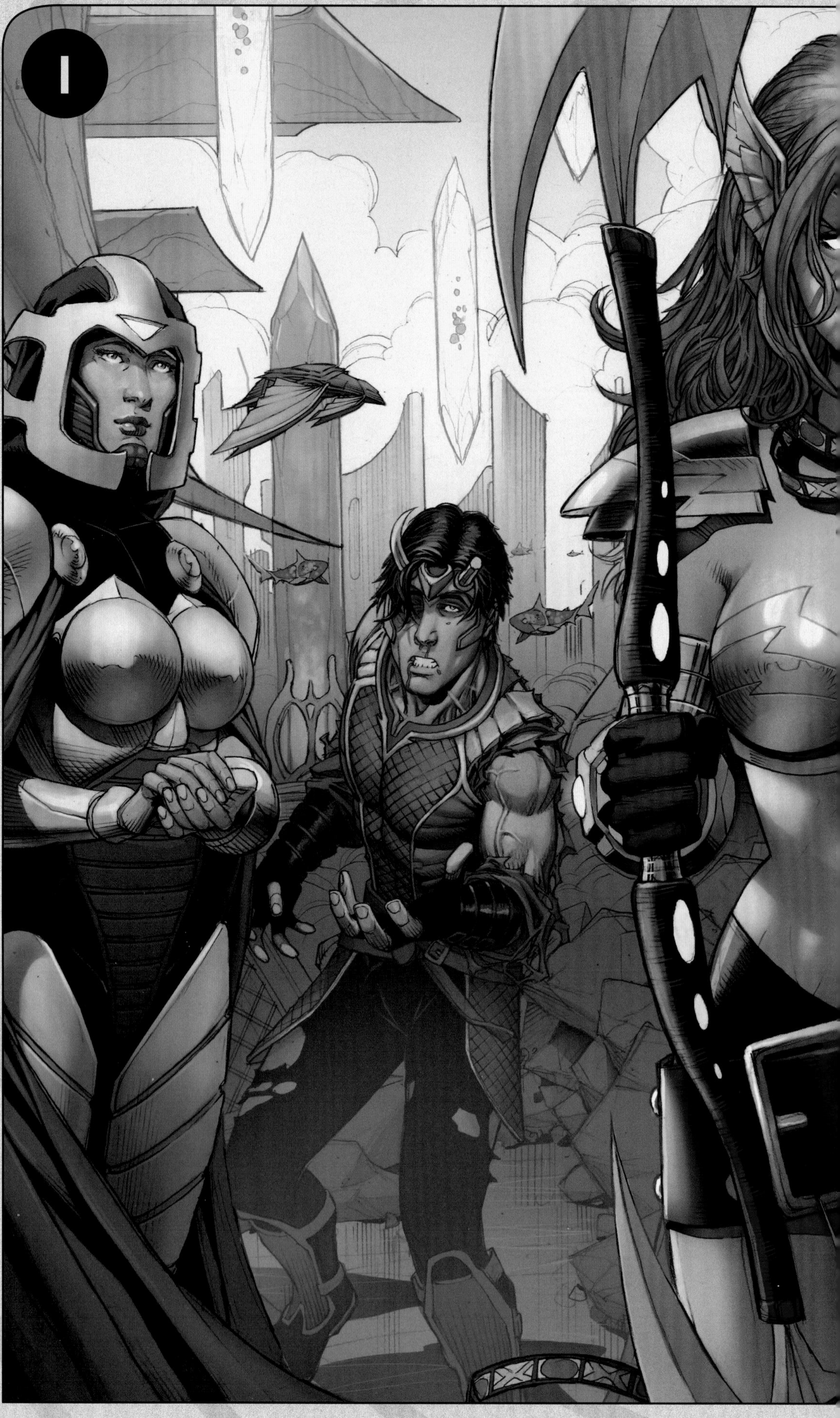
1

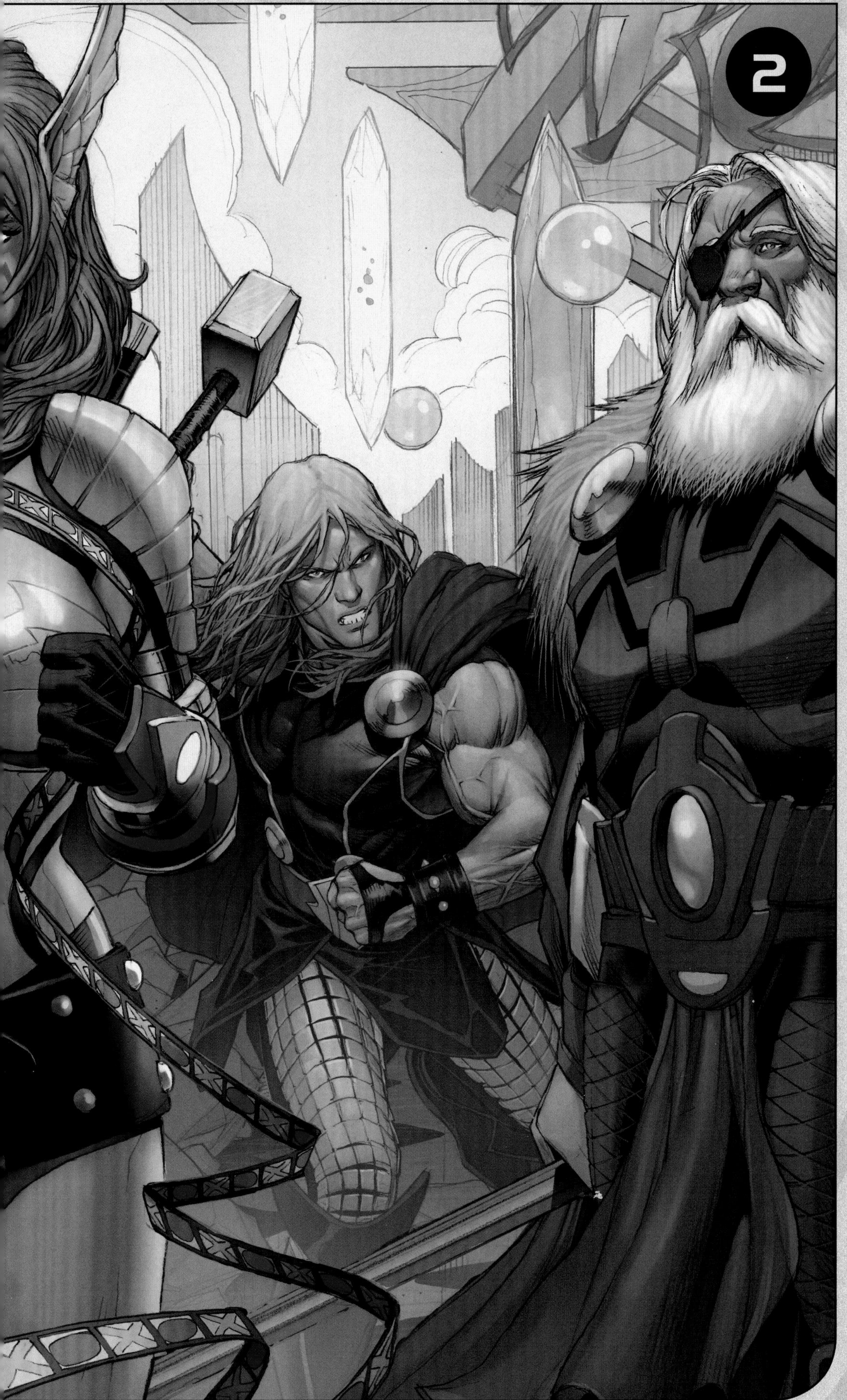
2

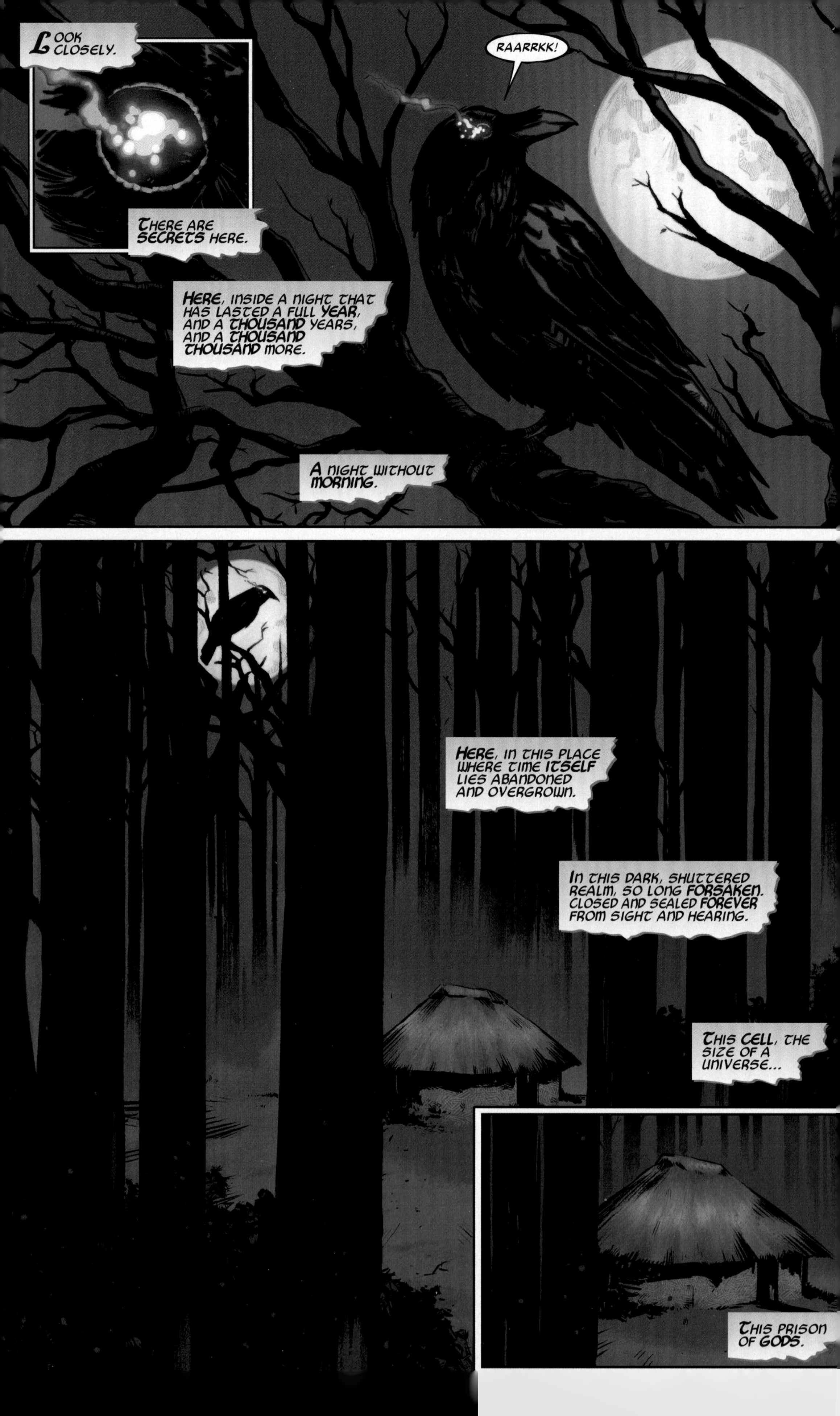
LOOK CLOSELY.
THERE ARE SECRETS HERE.
RAARRKK!
HERE, INSIDE A NIGHT THAT HAS LASTED A FULL YEAR, AND A THOUSAND YEARS, AND A THOUSAND THOUSAND MORE.
A NIGHT WITHOUT MORNING.
HERE, IN THIS PLACE WHERE TIME ITSELF LIES ABANDONED AND OVERGROWN.
IN THIS DARK, SHUTTERED REALM, SO LONG FORSAKEN. CLOSED AND SEALED FOREVER FROM SIGHT AND HEARING.
THIS CELL, THE SIZE OF A UNIVERSE...
THIS PRISON OF GODS.

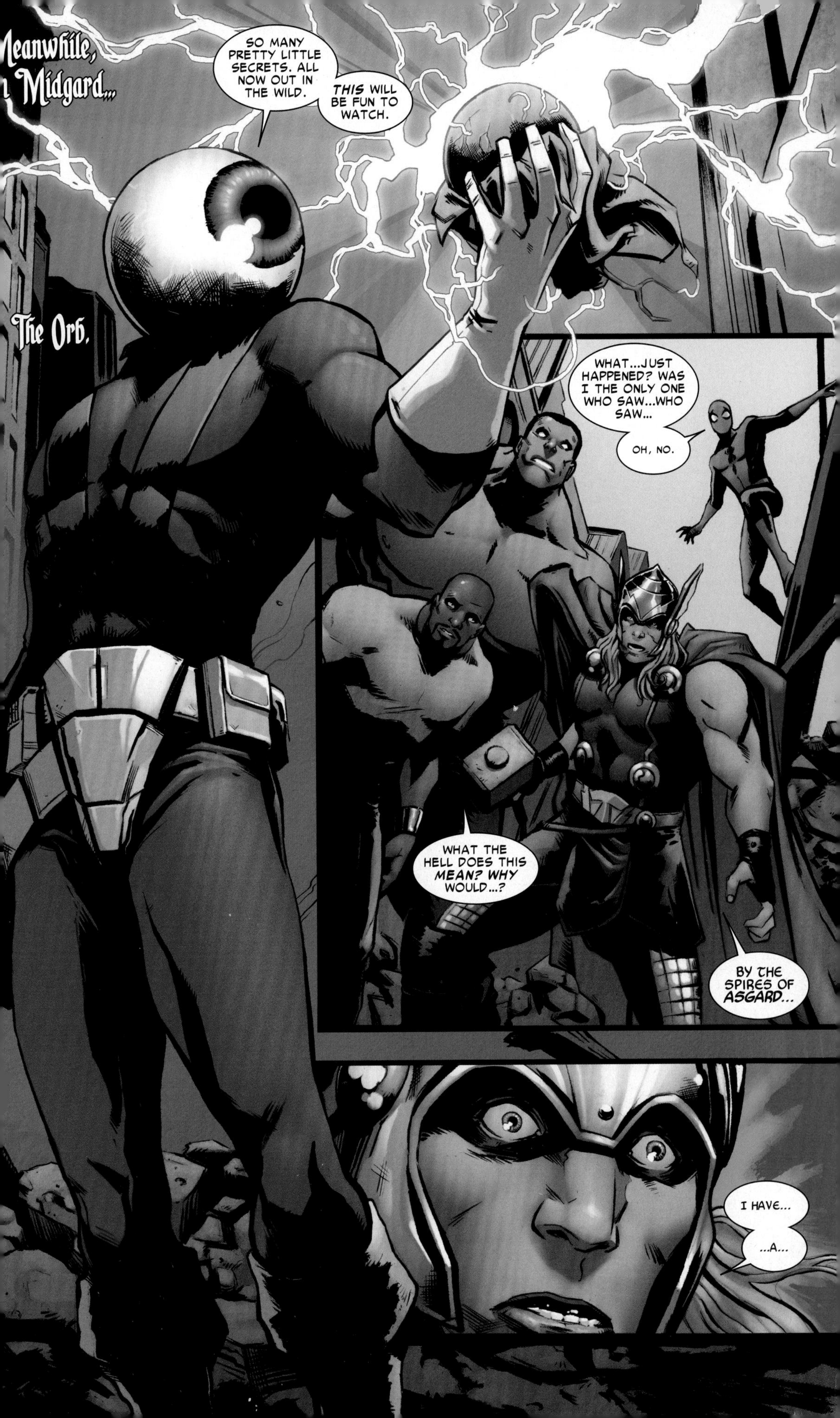
Meanwhile, in Midgard...
The Orb.
SO MANY PRETTY LITTLE SECRETS. ALL NOW OUT IN THE WILD.
THIS WILL BE FUN TO WATCH.
WHAT...JUST HAPPENED? WAS I THE ONLY ONE WHO SAW...WHO SAW...
OH, NO.
WHAT THE HELL DOES THIS MEAN? WHY WOULD...?
BY THE SPIRES OF ASGARD...
I HAVE...
...A...

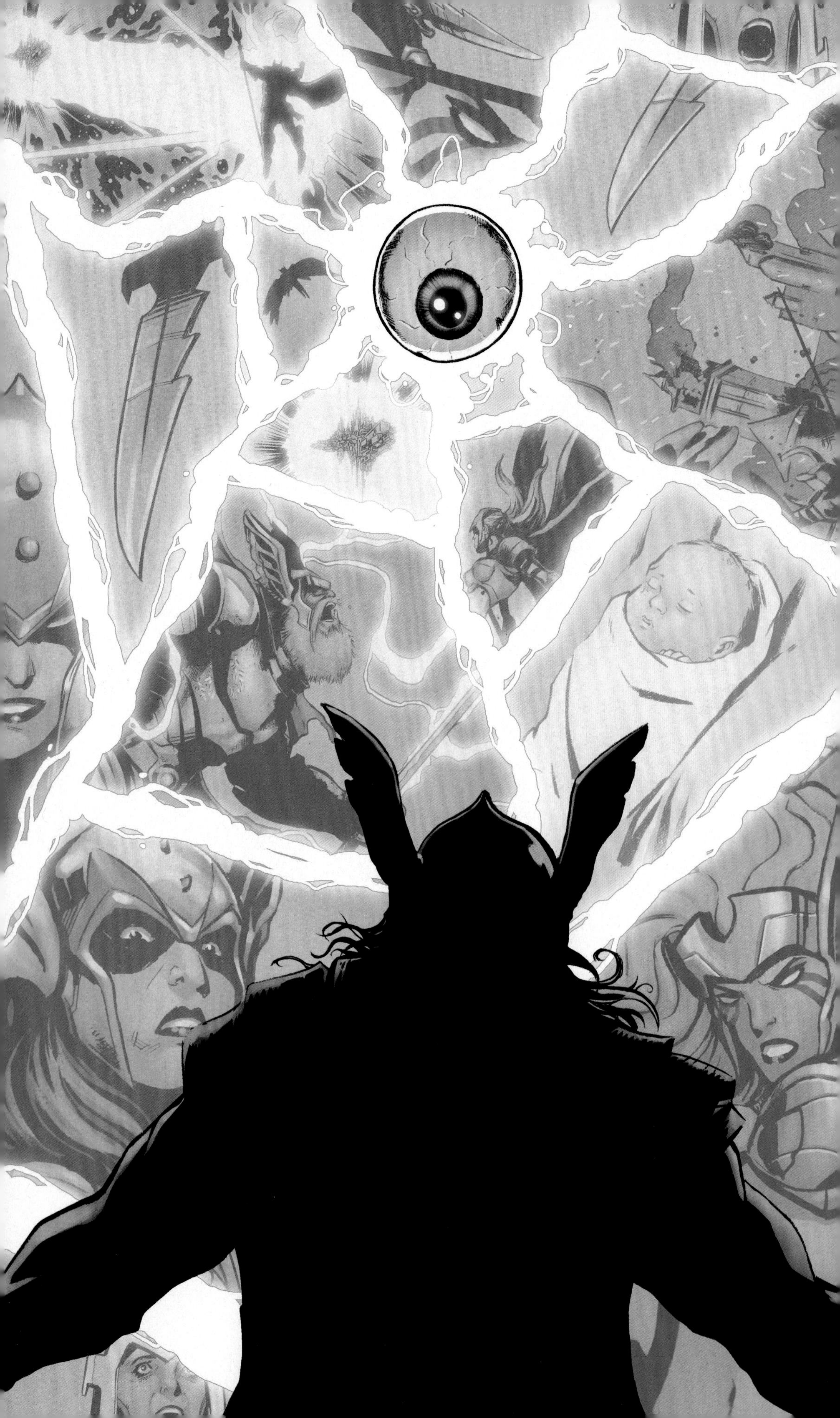

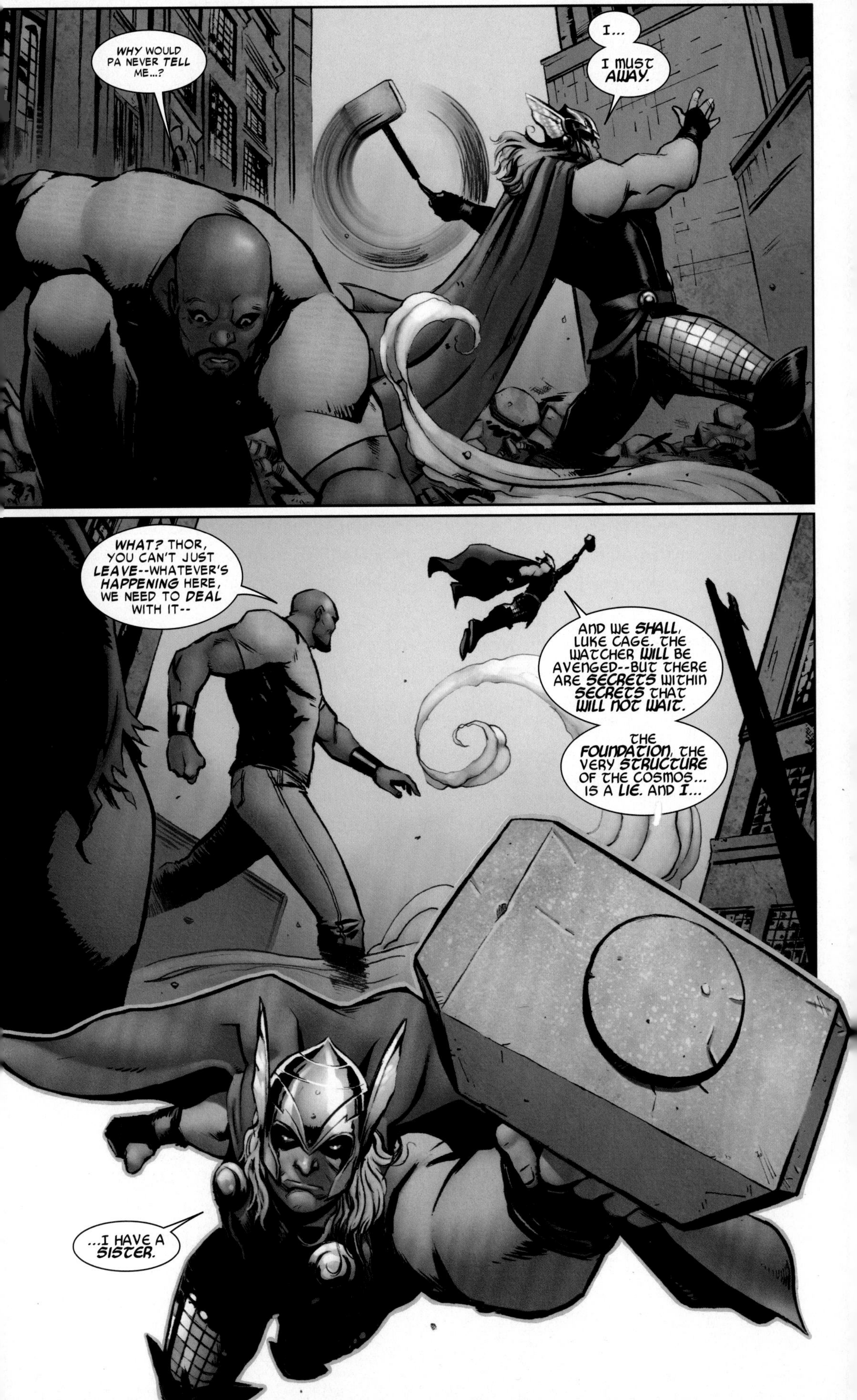
WHY WOULD PA NEVER TELL ME...?
I...
I MUST AWAY.
WHAT? THOR, YOU CAN'T JUST LEAVE--WHATEVER'S HAPPENING HERE, WE NEED TO DEAL WITH IT--
AND WE SHALL, LUKE CAGE. THE WATCHER WILL BE AVENGED--BUT THERE ARE SECRETS WITHIN SECRETS THAT WILL NOT WAIT.
THE FOUNDATION, THE VERY STRUCTURE OF THE COSMOS... IS A LIE. AND I...
...I HAVE A SISTER.

ORIGINAL SIN

THOR & LOKI: THE TENTH REALM

THE WATCHER HAS BEEN MURDERED!

A team of heroes tracked down a suspect in the murder, the Orb, who had one of the Watcher's eyes. During the conflict, the eye detonated, exposing secrets the Watcher had witnessed to everyone in the blast area — including Thor, the God of Thunder.

Thor is from Asgard, one of the Nine Realms (of which Earth — or, as Asgardians refer to it, Midgard — is also one). He is the son of Odin — the former ruler of Asgard, currently M.I.A. — and Freyja — the current ruler of Asgard. Thor also has an adopted brother named Loki.

Loki, as the trickster god, has more often than not found himself cast in the role of villain. But recently he has been trying to break free of that role and make his own destiny. This plan has been thwarted, however, by the arrival of a future version of Loki, evil as ever, whose very existence seemingly dooms the trickster god to a life of villainy. What's worse, Freyja — Loki's own foster-mother — is colluding with "Old Loki" to secure a bright future for Asgard at his younger self's expense.

So things among the royal family of Asgard have been a little rocky of late. And now comes a revelation that may potentially rip them apart entirely…

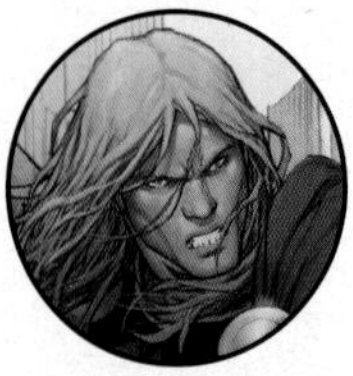

THOR

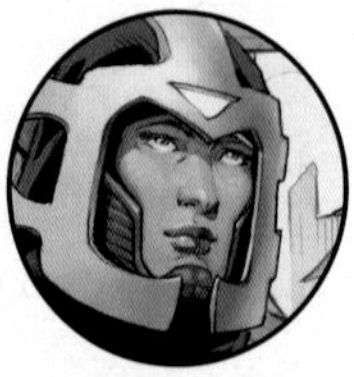

FREYJA

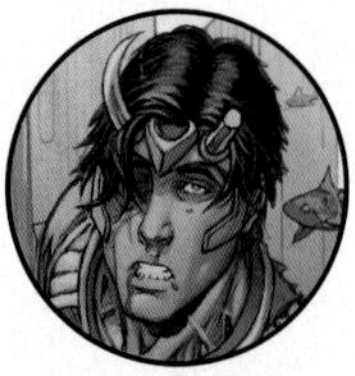

LOKI

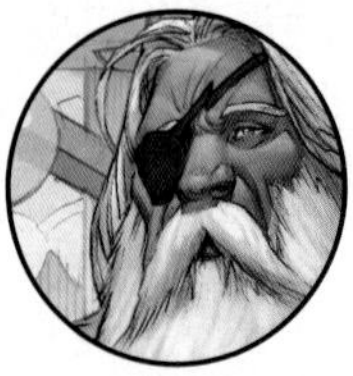

ODIN

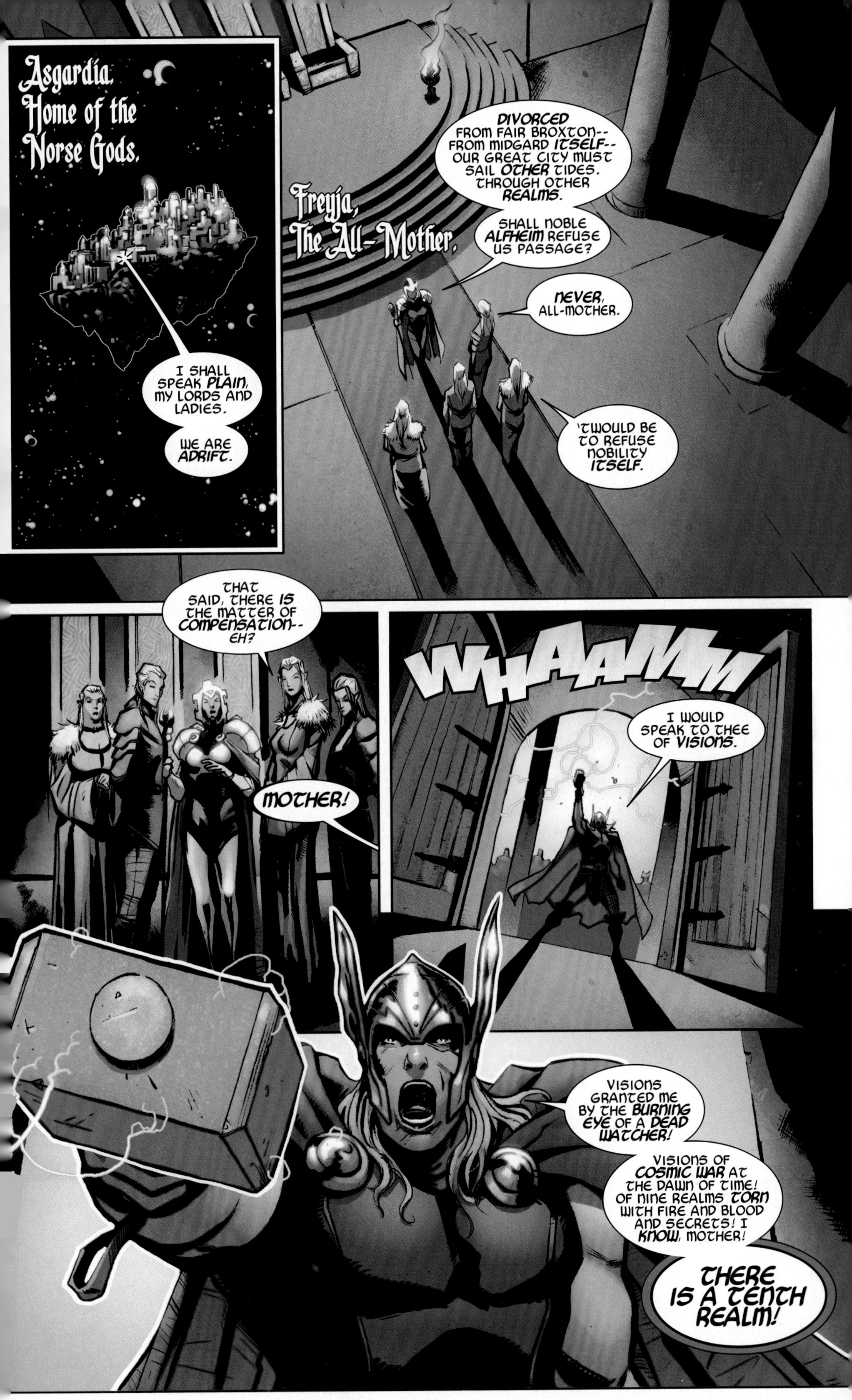

Asgardia. Home of the Norse Gods.
I SHALL SPEAK PLAIN, MY LORDS AND LADIES.
WE ARE ADRIFT.
Freyja, The All-Mother.
DIVORCED FROM FAIR BROXTON-- FROM MIDGARD ITSELF-- OUR GREAT CITY MUST SAIL OTHER TIDES. THROUGH OTHER REALMS.
SHALL NOBLE ALFHEIM REFUSE US PASSAGE?
NEVER, ALL-MOTHER.
'TWOULD BE TO REFUSE NOBILITY ITSELF.
THAT SAID, THERE IS THE MATTER OF COMPENSATION-- EH?
MOTHER!
WHAAMM
I WOULD SPEAK TO THEE OF VISIONS.
VISIONS GRANTED ME BY THE BURNING EYE OF A DEAD WATCHER!
VISIONS OF COSMIC WAR AT THE DAWN OF TIME! OF NINE REALMS TORN WITH FIRE AND BLOOD AND SECRETS! I KNOW, MOTHER!
THERE IS A TENTH REALM!

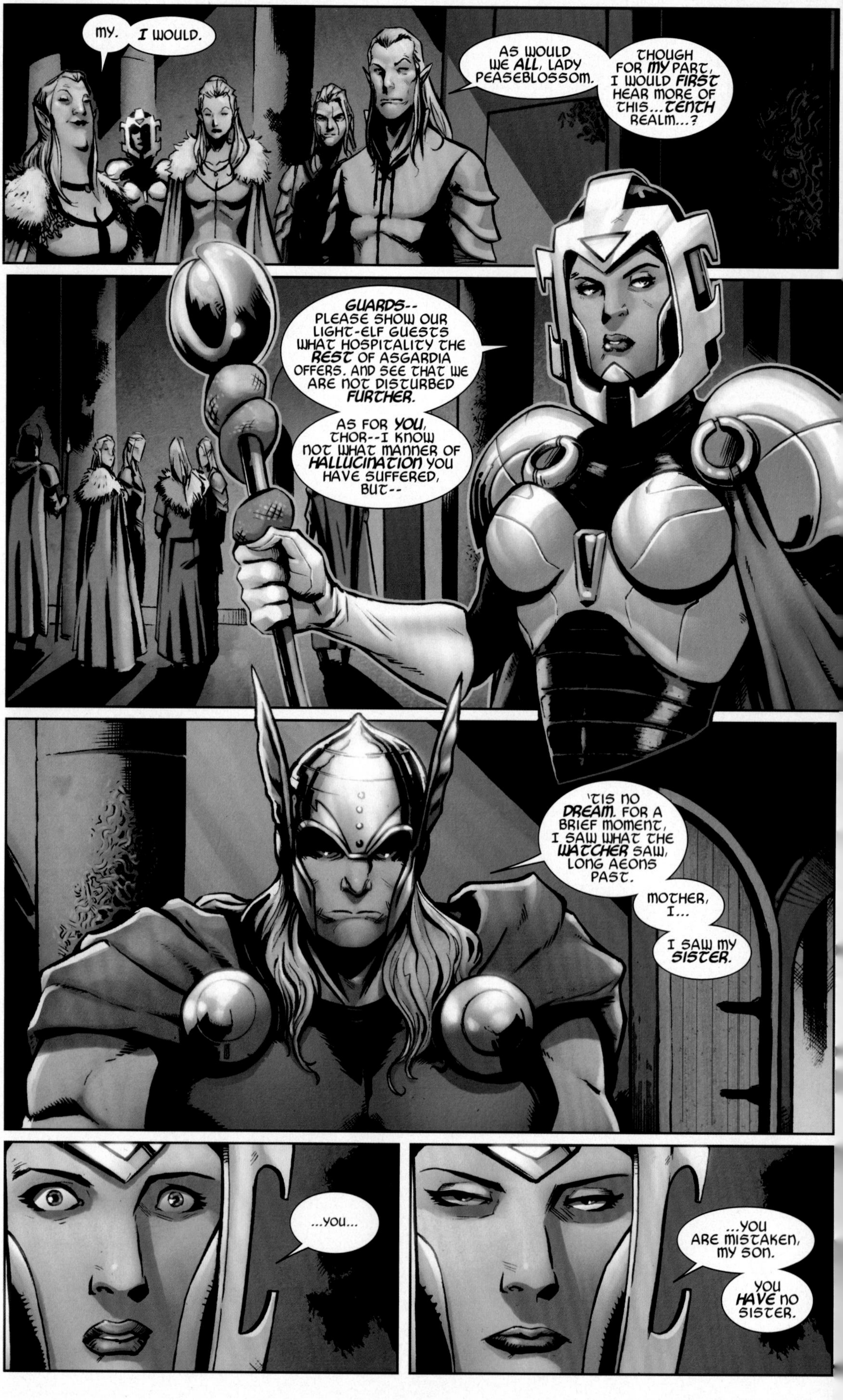
my.
I WOULD.
AS WOULD WE ALL, LADY PEASEBLOSSOM.
THOUGH FOR MY PART, I WOULD FIRST HEAR MORE OF THIS...TENTH REALM...?
GUARDS-- PLEASE SHOW OUR LIGHT-ELF GUESTS WHAT HOSPITALITY THE REST OF ASGARDIA OFFERS. AND SEE THAT WE ARE NOT DISTURBED FURTHER.
AS FOR YOU, THOR--I KNOW NOT WHAT MANNER OF HALLUCINATION YOU HAVE SUFFERED, BUT--
'TIS NO DREAM. FOR A BRIEF MOMENT, I SAW WHAT THE WATCHER SAW, LONG AEONS PAST.
MOTHER, I...
I SAW MY SISTER.
...YOU...
...YOU ARE MISTAKEN, MY SON.
YOU HAVE NO SISTER.

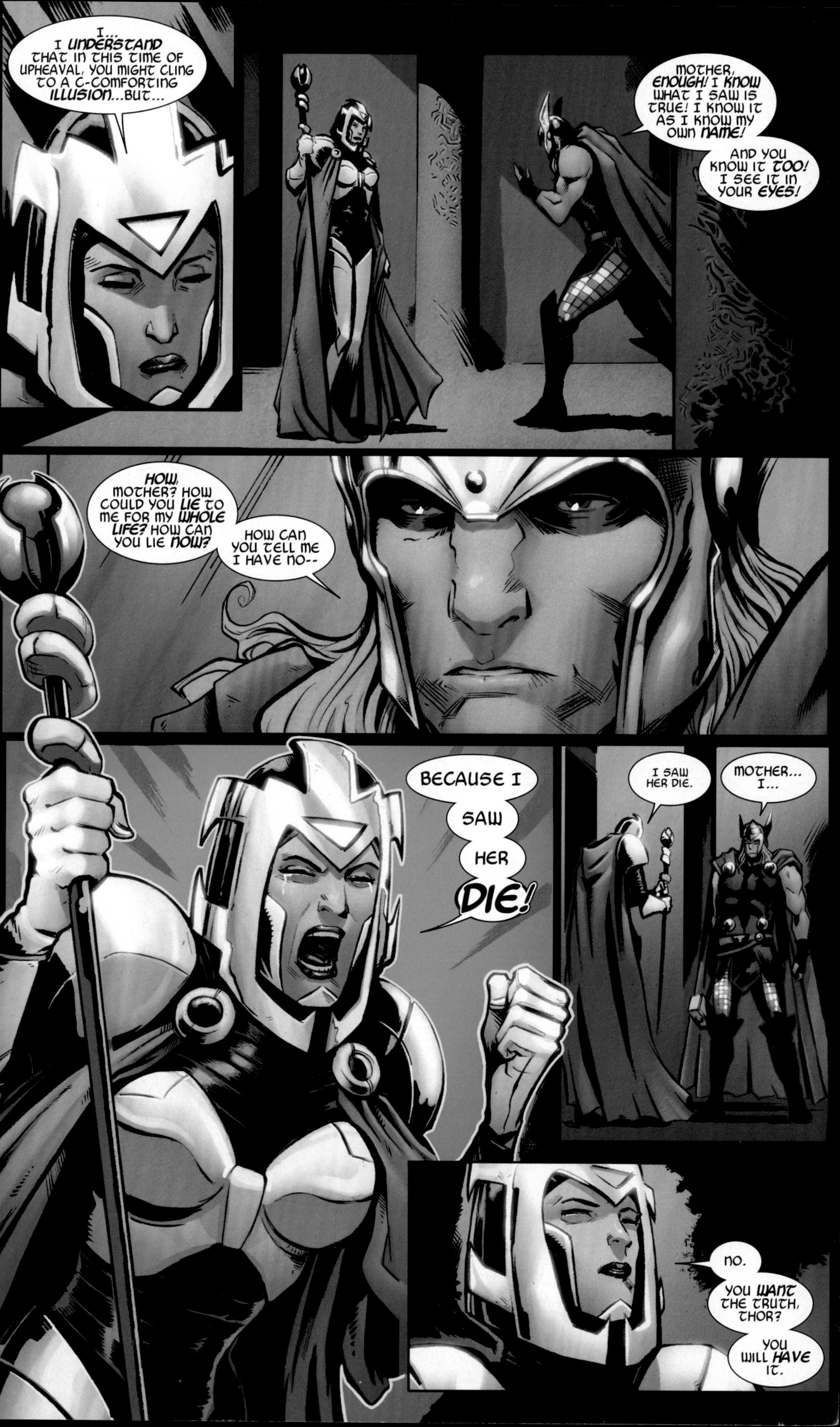
I... I UNDERSTAND THAT IN THIS TIME OF UPHEAVAL, YOU MIGHT CLING TO A C-COMFORTING ILLUSION...BUT...
MOTHER, ENOUGH! I KNOW WHAT I SAW IS TRUE! I KNOW IT AS I KNOW MY OWN NAME!
AND YOU KNOW IT TOO! I SEE IT IN YOUR EYES!
HOW, MOTHER? HOW COULD YOU LIE TO ME FOR MY WHOLE LIFE? HOW CAN YOU LIE NOW?
HOW CAN YOU TELL ME I HAVE NO--
BECAUSE I SAW HER DIE!
I SAW HER DIE.
MOTHER... I...
NO.
YOU WANT THE TRUTH, THOR?
YOU WILL HAVE IT.

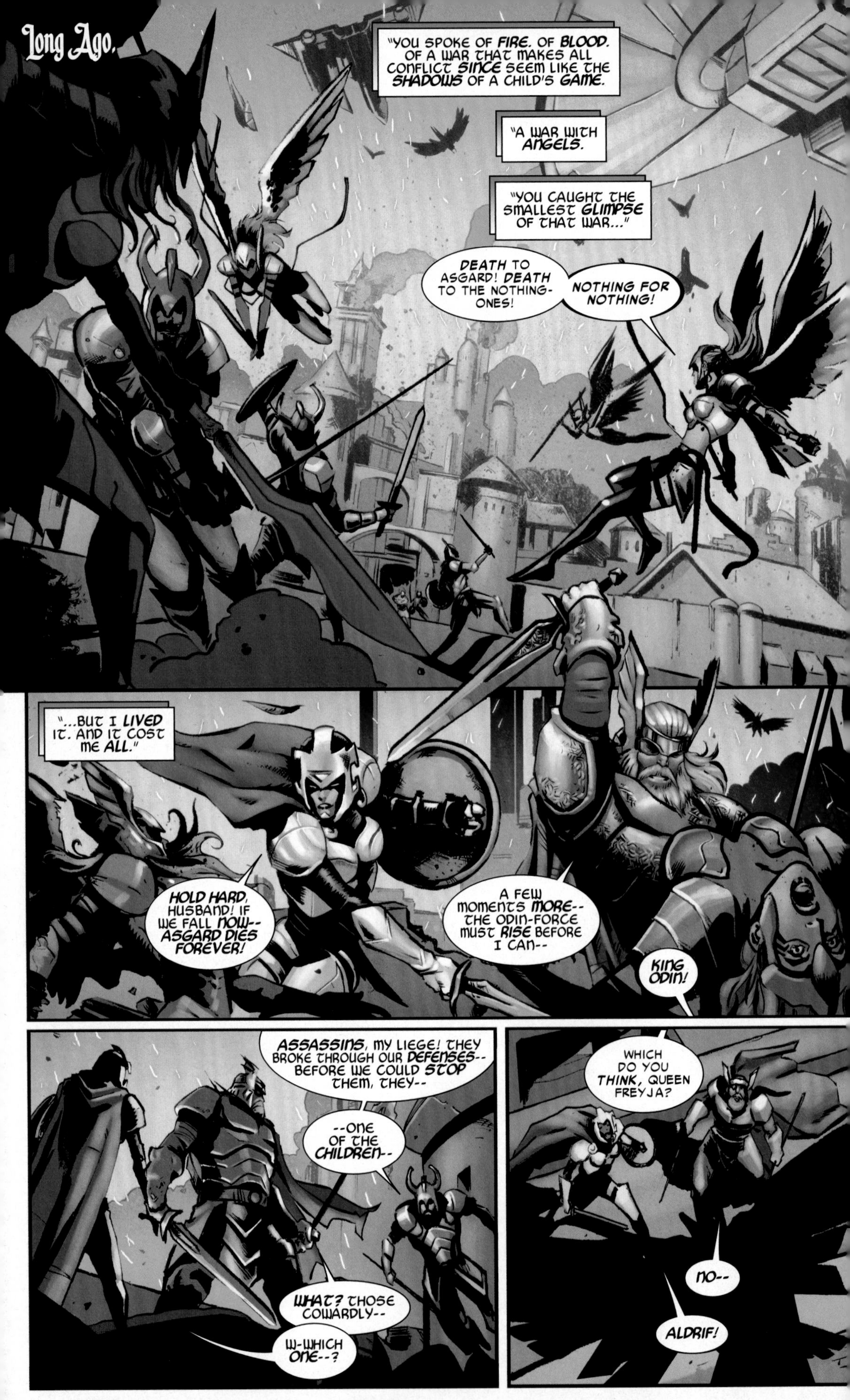
Long Ago.
"YOU SPOKE OF FIRE. OF BLOOD. OF A WAR THAT MAKES ALL CONFLICT SINCE SEEM LIKE THE SHADOWS OF A CHILD'S GAME.
"A WAR WITH ANGELS.
"YOU CAUGHT THE SMALLEST GLIMPSE OF THAT WAR..."
DEATH TO ASGARD! DEATH TO THE NOTHING-ONES!
NOTHING FOR NOTHING!
"...BUT I LIVED IT. AND IT COST ME ALL."
HOLD HARD, HUSBAND! IF WE FALL NOW-- ASGARD DIES FOREVER!
A FEW MOMENTS MORE-- THE ODIN-FORCE MUST RISE BEFORE I CAN--
KING ODIN!
ASSASSINS, MY LIEGE! THEY BROKE THROUGH OUR DEFENSES-- BEFORE WE COULD STOP THEM, THEY--
--ONE OF THE CHILDREN--
WHAT? THOSE COWARDLY--
W-WHICH ONE--?
WHICH DO YOU THINK, QUEEN FREYJA?
NO--
ALDRIF!

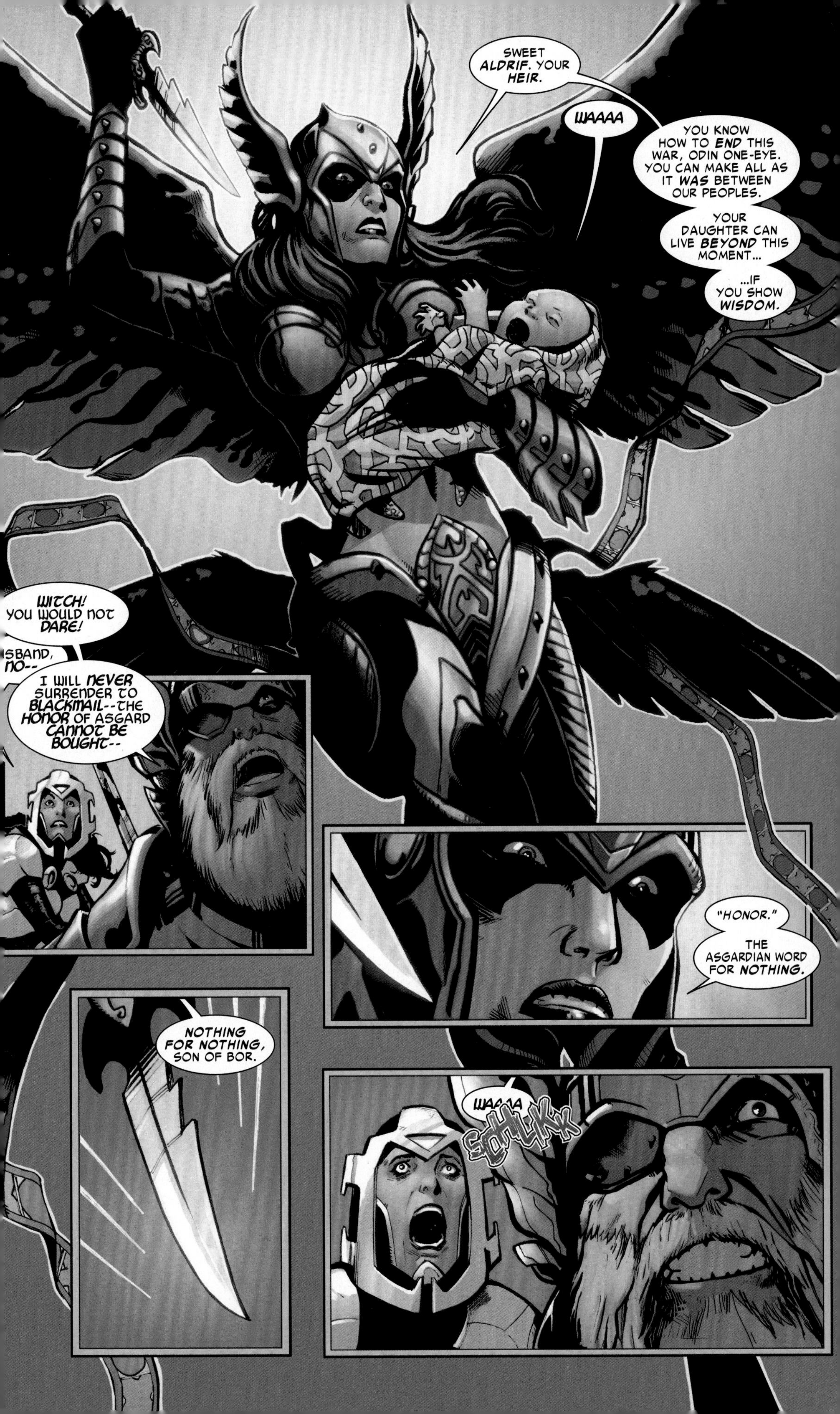
SWEET ALDRIF. YOUR HEIR.
WAAAA
YOU KNOW HOW TO END THIS WAR, ODIN ONE-EYE. YOU CAN MAKE ALL AS IT WAS BETWEEN OUR PEOPLES.
YOUR DAUGHTER CAN LIVE BEYOND THIS MOMENT...
...IF YOU SHOW WISDOM.
WITCH! YOU WOULD NOT DARE!
SBAND, NO--
I WILL NEVER SURRENDER TO BLACKMAIL--THE HONOR OF ASGARD CANNOT BE BOUGHT--
"HONOR."
THE ASGARDIAN WORD FOR NOTHING.
NOTHING FOR NOTHING, SON OF BOR.
WAAAA
SCHLUKK

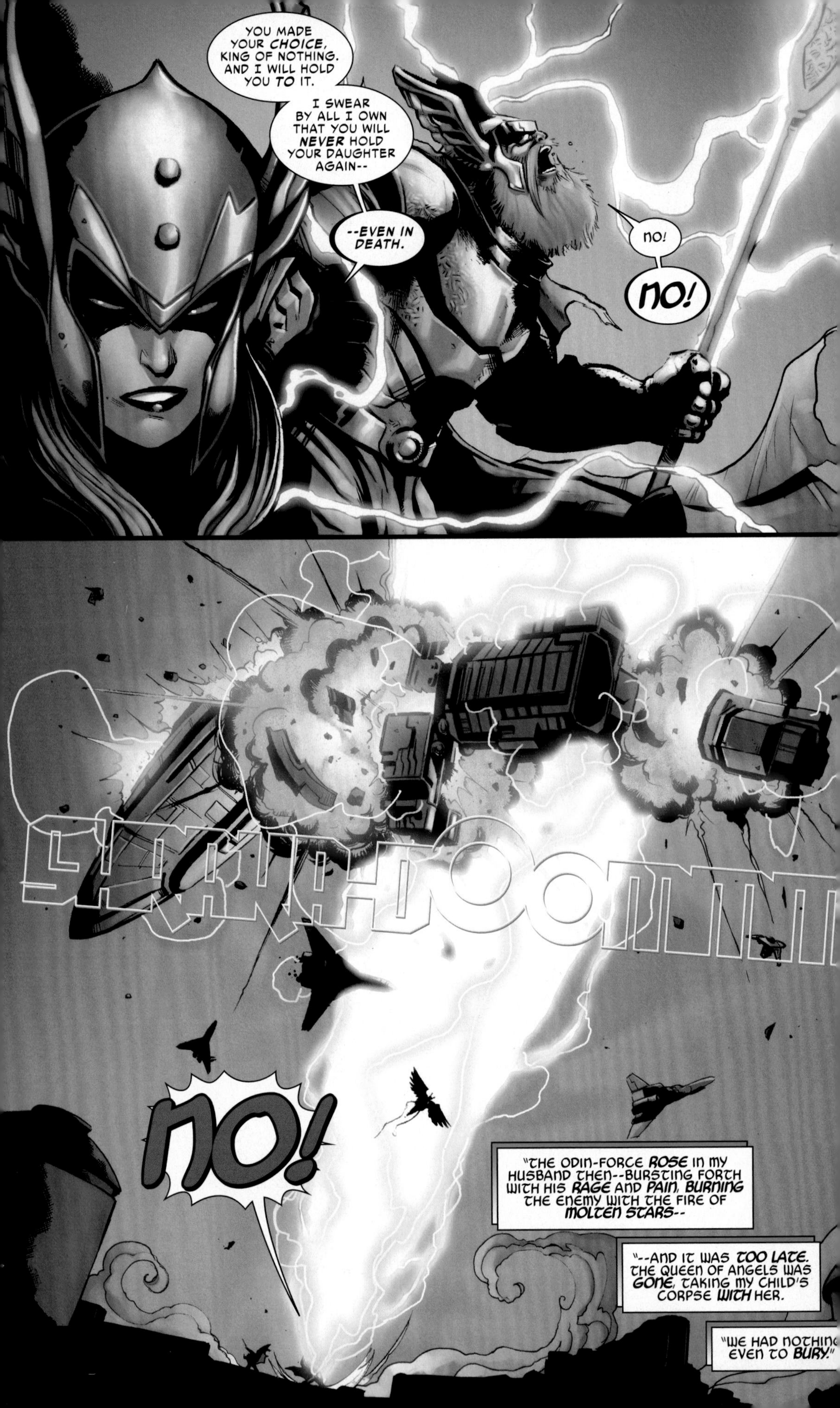
YOU MADE YOUR CHOICE, KING OF NOTHING. AND I WILL HOLD YOU TO IT.
I SWEAR BY ALL I OWN THAT YOU WILL NEVER HOLD YOUR DAUGHTER AGAIN--
--EVEN IN DEATH.
NO!
NO!
NO!
"THE ODIN-FORCE ROSE IN MY HUSBAND THEN--BURSTING FORTH WITH HIS RAGE AND PAIN, BURNING THE ENEMY WITH THE FIRE OF MOLTEN STARS--
"--AND IT WAS TOO LATE. THE QUEEN OF ANGELS WAS GONE, TAKING MY CHILD'S CORPSE WITH HER.
"WE HAD NOTHING EVEN TO BURY."

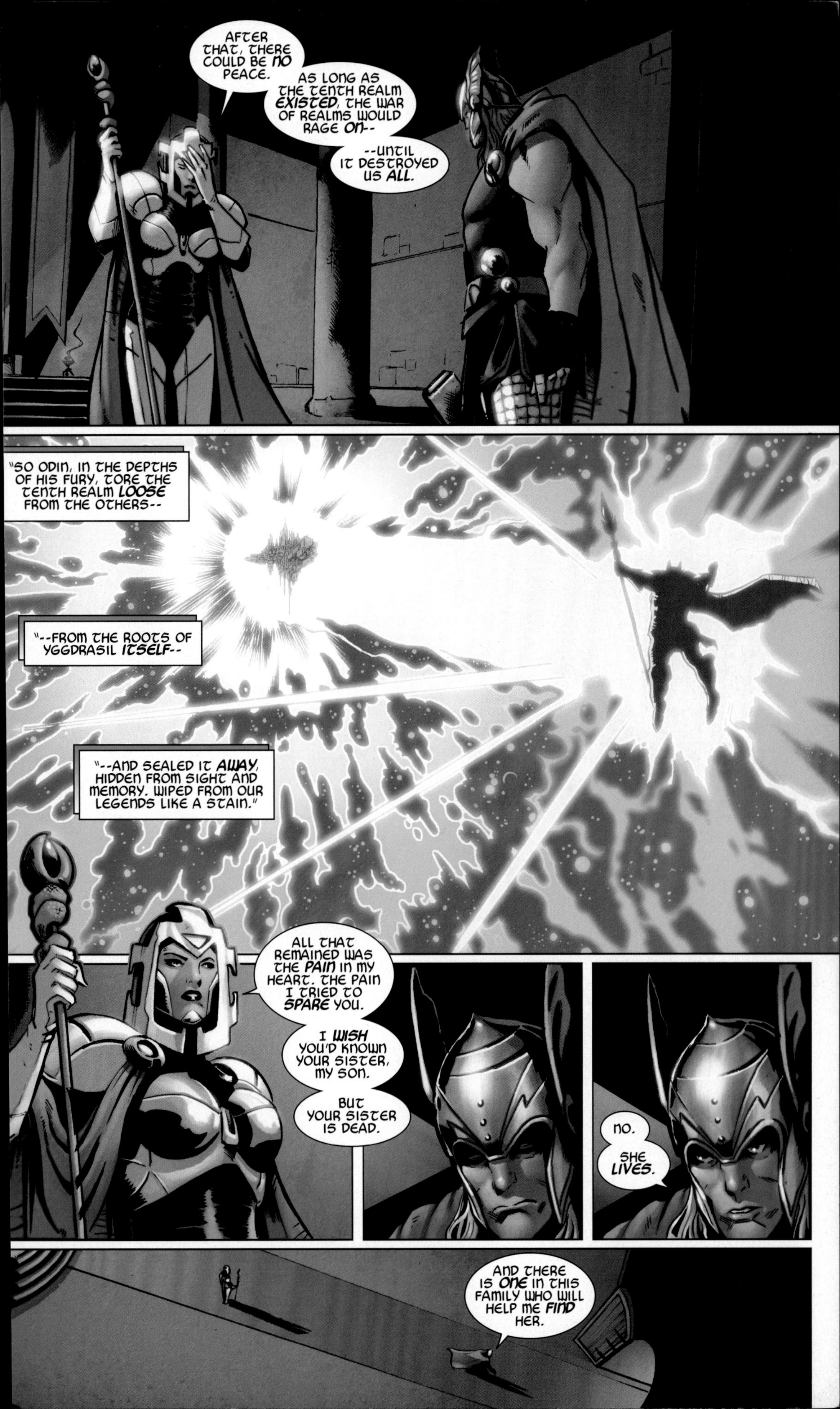
AFTER THAT, THERE COULD BE NO PEACE.
AS LONG AS THE TENTH REALM EXISTED, THE WAR OF REALMS WOULD RAGE ON--
--UNTIL IT DESTROYED US ALL.
"SO ODIN, IN THE DEPTHS OF HIS FURY, TORE THE TENTH REALM LOOSE FROM THE OTHERS--
"--FROM THE ROOTS OF YGGDRASIL ITSELF--
"--AND SEALED IT AWAY, HIDDEN FROM SIGHT AND MEMORY. WIPED FROM OUR LEGENDS LIKE A STAIN."
ALL THAT REMAINED WAS THE PAIN IN MY HEART. THE PAIN I TRIED TO SPARE YOU.
I WISH YOU'D KNOWN YOUR SISTER, MY SON.
BUT YOUR SISTER IS DEAD.
NO.
SHE LIVES.
AND THERE IS ONE IN THIS FAMILY WHO WILL HELP ME FIND HER.

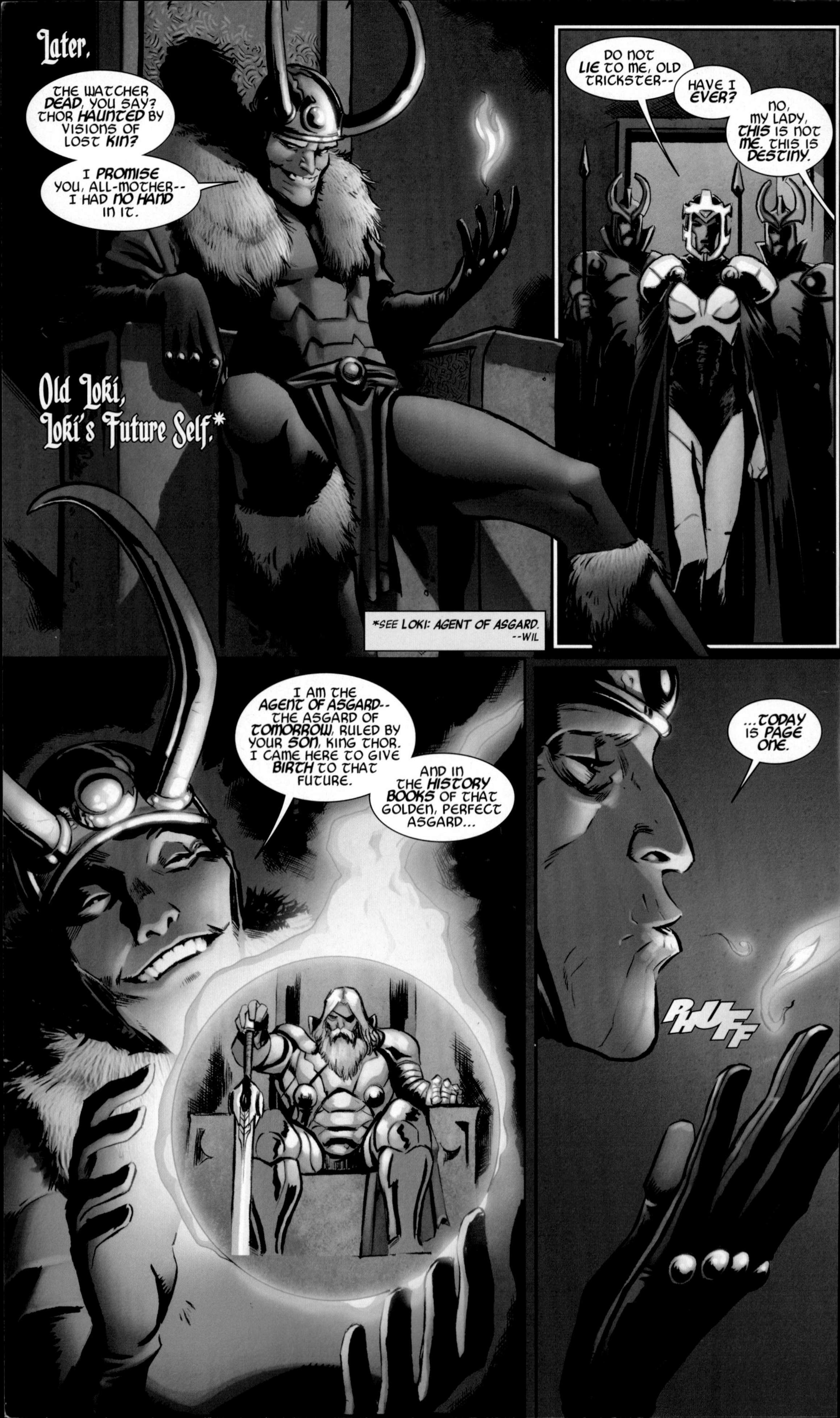
Later.
THE WATCHER DEAD, YOU SAY? THOR HAUNTED BY VISIONS OF LOST KIN?
I PROMISE YOU, ALL-MOTHER-- I HAD NO HAND IN IT.
DO NOT LIE TO ME, OLD TRICKSTER--
HAVE I EVER?
NO, MY LADY, THIS IS NOT ME. THIS IS DESTINY.
Old Loki, Loki's Future Self.*
*SEE LOKI: AGENT OF ASGARD. --WIL
I AM THE AGENT OF ASGARD-- THE ASGARD OF TOMORROW, RULED BY YOUR SON, KING THOR. I CAME HERE TO GIVE BIRTH TO THAT FUTURE.
AND IN THE HISTORY BOOKS OF THAT GOLDEN, PERFECT ASGARD...
...TODAY IS PAGE ONE.
RHUFF

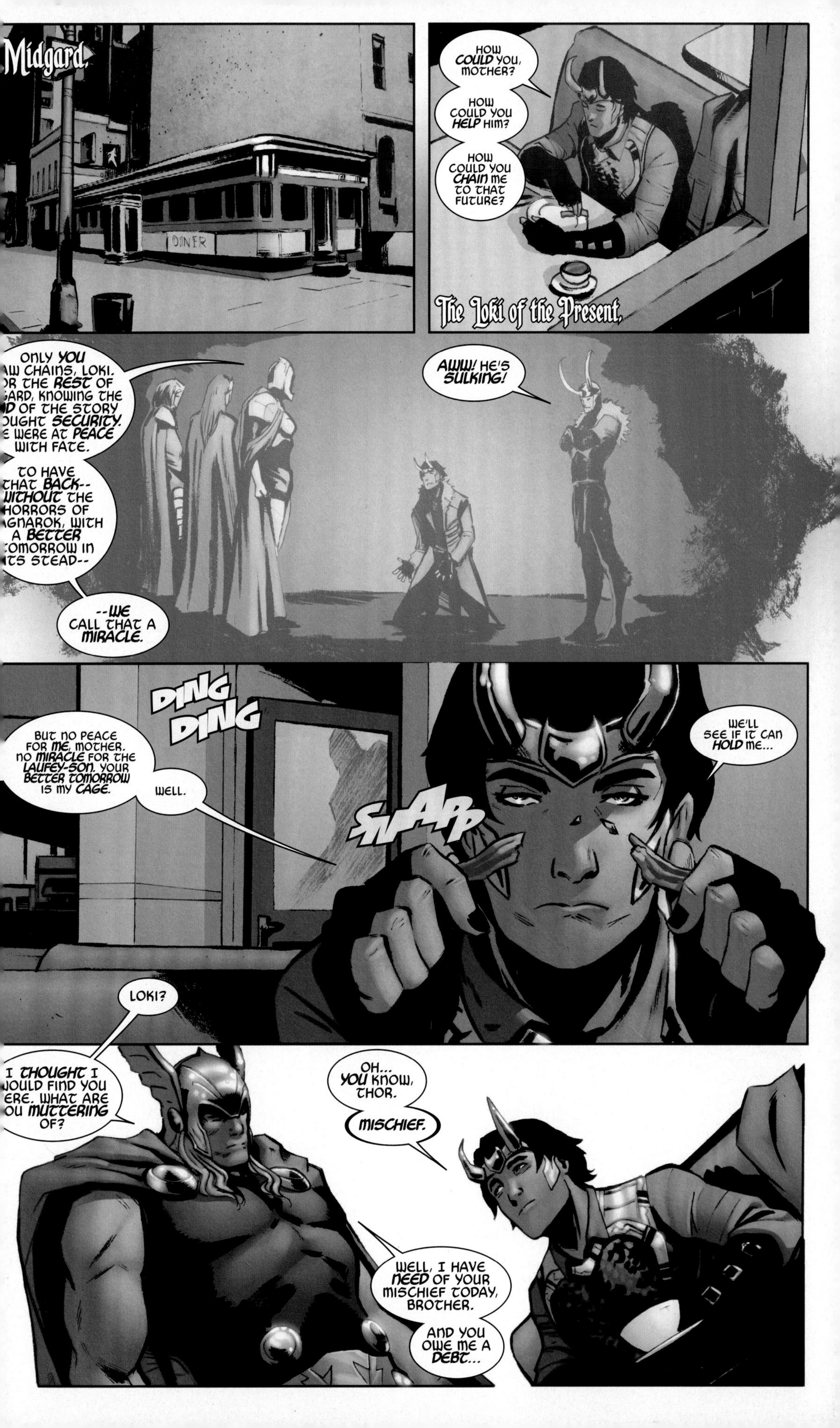
Midgard.
HOW COULD YOU, MOTHER?
HOW COULD YOU HELP HIM?
HOW COULD YOU CHAIN ME TO THAT FUTURE?
The Loki of the Present.
ONLY YOU SAW CHAINS, LOKI. FOR THE REST OF ASGARD, KNOWING THE END OF THE STORY BROUGHT SECURITY. WE WERE AT PEACE WITH FATE.
TO HAVE THAT BACK-- WITHOUT THE HORRORS OF RAGNAROK, WITH A BETTER TOMORROW IN ITS STEAD--
--WE CALL THAT A MIRACLE.
AWW! HE'S SULKING!
DING DING
BUT NO PEACE FOR ME, MOTHER. NO MIRACLE FOR THE LAUFEY-SON. YOUR BETTER TOMORROW IS MY CAGE.
WELL.
WE'LL SEE IF IT CAN HOLD ME...
SNAP
LOKI?
I THOUGHT I WOULD FIND YOU HERE. WHAT ARE YOU MUTTERING OF?
OH... YOU KNOW, THOR.
MISCHIEF.
WELL, I HAVE NEED OF YOUR MISCHIEF TODAY, BROTHER.
AND YOU OWE ME A DEBT...

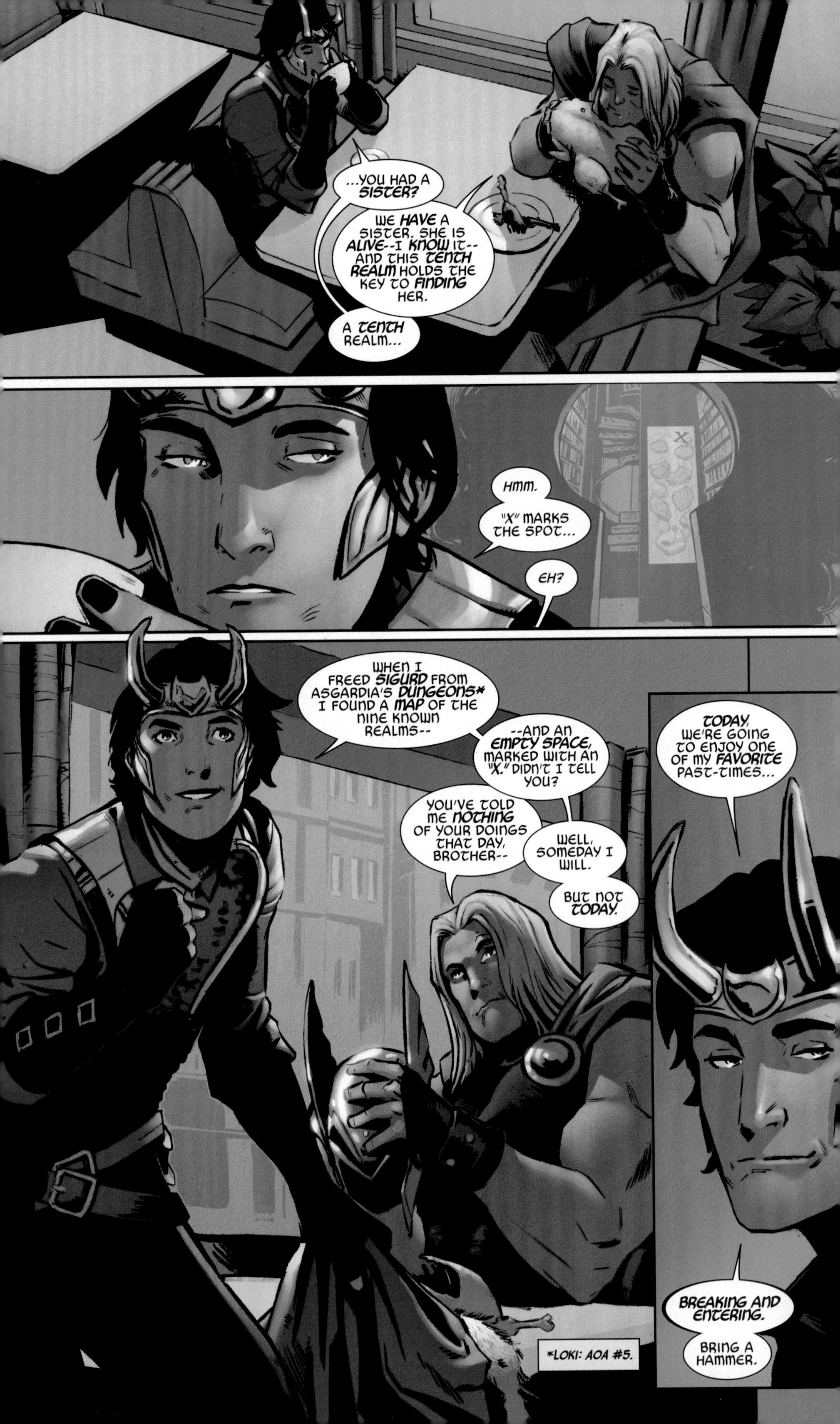
...YOU HAD A SISTER?
WE HAVE A SISTER. SHE IS ALIVE--I KNOW IT--AND THIS TENTH REALM HOLDS THE KEY TO FINDING HER.
A TENTH REALM...
HMM.
"X" MARKS THE SPOT...
EH?
WHEN I FREED SIGURD FROM ASGARDIA'S DUNGEONS* I FOUND A MAP OF THE NINE KNOWN REALMS--
--AND AN EMPTY SPACE, MARKED WITH AN "X." DIDN'T I TELL YOU?
YOU'VE TOLD ME NOTHING OF YOUR DOINGS THAT DAY, BROTHER--
WELL, SOMEDAY I WILL.
BUT NOT TODAY.
TODAY, WE'RE GOING TO ENJOY ONE OF MY FAVORITE PAST-TIMES...
BREAKING AND ENTERING.
BRING A HAMMER.
*LOKI: AOA #5.

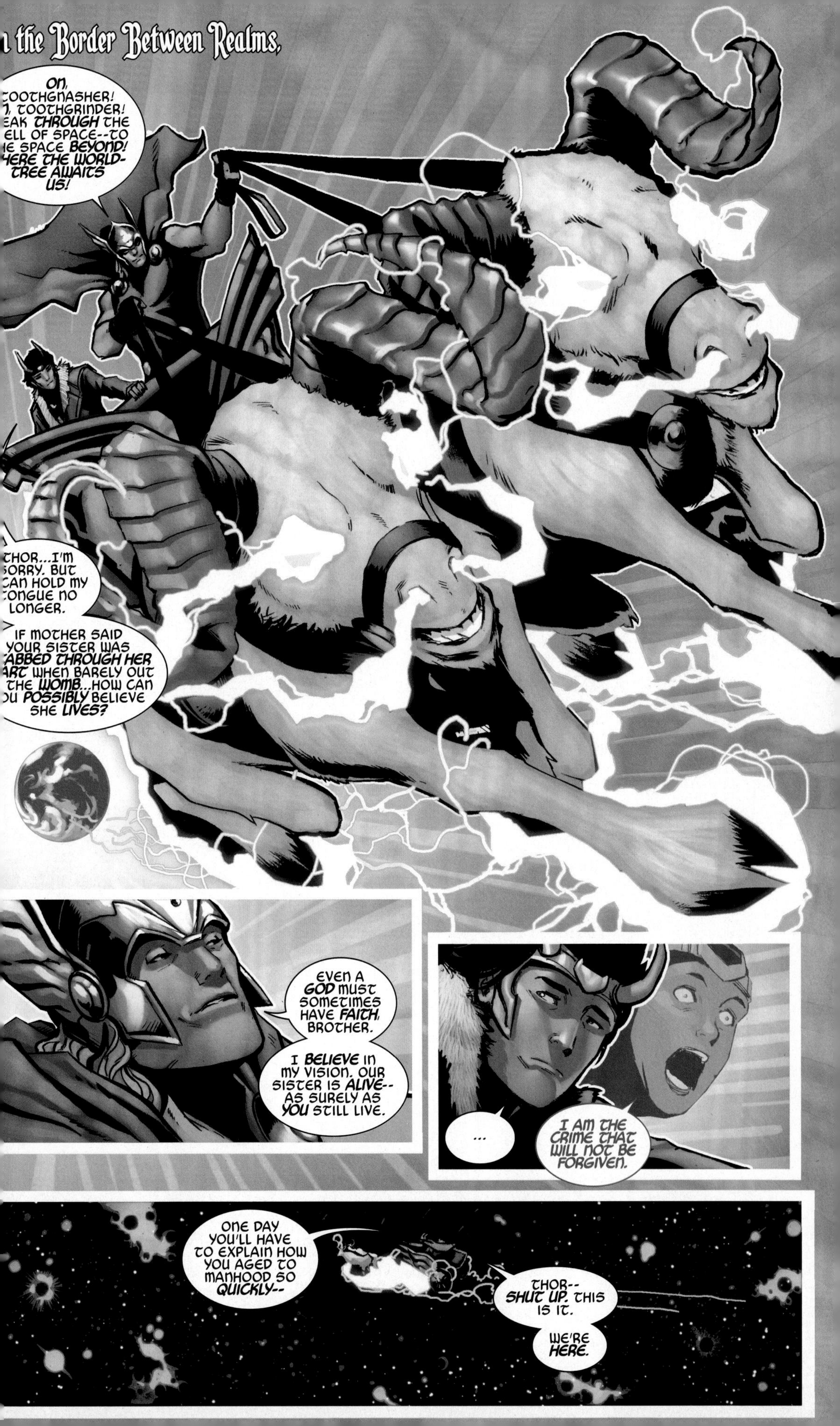
n the Border Between Realms,
ON, TOOTHGNASHER! N, TOOTHGRINDER! EAK THROUGH THE ELL OF SPACE--TO IE SPACE BEYOND! HERE THE WORLD-TREE AWAITS US!
THOR...I'M SORRY. BUT CAN HOLD MY TONGUE NO LONGER.
IF MOTHER SAID YOUR SISTER WAS TABBED THROUGH HER ART WHEN BARELY OUT THE WOMB...HOW CAN OU POSSIBLY BELIEVE SHE LIVES?
EVEN A GOD MUST SOMETIMES HAVE FAITH, BROTHER.
I BELIEVE IN MY VISION. OUR SISTER IS ALIVE--AS SURELY AS YOU STILL LIVE.
...
I AM THE CRIME THAT WILL NOT BE FORGIVEN.
ONE DAY YOU'LL HAVE TO EXPLAIN HOW YOU AGED TO MANHOOD SO QUICKLY--
THOR--SHUT UP. THIS IS IT.
WE'RE HERE.

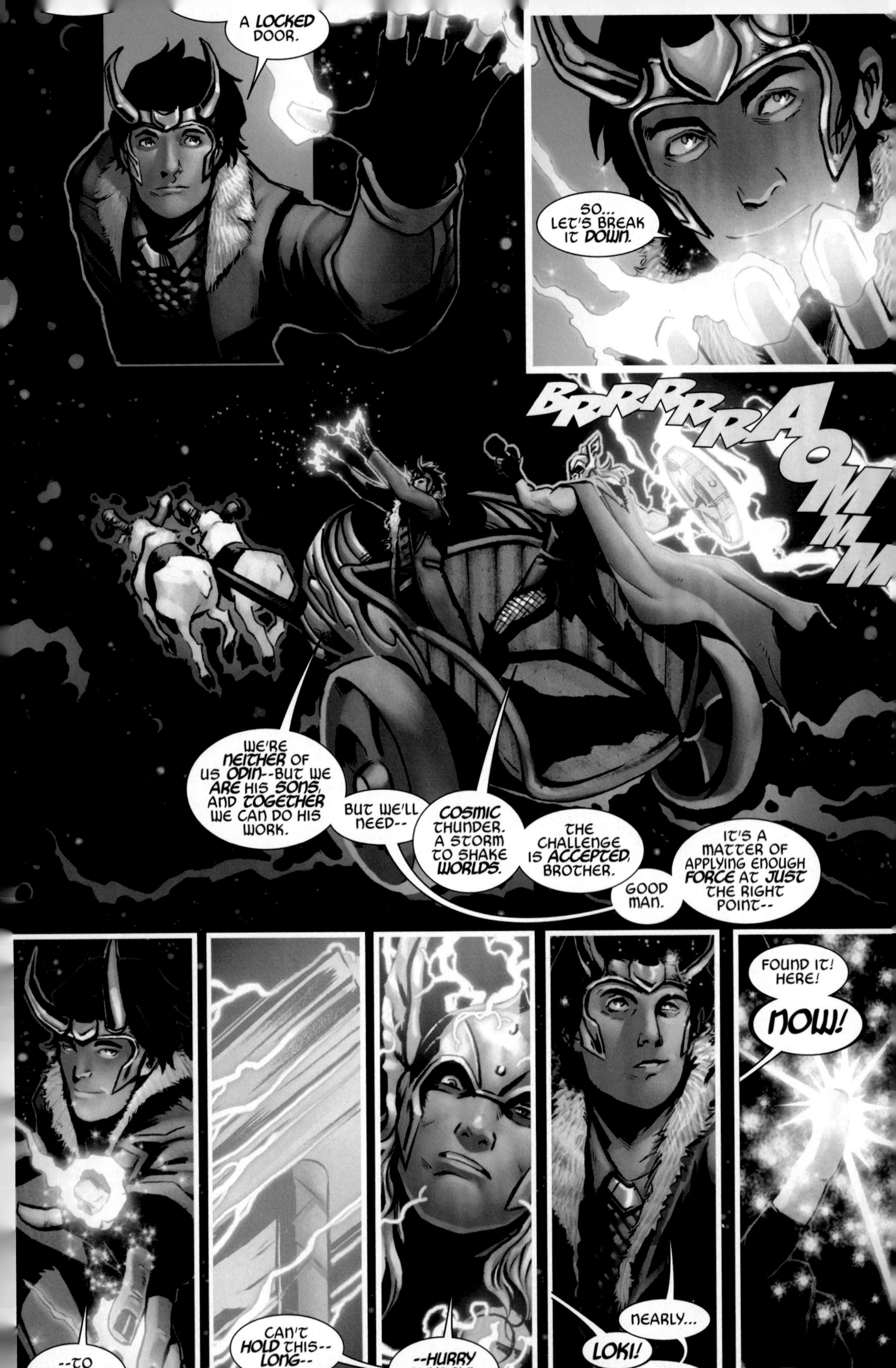
A LOCKED DOOR.
SO... LET'S BREAK IT DOWN.
BRRRRRRAOOMMMM
WE'RE NEITHER OF US ODIN--BUT WE ARE HIS SONS, AND TOGETHER WE CAN DO HIS WORK.
BUT WE'LL NEED--
COSMIC THUNDER. A STORM TO SHAKE WORLDS.
THE CHALLENGE IS ACCEPTED, BROTHER.
GOOD MAN.
IT'S A MATTER OF APPLYING ENOUGH FORCE AT JUST THE RIGHT POINT--
--TO SHATTER THE LOCK.
CAN'T HOLD THIS--LONG--
--HURRY THYSELF, BROTHER--
NEARLY...
LOKI!
NEEEARLYY...
FOUND IT! HERE!
NOW!

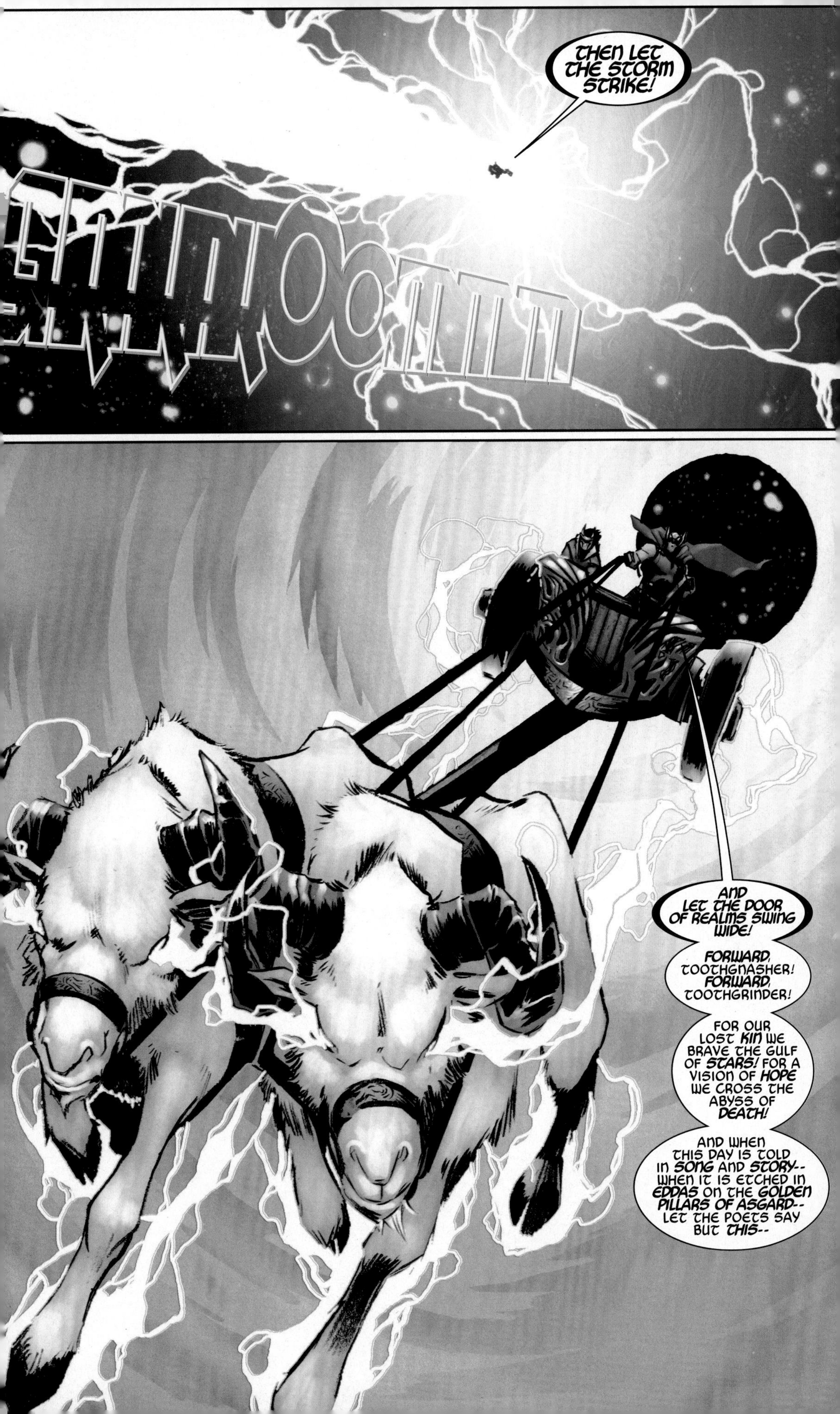
THEN LET THE STORM STRIKE!
AND LET THE DOOR OF REALMS SWING WIDE!
FORWARD, TOOTHGNASHER! FORWARD, TOOTHGRINDER!
FOR OUR LOST KIN WE BRAVE THE GULF OF STARS! FOR A VISION OF HOPE WE CROSS THE ABYSS OF DEATH!
AND WHEN THIS DAY IS TOLD IN SONG AND STORY-- WHEN IT IS ETCHED IN EDDAS ON THE GOLDEN PILLARS OF ASGARD-- LET THE POETS SAY BUT THIS--

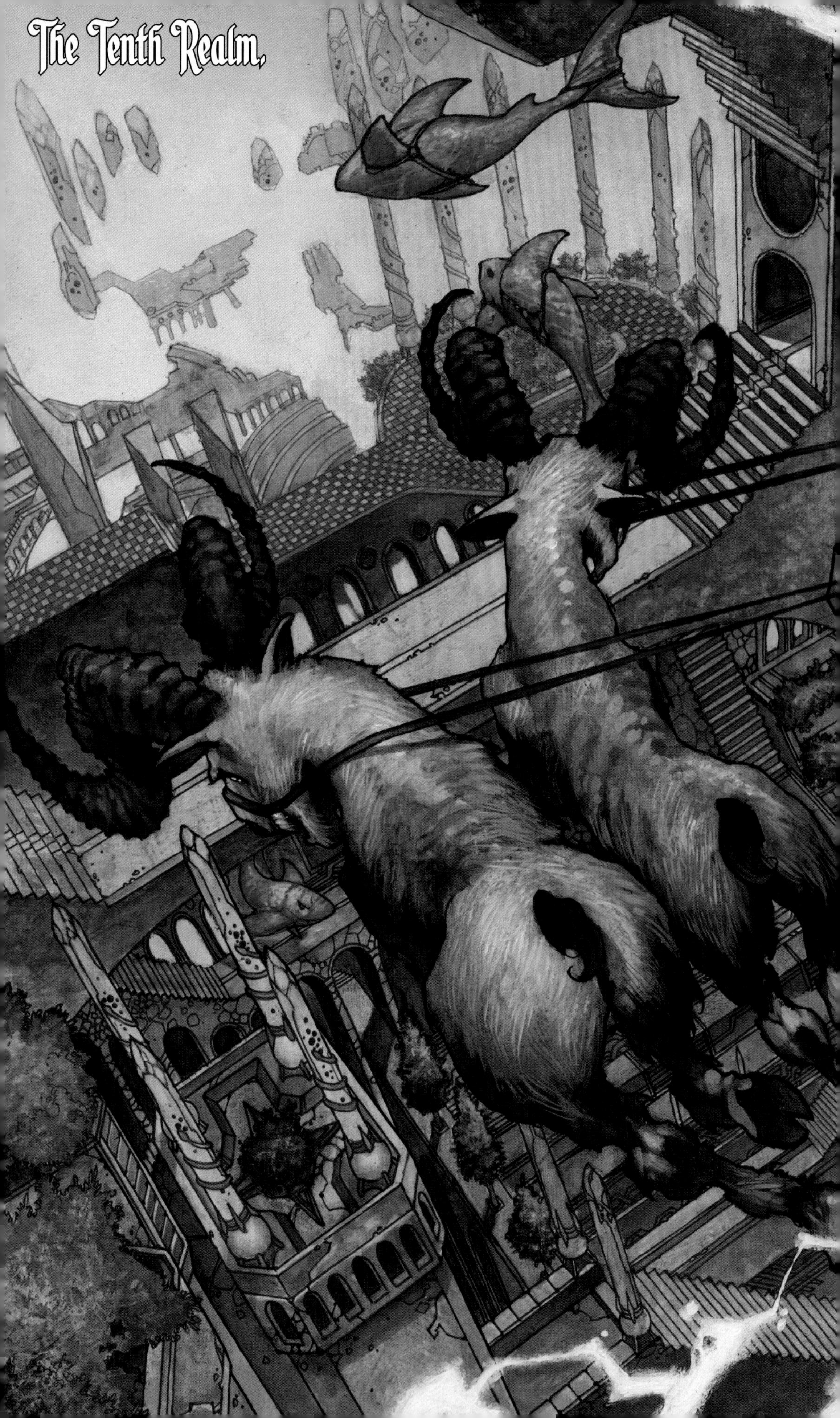
The Tenth Realm,

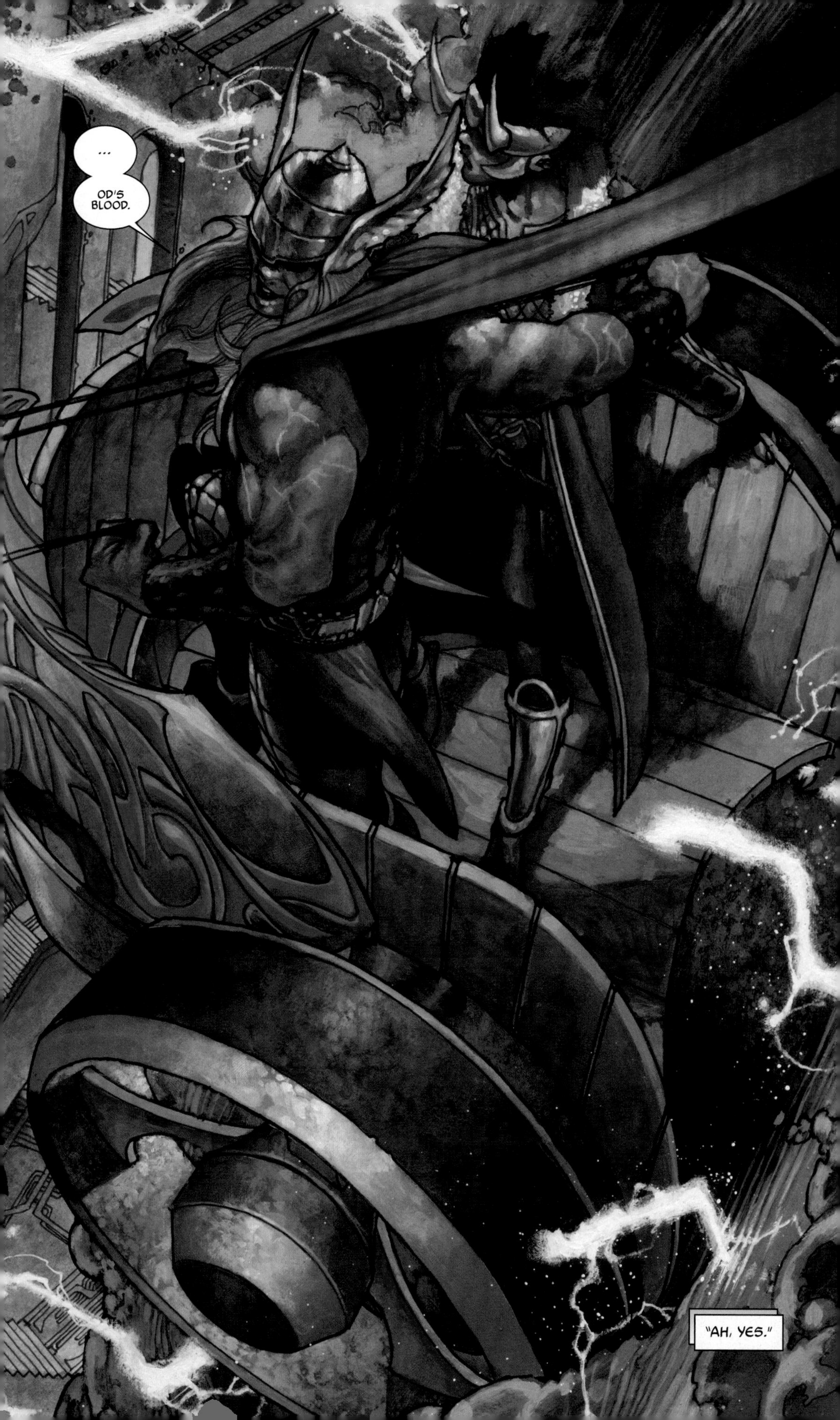
...
OD'S BLOOD.
"AH, YES."

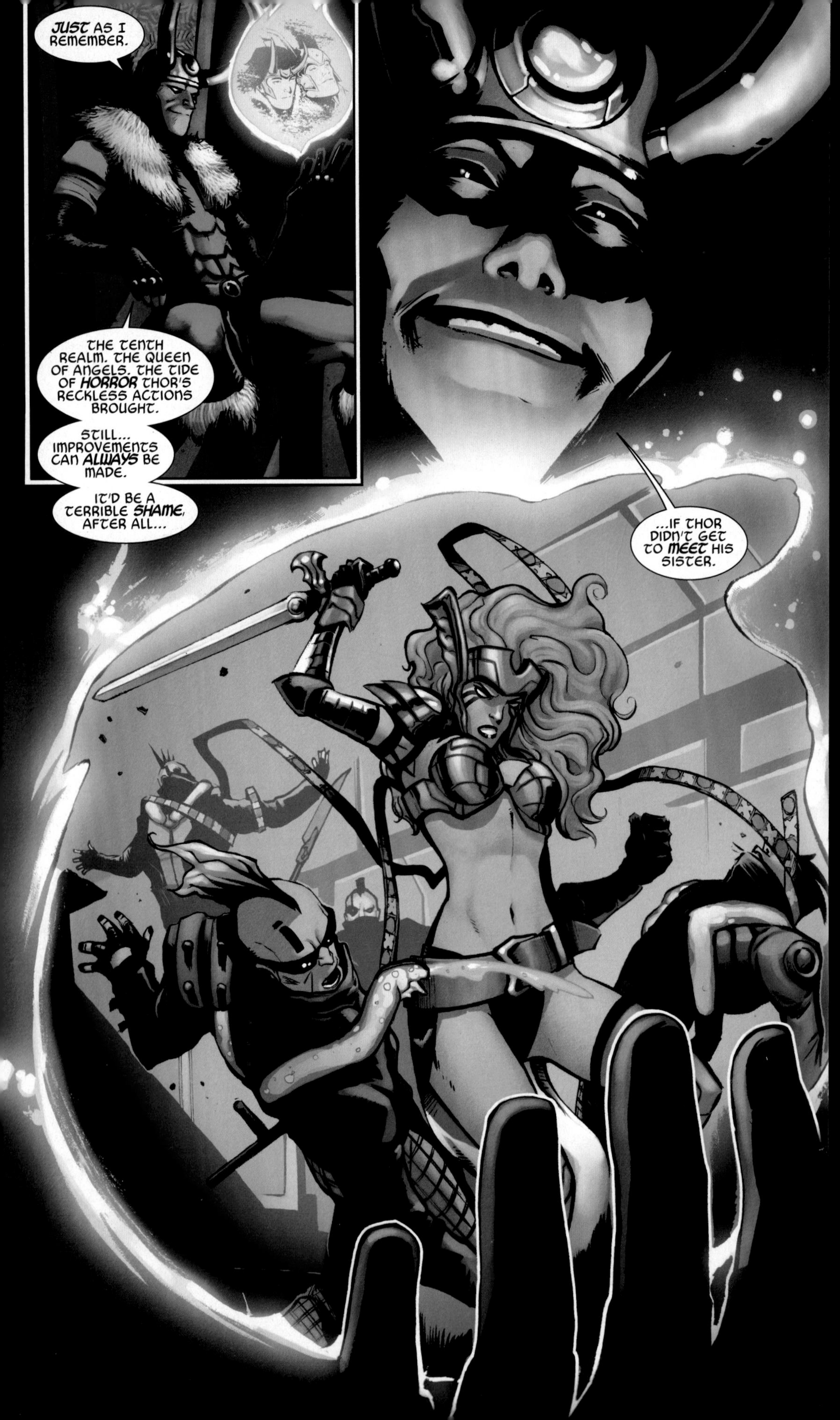
JUST AS I REMEMBER.
THE TENTH REALM. THE QUEEN OF ANGELS. THE TIDE OF HORROR THOR'S RECKLESS ACTIONS BROUGHT.
STILL... IMPROVEMENTS CAN ALWAYS BE MADE.
IT'D BE A TERRIBLE SHAME, AFTER ALL...
...IF THOR DIDN'T GET TO MEET HIS SISTER.

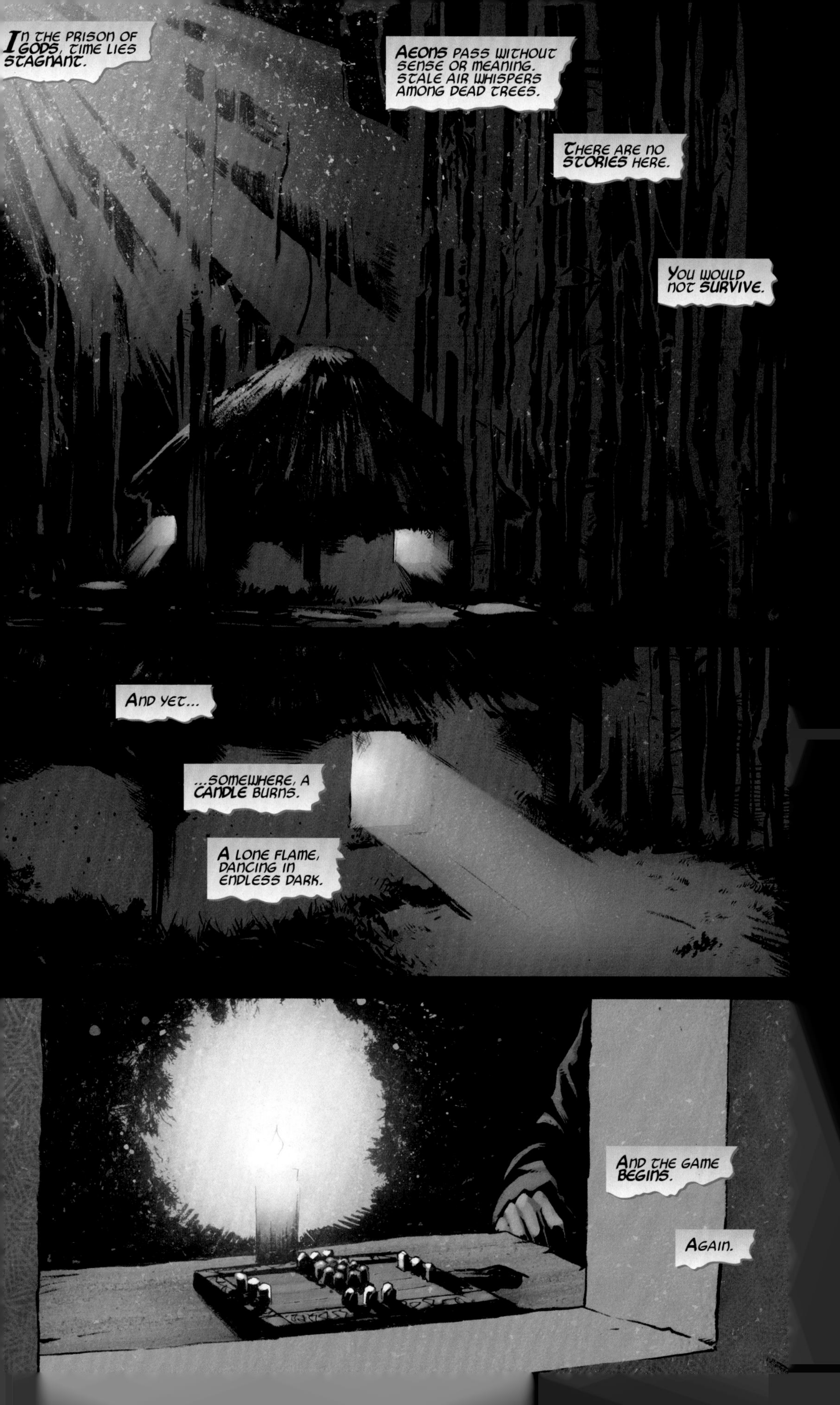
In the prison of gods, time lies stagnant.
Aeons pass without sense or meaning. Stale air whispers among dead trees.
There are no stories here.
You would not survive.
And yet...
...somewhere, a candle burns.
A lone flame, dancing in endless dark.
And the game begins.
Again.

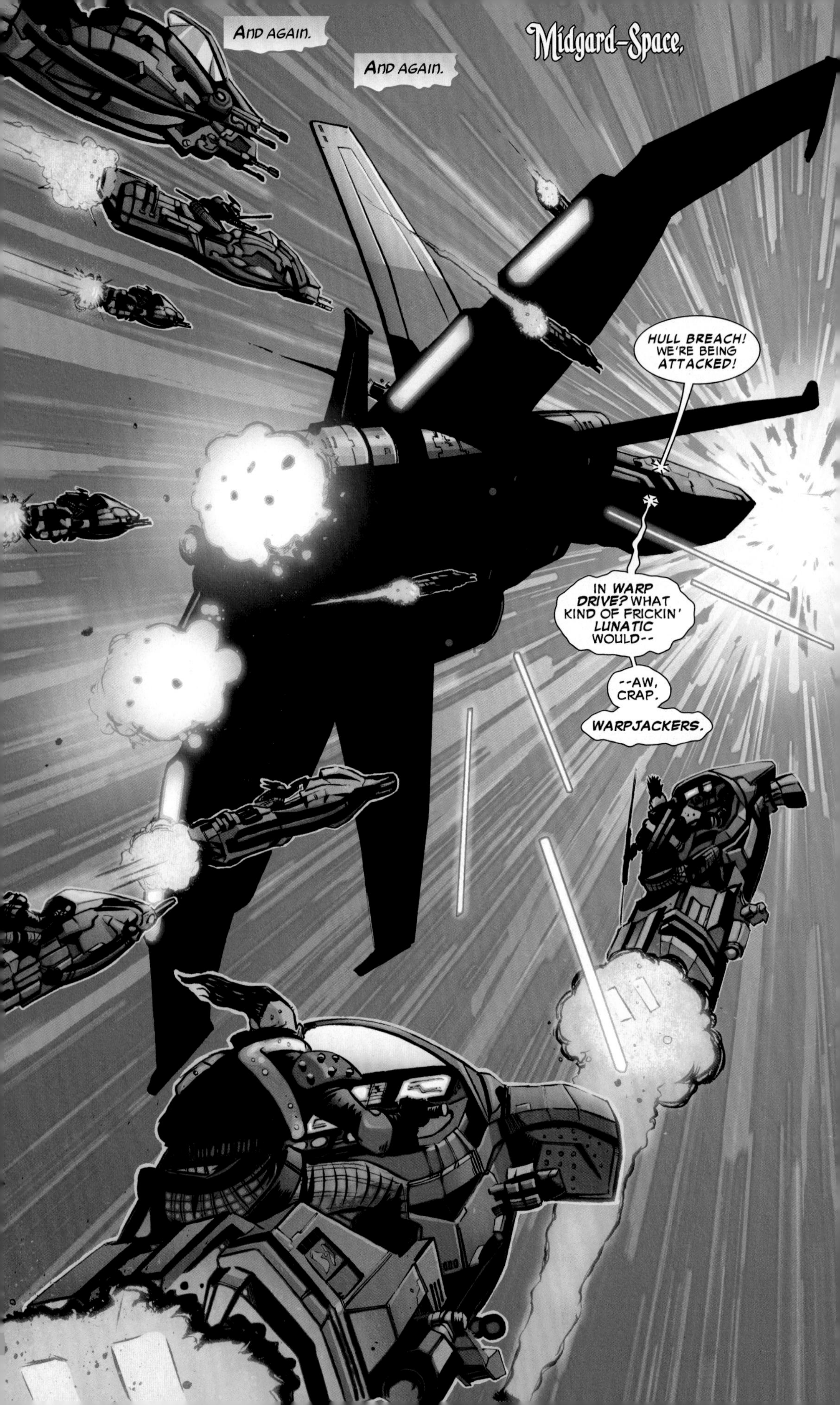
And again.
And again.
Midgard-Space,
HULL BREACH! WE'RE BEING ATTACKED!
IN WARP DRIVE? WHAT KIND OF FRICKIN' LUNATIC WOULD--
--AW, CRAP.
WARPJACKERS.

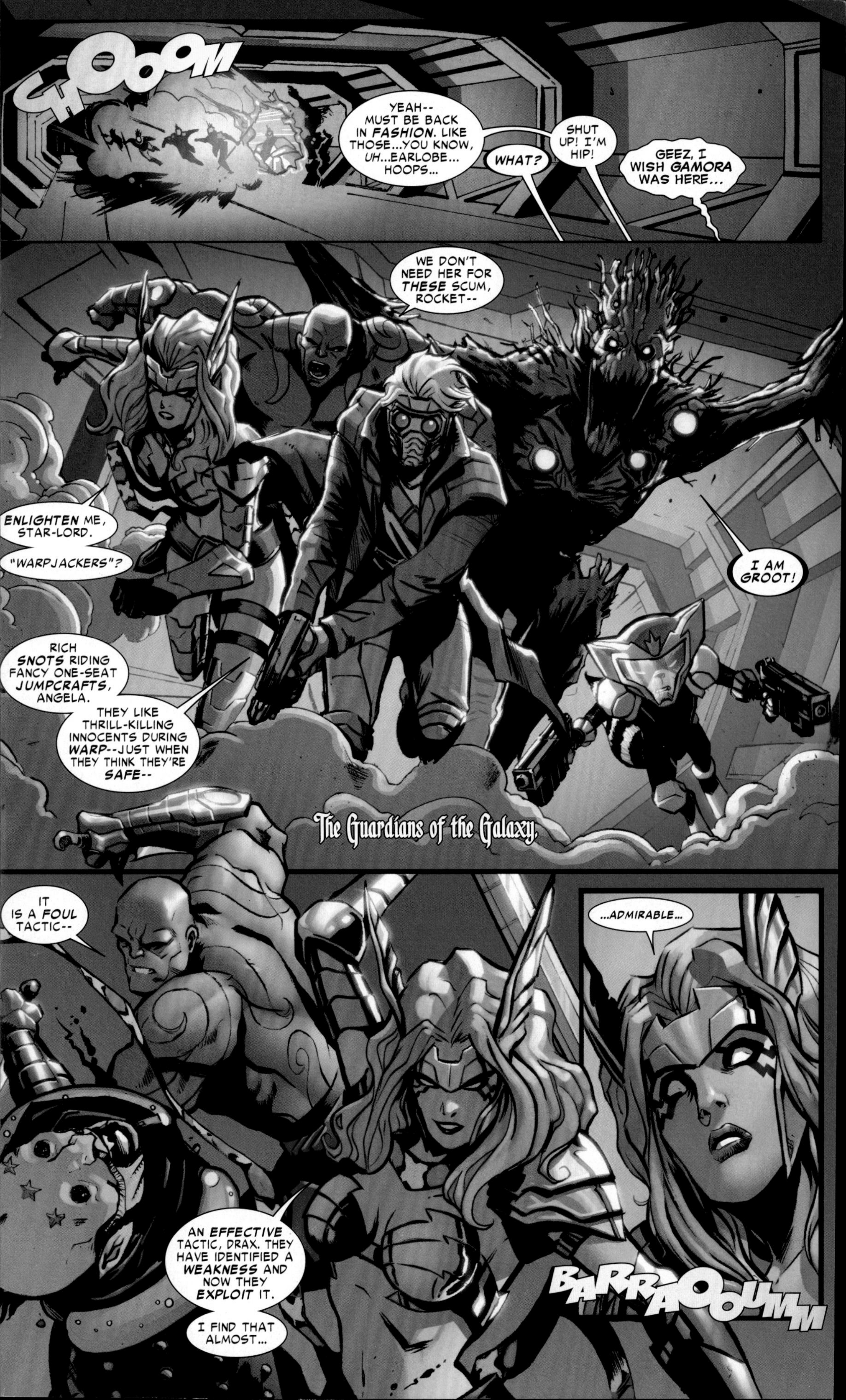

CHOOOOM
YEAH-- MUST BE BACK IN FASHION. LIKE THOSE...YOU KNOW, UH...EARLOBE... HOOPS...
WHAT?
SHUT UP! I'M HIP!
GEEZ, I WISH GAMORA WAS HERE...
WE DON'T NEED HER FOR THESE SCUM, ROCKET--
ENLIGHTEN ME, STAR-LORD.
"WARPJACKERS"?
I AM GROOT!
RICH SNOTS RIDING FANCY ONE-SEAT JUMPCRAFTS, ANGELA.
THEY LIKE THRILL-KILLING INNOCENTS DURING WARP--JUST WHEN THEY THINK THEY'RE SAFE--
The Guardians of the Galaxy.
IT IS A FOUL TACTIC--
AN EFFECTIVE TACTIC, DRAX. THEY HAVE IDENTIFIED A WEAKNESS AND NOW THEY EXPLOIT IT.
I FIND THAT ALMOST...
...ADMIRABLE...
BARRAOOUMM

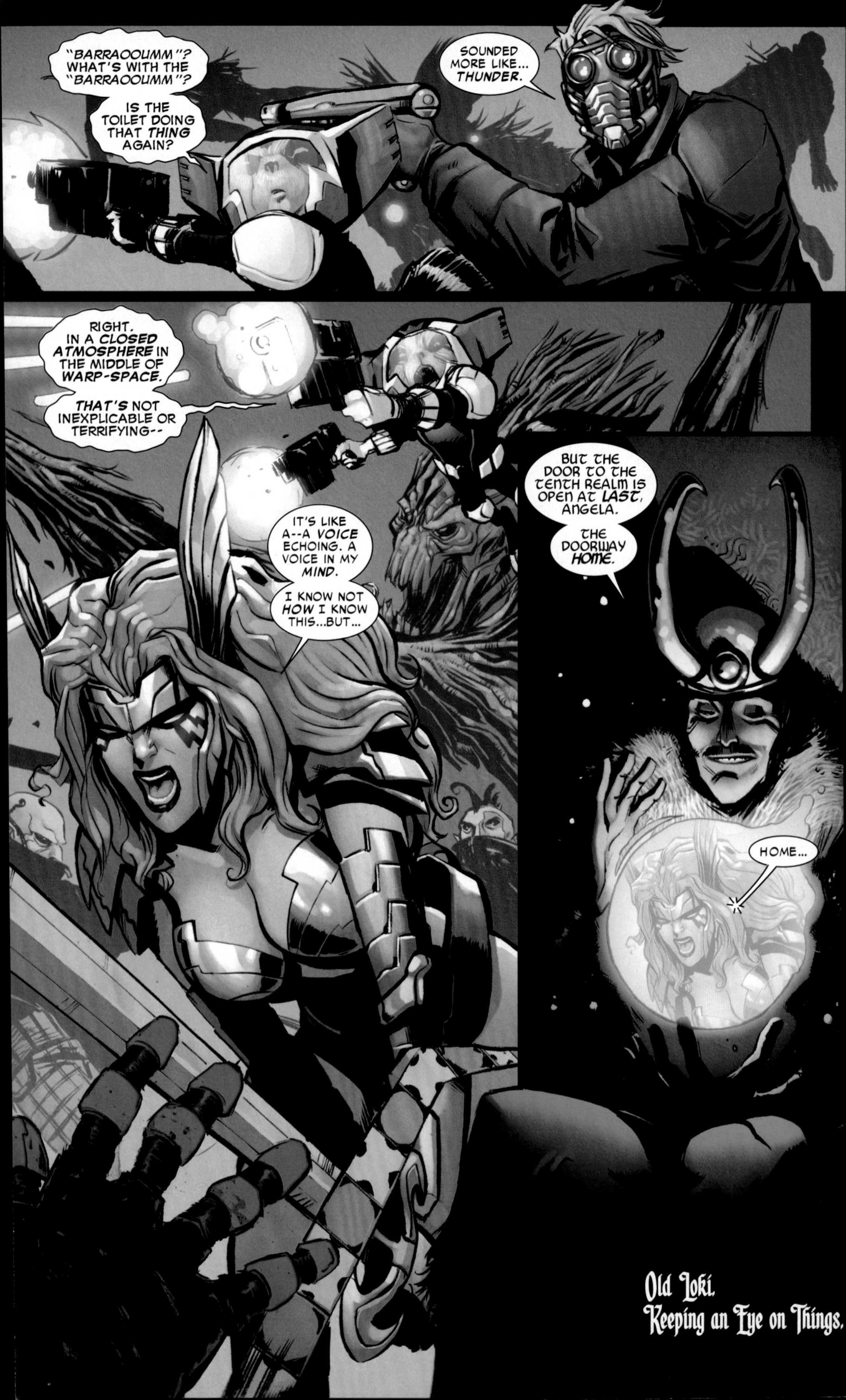
"BARRAOOUMM"? WHAT'S WITH THE "BARRAOOUMM"?
IS THE TOILET DOING THAT THING AGAIN?
SOUNDED MORE LIKE... THUNDER.
RIGHT. IN A CLOSED ATMOSPHERE IN THE MIDDLE OF WARP-SPACE.
THAT'S NOT INEXPLICABLE OR TERRIFYING--
IT'S LIKE A--A VOICE ECHOING. A VOICE IN MY MIND.
I KNOW NOT HOW I KNOW THIS...BUT...
BUT THE DOOR TO THE TENTH REALM IS OPEN AT LAST, ANGELA.
THE DOORWAY HOME.
HOME...
Old Loki.
Keeping an Eye on Things.

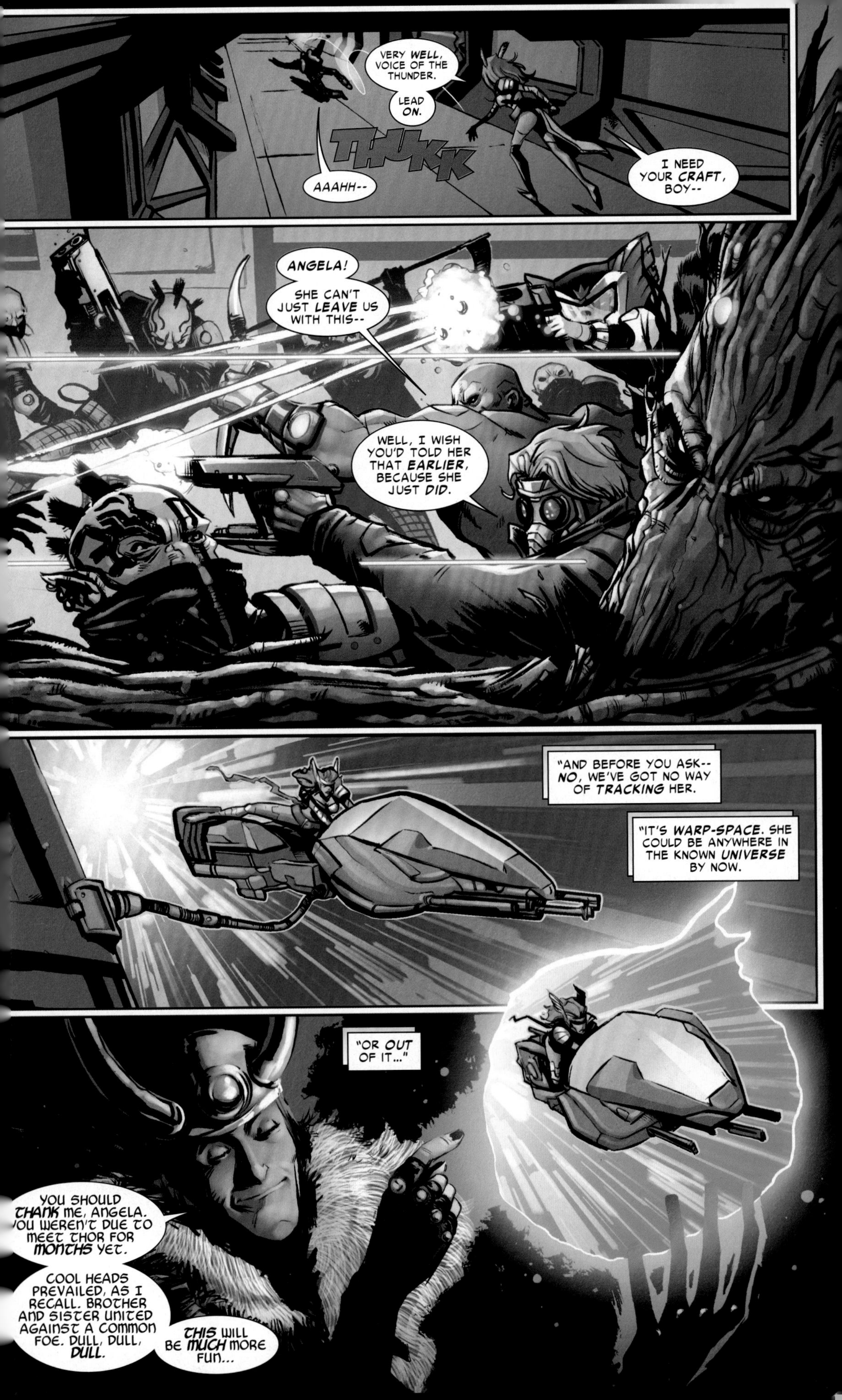
VERY WELL, VOICE OF THE THUNDER.
LEAD ON.
THUKK
AAAHH--
I NEED YOUR CRAFT, BOY--
ANGELA!
SHE CAN'T JUST LEAVE US WITH THIS--
WELL, I WISH YOU'D TOLD HER THAT EARLIER, BECAUSE SHE JUST DID.
"AND BEFORE YOU ASK-- NO, WE'VE GOT NO WAY OF TRACKING HER.
"IT'S WARP-SPACE. SHE COULD BE ANYWHERE IN THE KNOWN UNIVERSE BY NOW.
"OR OUT OF IT..."
YOU SHOULD THANK ME, ANGELA. YOU WEREN'T DUE TO MEET THOR FOR MONTHS YET.
COOL HEADS PREVAILED, AS I RECALL. BROTHER AND SISTER UNITED AGAINST A COMMON FOE. DULL, DULL, DULL.
THIS WILL BE MUCH MORE FUN...

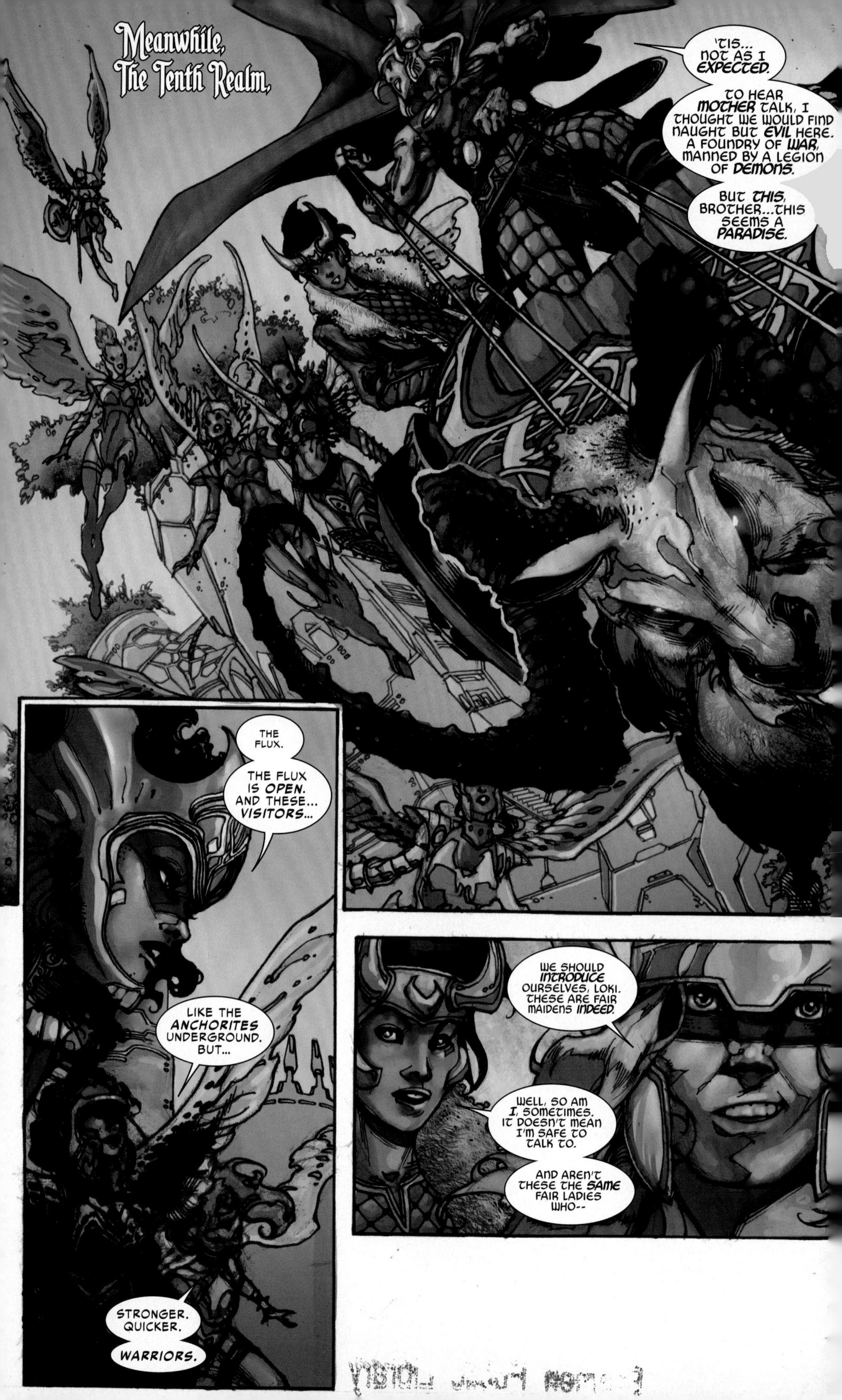

Meanwhile, The Tenth Realm,
'TIS... NOT AS I EXPECTED.
TO HEAR MOTHER TALK, I THOUGHT WE WOULD FIND NAUGHT BUT EVIL HERE. A FOUNDRY OF WAR, MANNED BY A LEGION OF DEMONS.
BUT THIS, BROTHER...THIS SEEMS A PARADISE.
THE FLUX.
THE FLUX IS OPEN. AND THESE... VISITORS...
LIKE THE ANCHORITES UNDERGROUND. BUT...
STRONGER. QUICKER.
WARRIORS.
WE SHOULD INTRODUCE OURSELVES, LOKI. THESE ARE FAIR MAIDENS INDEED.
WELL, SO AM I, SOMETIMES. IT DOESN'T MEAN I'M SAFE TO TALK TO.
AND AREN'T THESE THE SAME FAIR LADIES WHO--

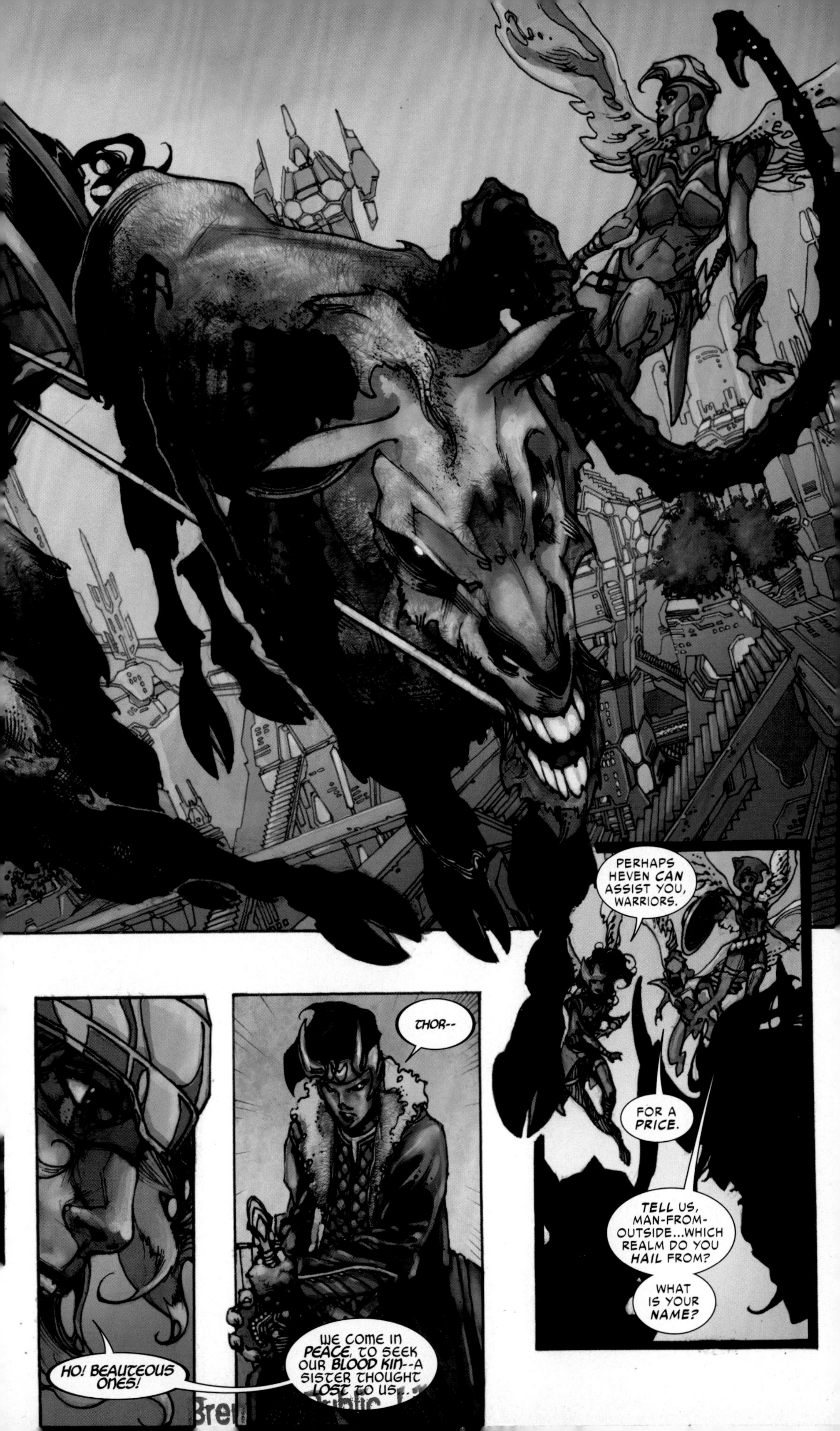
HO! BEAUTEOUS ONES!
WE COME IN PEACE, TO SEEK OUR BLOOD KIN--A SISTER THOUGHT LOST TO US.
THOR--
PERHAPS HEVEN CAN ASSIST YOU, WARRIORS.
FOR A PRICE.
TELL US, MAN-FROM-OUTSIDE...WHICH REALM DO YOU HAIL FROM?
WHAT IS YOUR NAME?

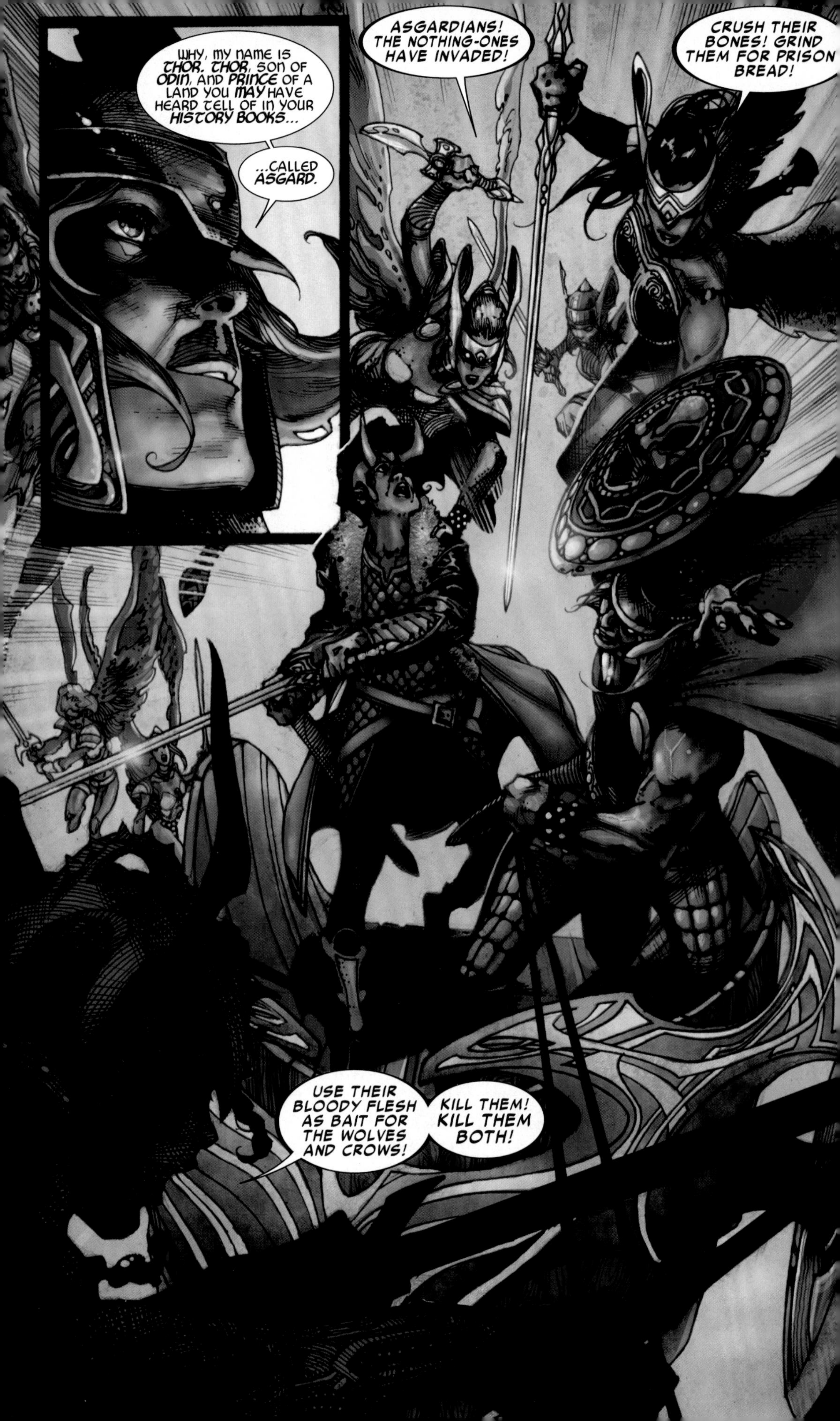
WHY, MY NAME IS THOR. THOR, SON OF ODIN, AND PRINCE OF A LAND YOU MAY HAVE HEARD TELL OF IN YOUR HISTORY BOOKS...
...CALLED ASGARD.
ASGARDIANS! THE NOTHING-ONES HAVE INVADED!
CRUSH THEIR BONES! GRIND THEM FOR PRISON BREAD!
USE THEIR BLOODY FLESH AS BAIT FOR THE WOLVES AND CROWS!
KILL THEM! KILL THEM BOTH!

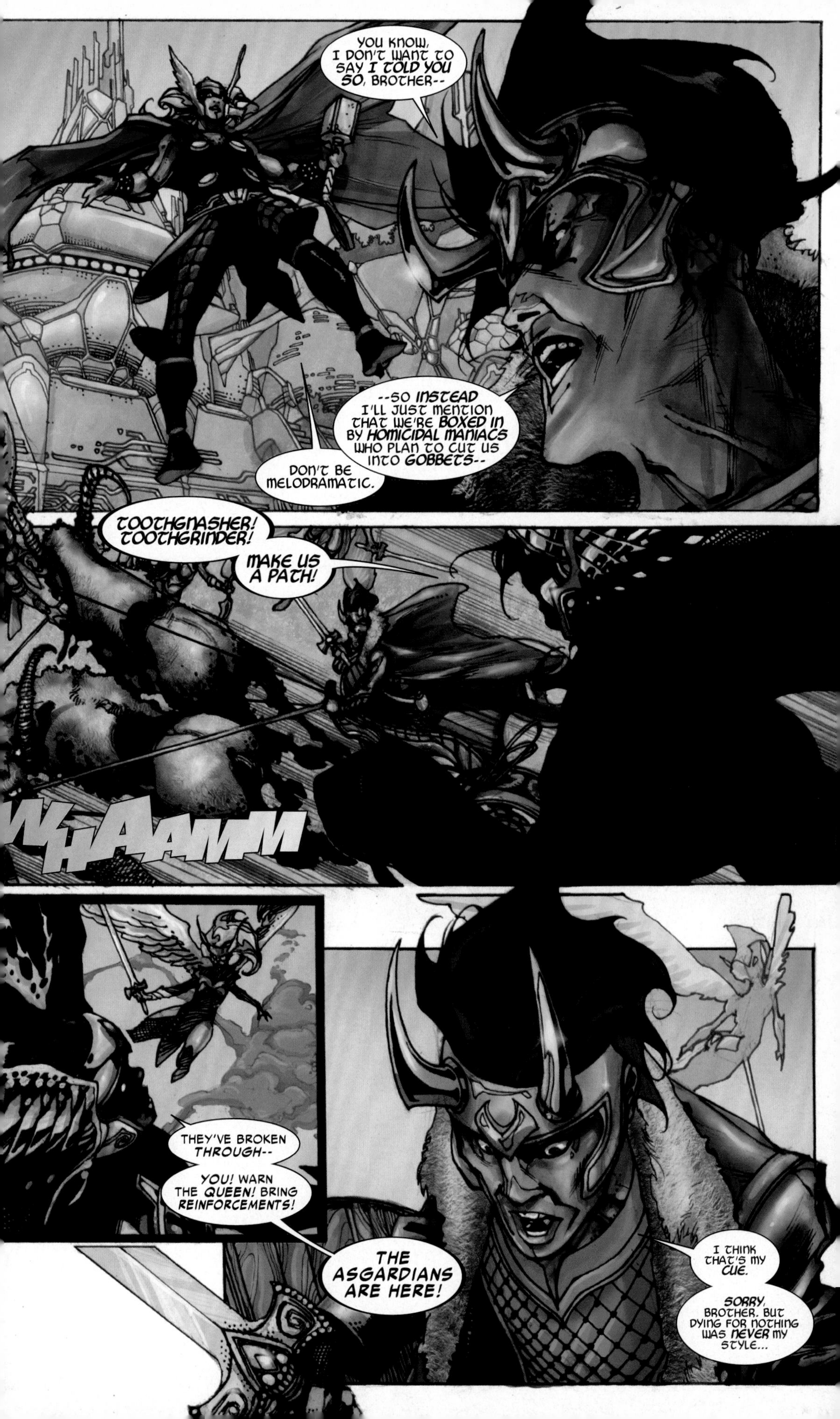

YOU KNOW, I DON'T WANT TO SAY I TOLD YOU SO, BROTHER--
--SO INSTEAD I'LL JUST MENTION THAT WE'RE BOXED IN BY HOMICIDAL MANIACS WHO PLAN TO CUT US INTO GOBBETS--
DON'T BE MELODRAMATIC.
TOOTHGNASHER! TOOTHGRINDER!
MAKE US A PATH!
WHAAMM
THEY'VE BROKEN THROUGH--
YOU! WARN THE QUEEN! BRING REINFORCEMENTS!
THE ASGARDIANS ARE HERE!
I THINK THAT'S MY CUE.
SORRY, BROTHER. BUT DYING FOR NOTHING WAS NEVER MY STYLE...

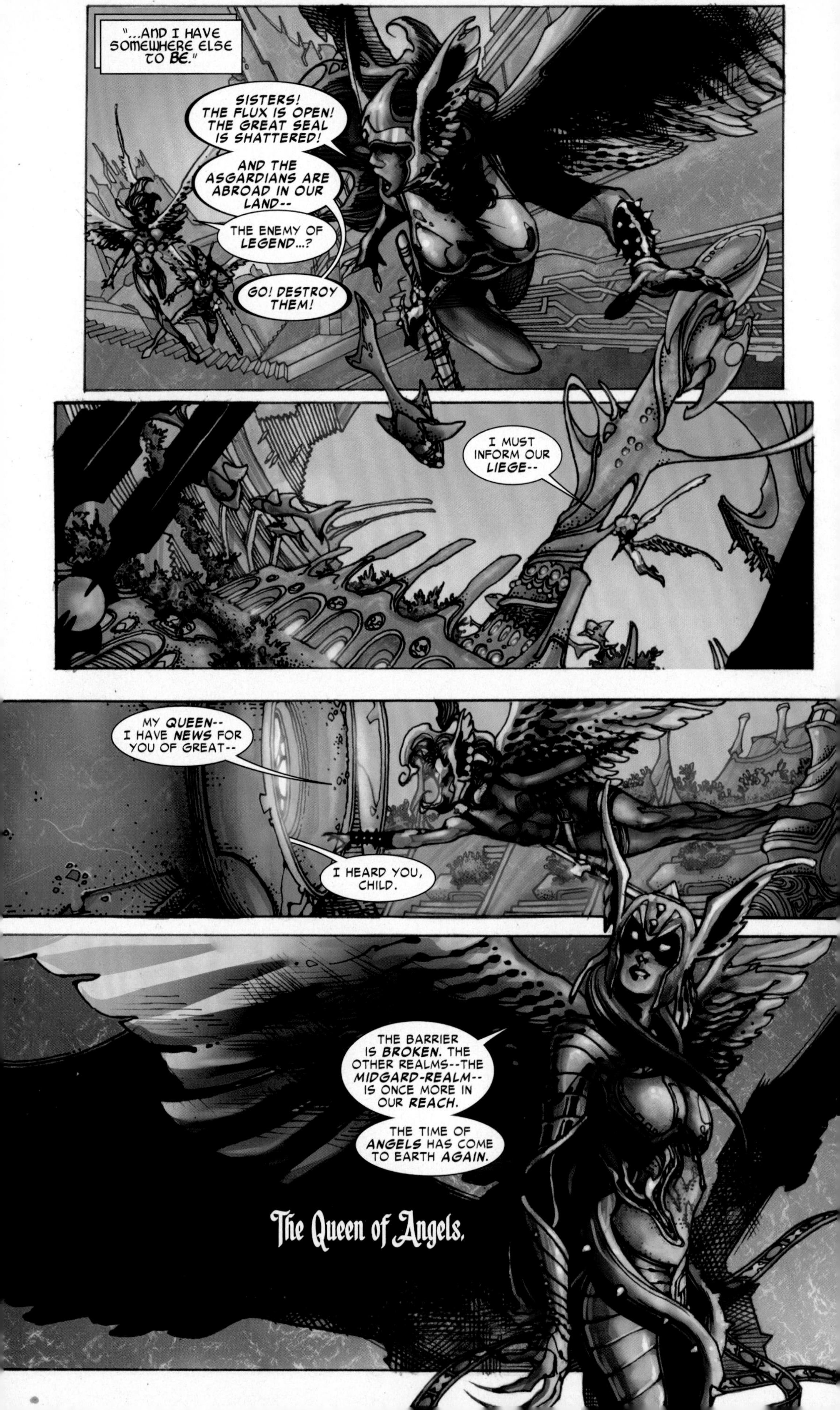
"...AND I HAVE SOMEWHERE ELSE TO BE."
SISTERS! THE FLUX IS OPEN! THE GREAT SEAL IS SHATTERED!
AND THE ASGARDIANS ARE ABROAD IN OUR LAND--
THE ENEMY OF LEGEND...?
GO! DESTROY THEM!
I MUST INFORM OUR LIEGE--
MY QUEEN-- I HAVE NEWS FOR YOU OF GREAT--
I HEARD YOU, CHILD.
THE BARRIER IS BROKEN. THE OTHER REALMS--THE MIDGARD-REALM-- IS ONCE MORE IN OUR REACH.
THE TIME OF ANGELS HAS COME TO EARTH AGAIN.
The Queen of Angels.

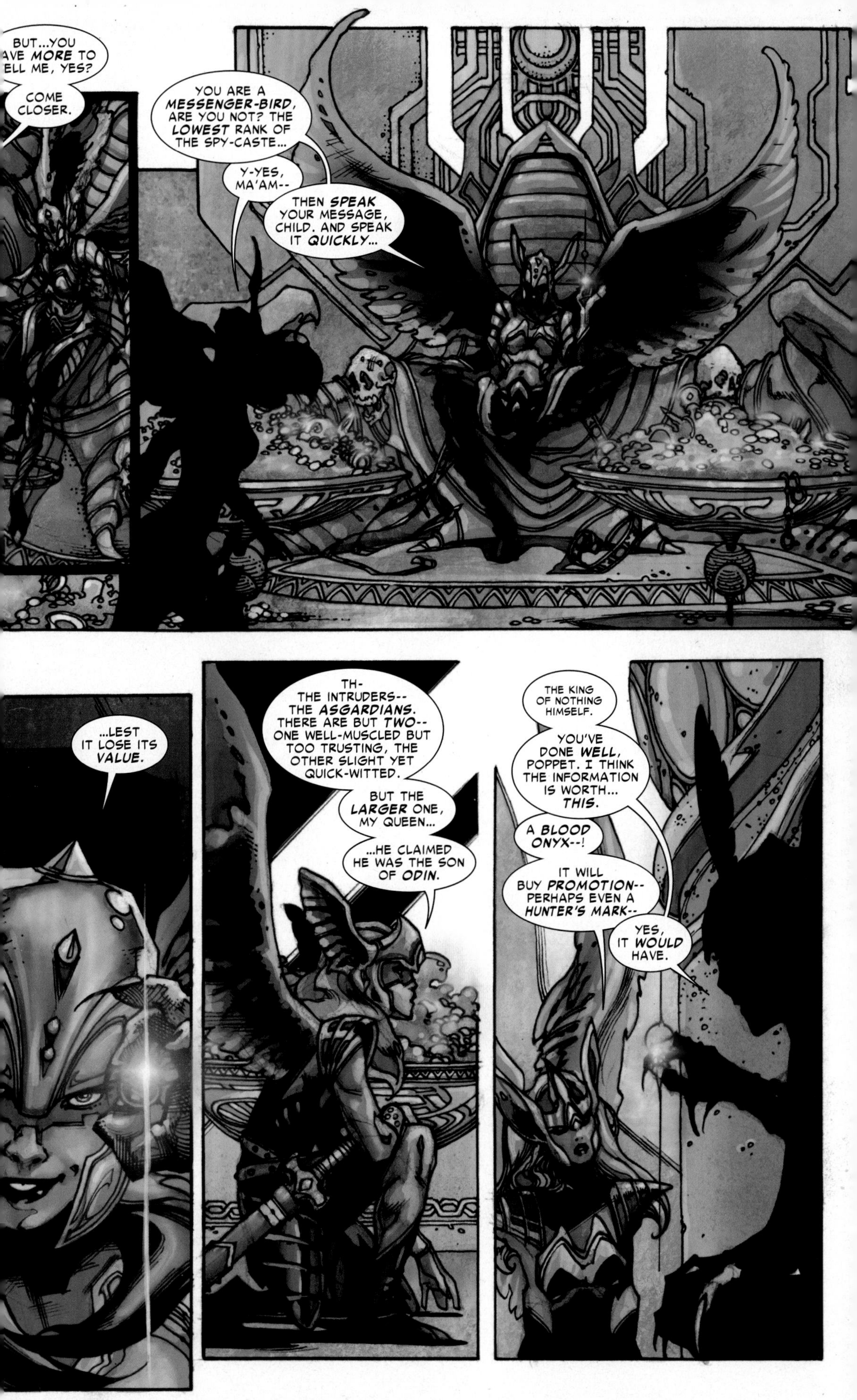
BUT...YOU AVE MORE TO ELL ME, YES?
COME CLOSER.
YOU ARE A MESSENGER-BIRD, ARE YOU NOT? THE LOWEST RANK OF THE SPY-CASTE...
Y-YES, MA'AM--
THEN SPEAK YOUR MESSAGE, CHILD. AND SPEAK IT QUICKLY...
...LEST IT LOSE ITS VALUE.
TH- THE INTRUDERS-- THE ASGARDIANS. THERE ARE BUT TWO-- ONE WELL-MUSCLED BUT TOO TRUSTING, THE OTHER SLIGHT YET QUICK-WITTED.
BUT THE LARGER ONE, MY QUEEN...
...HE CLAIMED HE WAS THE SON OF ODIN.
THE KING OF NOTHING HIMSELF.
YOU'VE DONE WELL, POPPET. I THINK THE INFORMATION IS WORTH... THIS.
A BLOOD ONYX--!
IT WILL BUY PROMOTION-- PERHAPS EVEN A HUNTER'S MARK--
YES, IT WOULD HAVE.

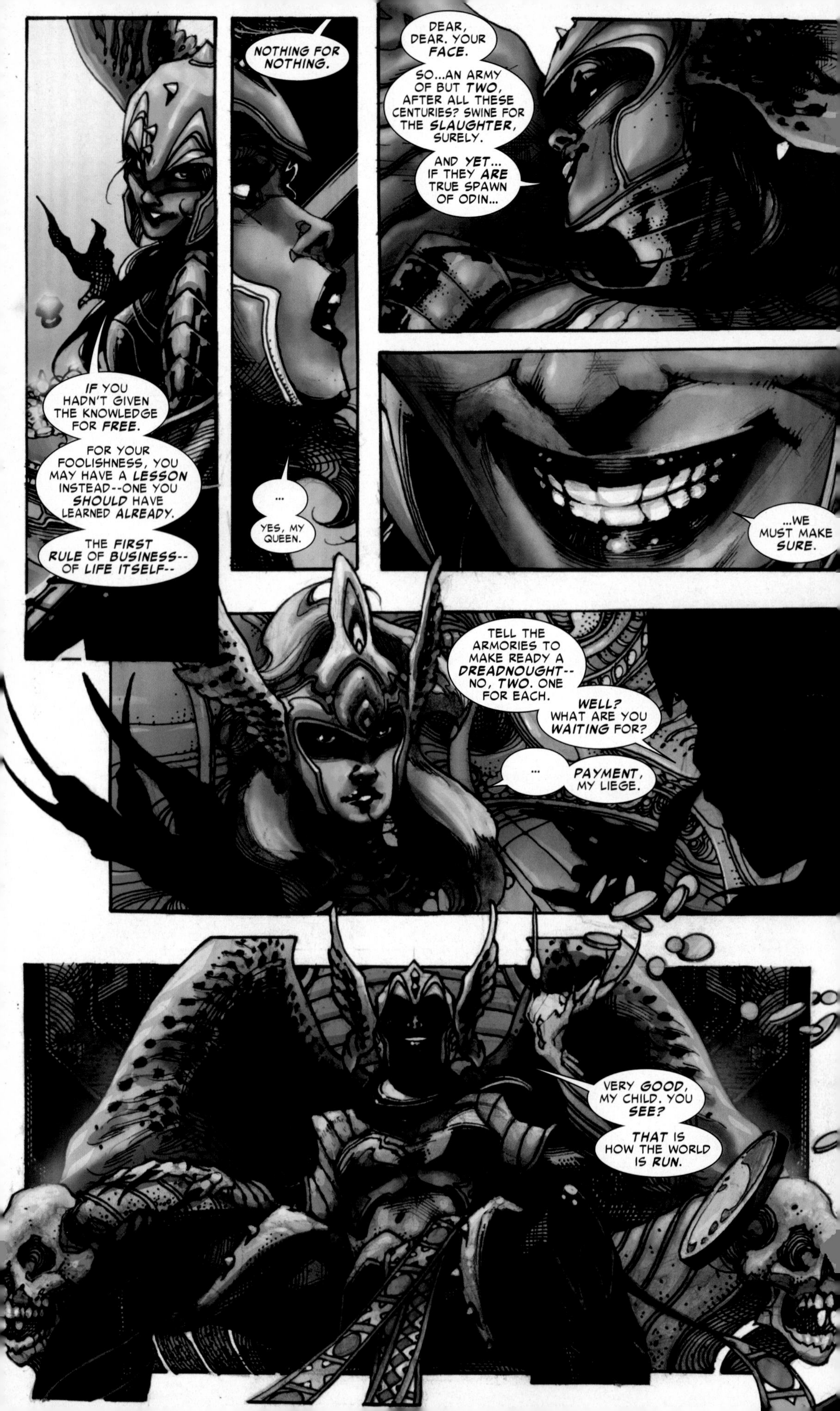
NOTHING FOR NOTHING.
IF YOU HADN'T GIVEN THE KNOWLEDGE FOR FREE.
FOR YOUR FOOLISHNESS, YOU MAY HAVE A LESSON INSTEAD--ONE YOU SHOULD HAVE LEARNED ALREADY.
THE FIRST RULE OF BUSINESS-- OF LIFE ITSELF--
...
YES, MY QUEEN.
DEAR, DEAR. YOUR FACE.
SO...AN ARMY OF BUT TWO, AFTER ALL THESE CENTURIES? SWINE FOR THE SLAUGHTER, SURELY.
AND YET... IF THEY ARE TRUE SPAWN OF ODIN...
...WE MUST MAKE SURE.
TELL THE ARMORIES TO MAKE READY A DREADNOUGHT-- NO, TWO. ONE FOR EACH.
WELL? WHAT ARE YOU WAITING FOR?
...
PAYMENT, MY LIEGE.
VERY GOOD, MY CHILD. YOU SEE?
THAT IS HOW THE WORLD IS RUN.

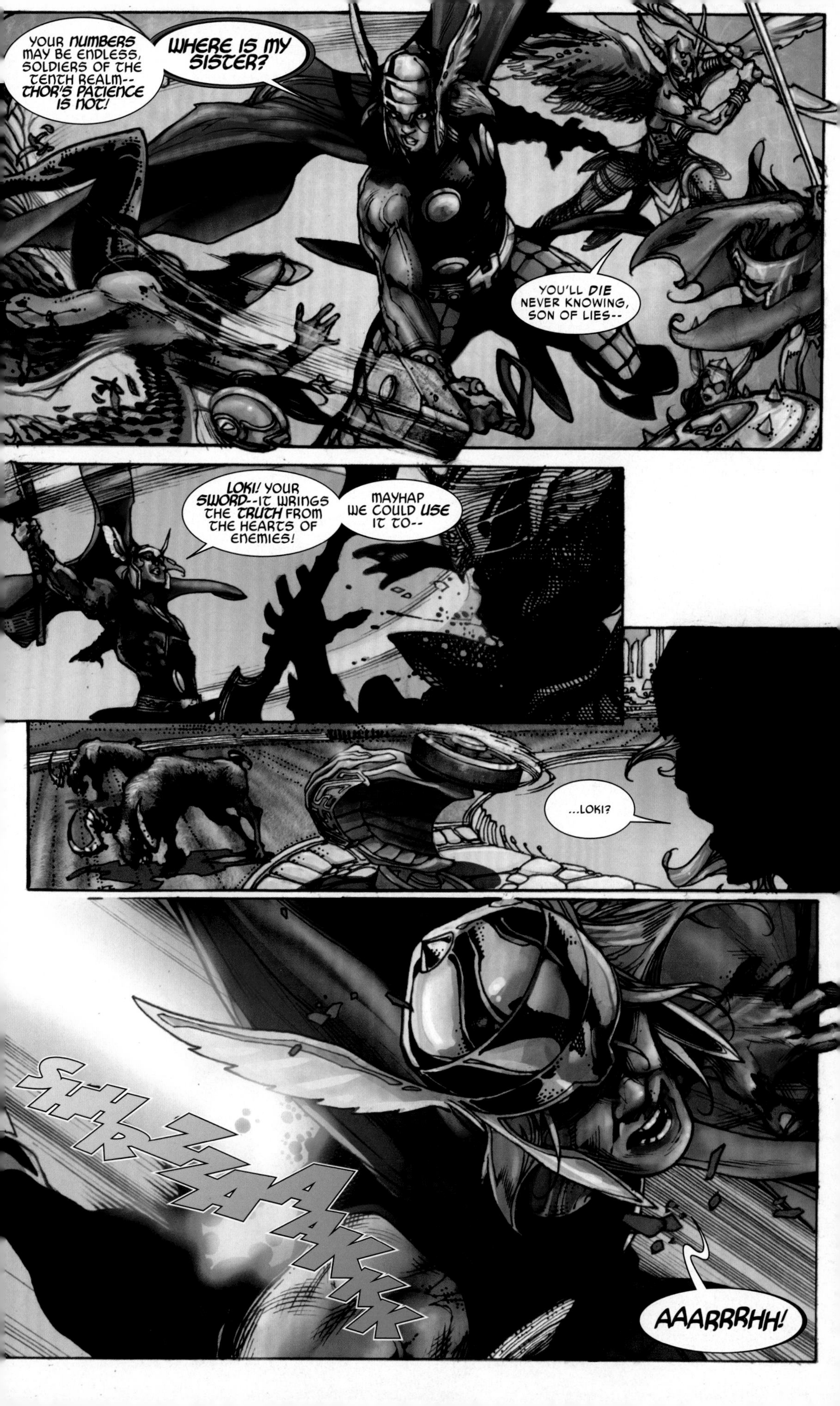
YOUR NUMBERS MAY BE ENDLESS, SOLDIERS OF THE TENTH REALM-- THOR'S PATIENCE IS NOT!
WHERE IS MY SISTER?
YOU'LL DIE NEVER KNOWING, SON OF LIES--
LOKI! YOUR SWORD--IT WRINGS THE TRUTH FROM THE HEARTS OF ENEMIES!
MAYHAP WE COULD USE IT TO--
...LOKI?
SHHZZAAKKK
AAARRRHH!

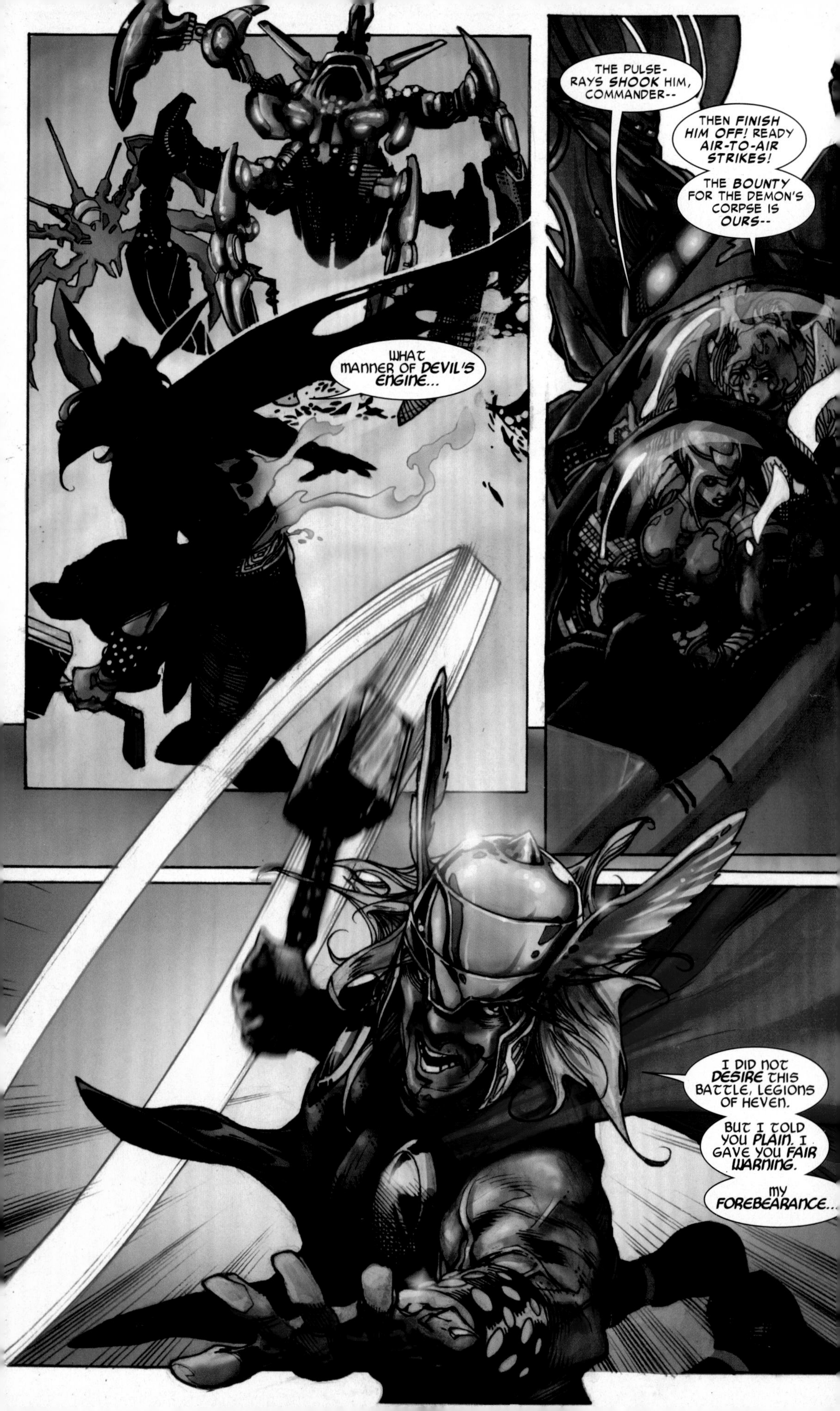
WHAT MANNER OF DEVIL'S ENGINE...
THE PULSE-RAYS SHOOK HIM, COMMANDER--
THEN FINISH HIM OFF! READY AIR-TO-AIR STRIKES!
THE BOUNTY FOR THE DEMON'S CORPSE IS OURS--
I DID NOT DESIRE THIS BATTLE, LEGIONS OF HEVEN.
BUT I TOLD YOU PLAIN. I GAVE YOU FAIR WARNING.
MY FOREBEARANCE...

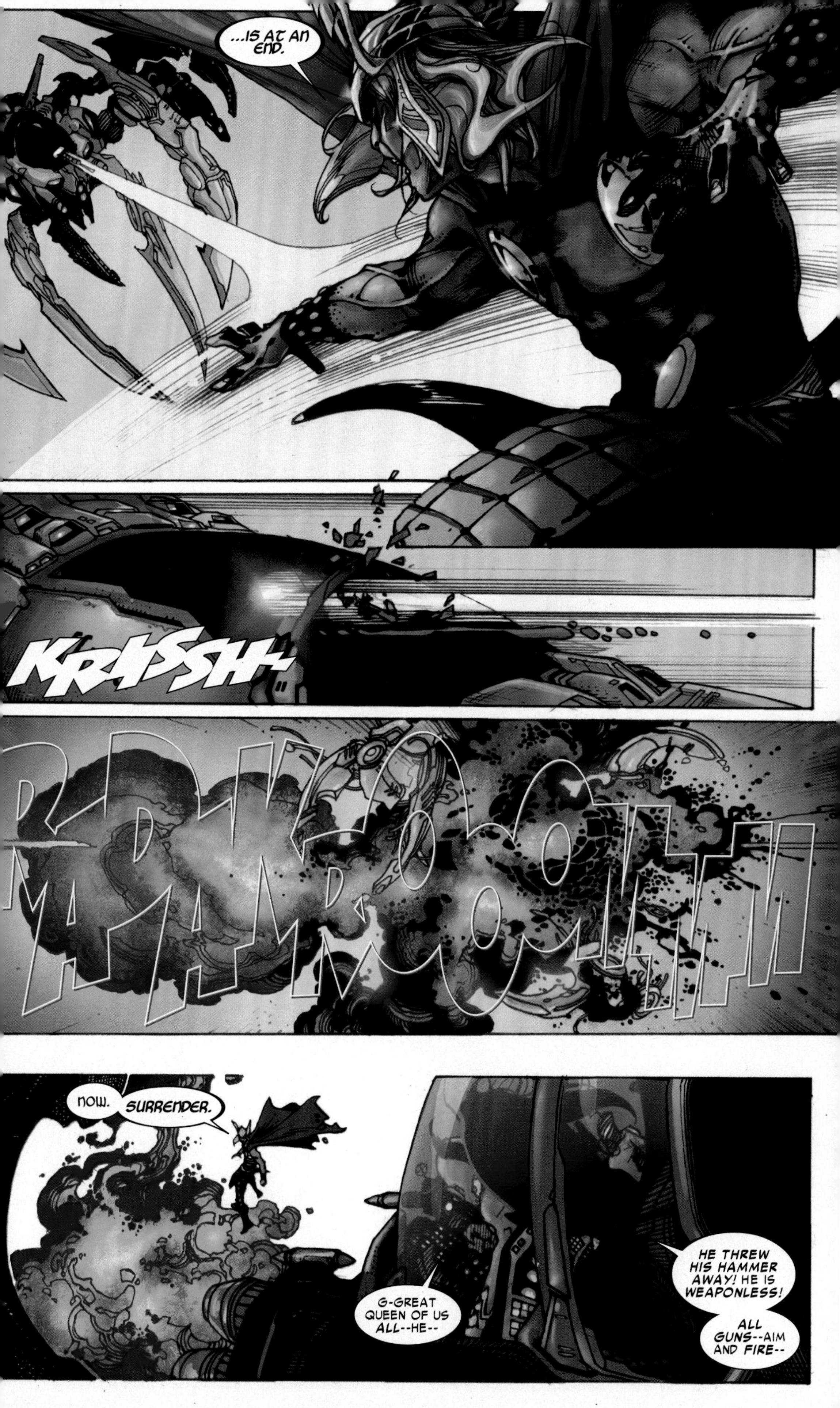
...IS AT AN END.
KRASH
DRAKOOOOM
NOW.
SURRENDER.
G-GREAT QUEEN OF US ALL--HE--
HE THREW HIS HAMMER AWAY! HE IS WEAPONLESS!
ALL GUNS--AIM AND FIRE--

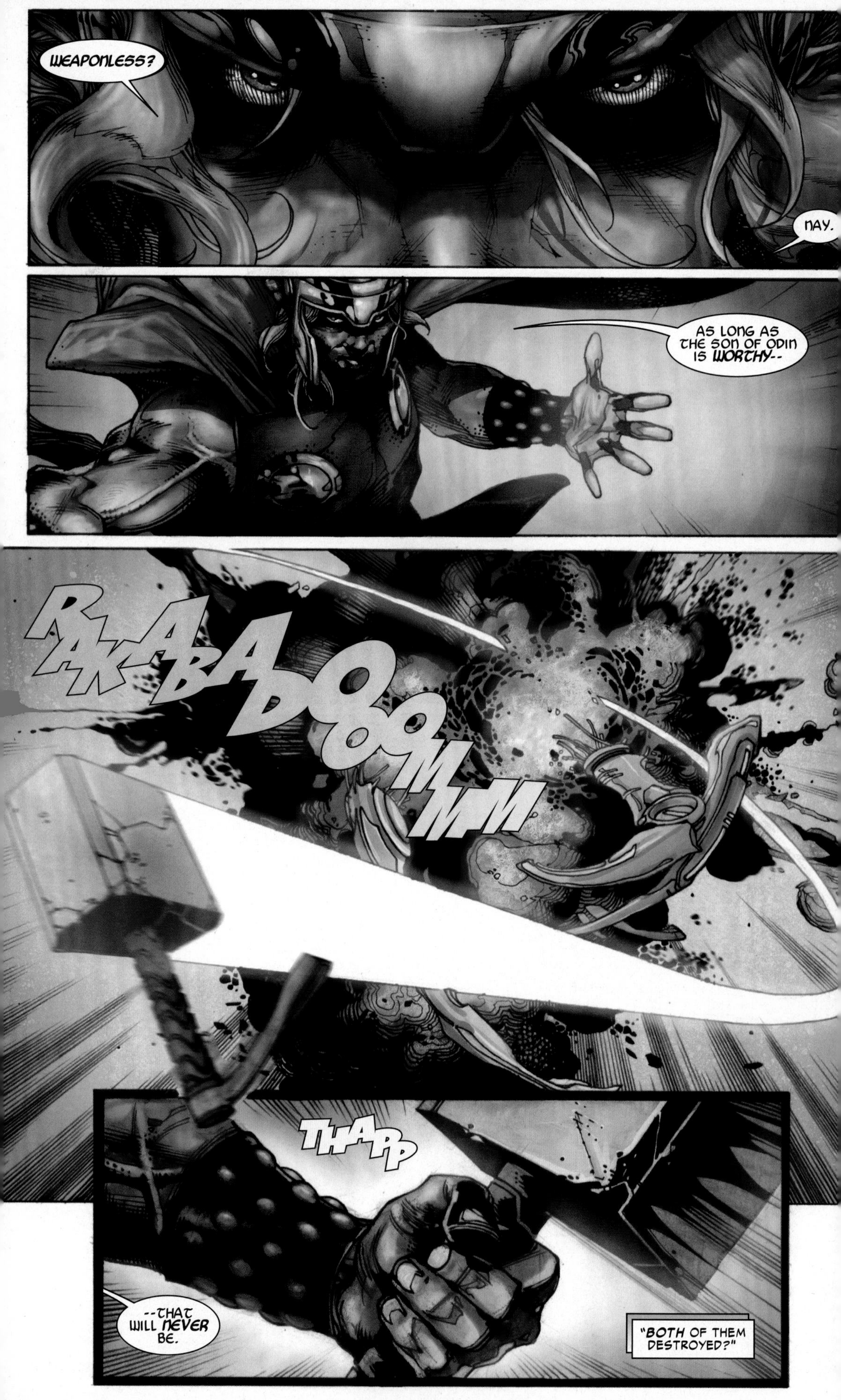
WEAPONLESS?
NAY.
AS LONG AS THE SON OF ODIN IS WORTHY--
RAKABADOOMMM
THAPP
--THAT WILL NEVER BE.
"BOTH OF THEM DESTROYED?"

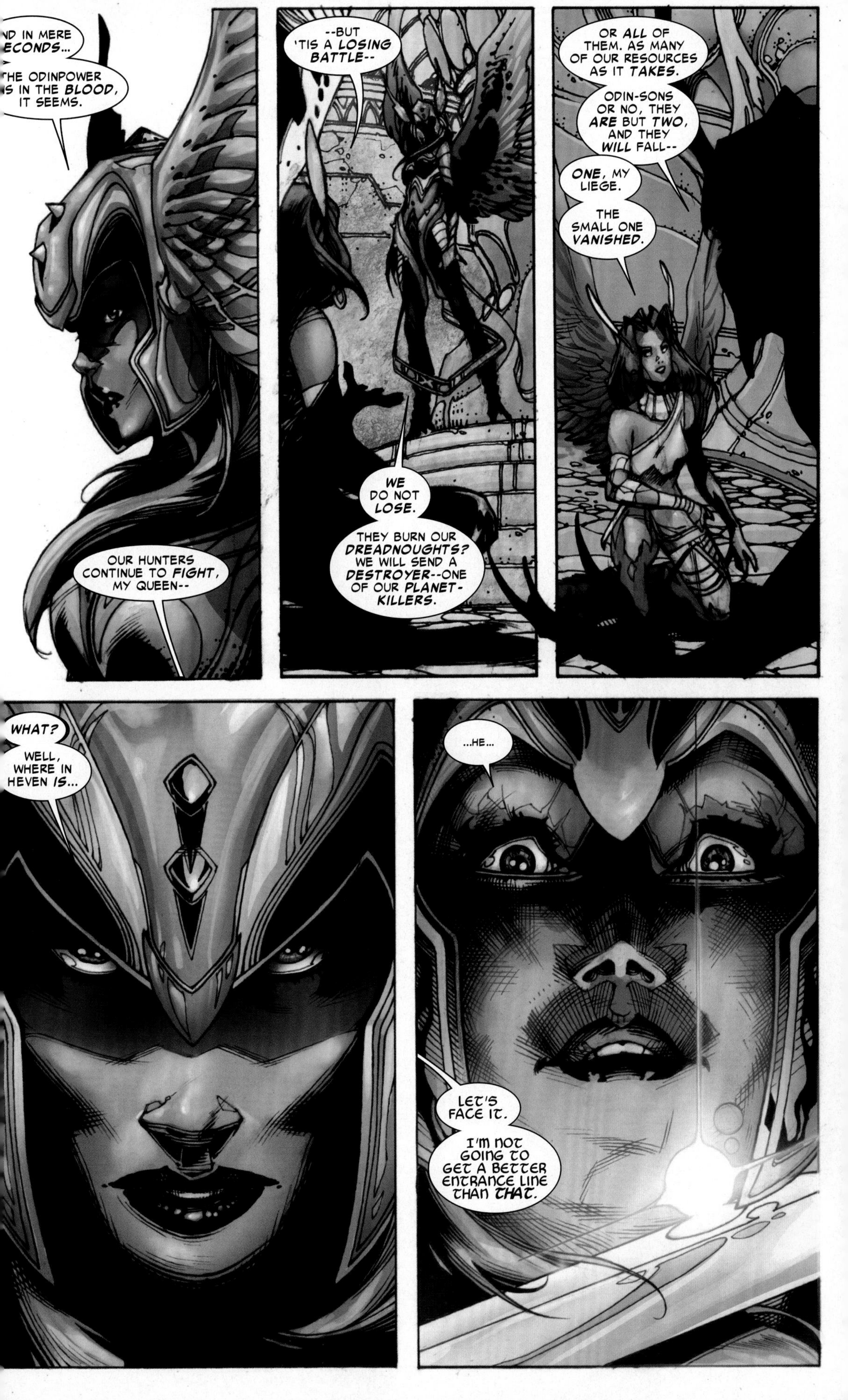
ND IN MERE ECONDS...
THE ODINPOWER S IN THE BLOOD, IT SEEMS.
OUR HUNTERS CONTINUE TO FIGHT, MY QUEEN--
--BUT 'TIS A LOSING BATTLE--
WE DO NOT LOSE.
THEY BURN OUR DREADNOUGHTS? WE WILL SEND A DESTROYER--ONE OF OUR PLANET-KILLERS.
OR ALL OF THEM. AS MANY OF OUR RESOURCES AS IT TAKES.
ODIN-SONS OR NO, THEY ARE BUT TWO, AND THEY WILL FALL--
ONE, MY LIEGE.
THE SMALL ONE VANISHED.
WHAT?
WELL, WHERE IN HEVEN IS...
...HE...
LET'S FACE IT.
I'M NOT GOING TO GET A BETTER ENTRANCE LINE THAN THAT.

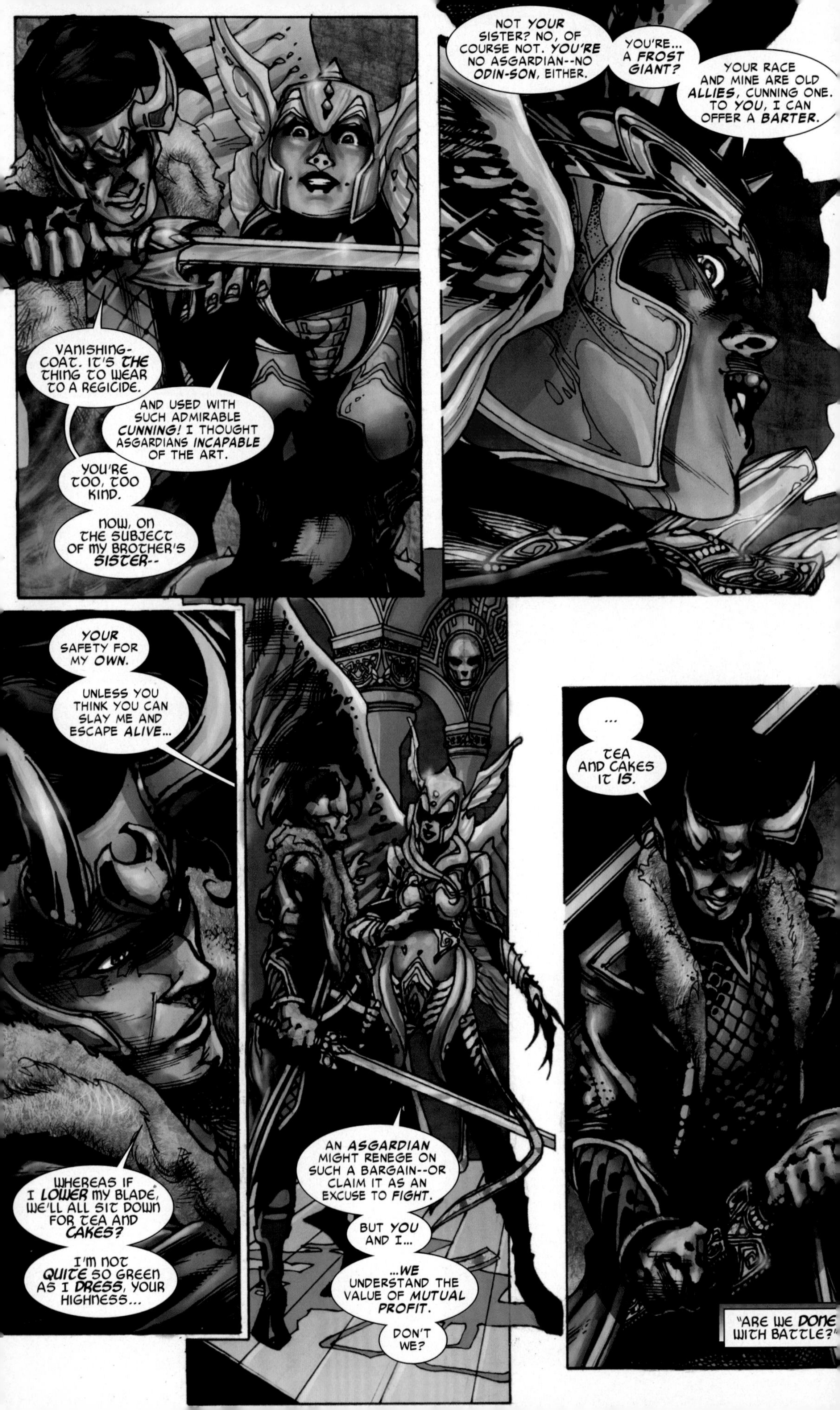

VANISHING-COAT. IT'S THE THING TO WEAR TO A REGICIDE.
AND USED WITH SUCH ADMIRABLE CUNNING! I THOUGHT ASGARDIANS INCAPABLE OF THE ART.
YOU'RE TOO, TOO KIND.
NOW, ON THE SUBJECT OF MY BROTHER'S SISTER--
NOT YOUR SISTER? NO, OF COURSE NOT. YOU'RE NO ASGARDIAN--NO ODIN-SON, EITHER.
YOU'RE... A FROST GIANT?
YOUR RACE AND MINE ARE OLD ALLIES, CUNNING ONE. TO YOU, I CAN OFFER A BARTER.
YOUR SAFETY FOR MY OWN.
UNLESS YOU THINK YOU CAN SLAY ME AND ESCAPE ALIVE...
WHEREAS IF I LOWER MY BLADE, WE'LL ALL SIT DOWN FOR TEA AND CAKES?
I'M NOT QUITE SO GREEN AS I DRESS, YOUR HIGHNESS...
AN ASGARDIAN MIGHT RENEGE ON SUCH A BARGAIN--OR CLAIM IT AS AN EXCUSE TO FIGHT.
BUT YOU AND I...
...WE UNDERSTAND THE VALUE OF MUTUAL PROFIT.
DON'T WE?
...
TEA AND CAKES IT IS.
"ARE WE DONE WITH BATTLE?"

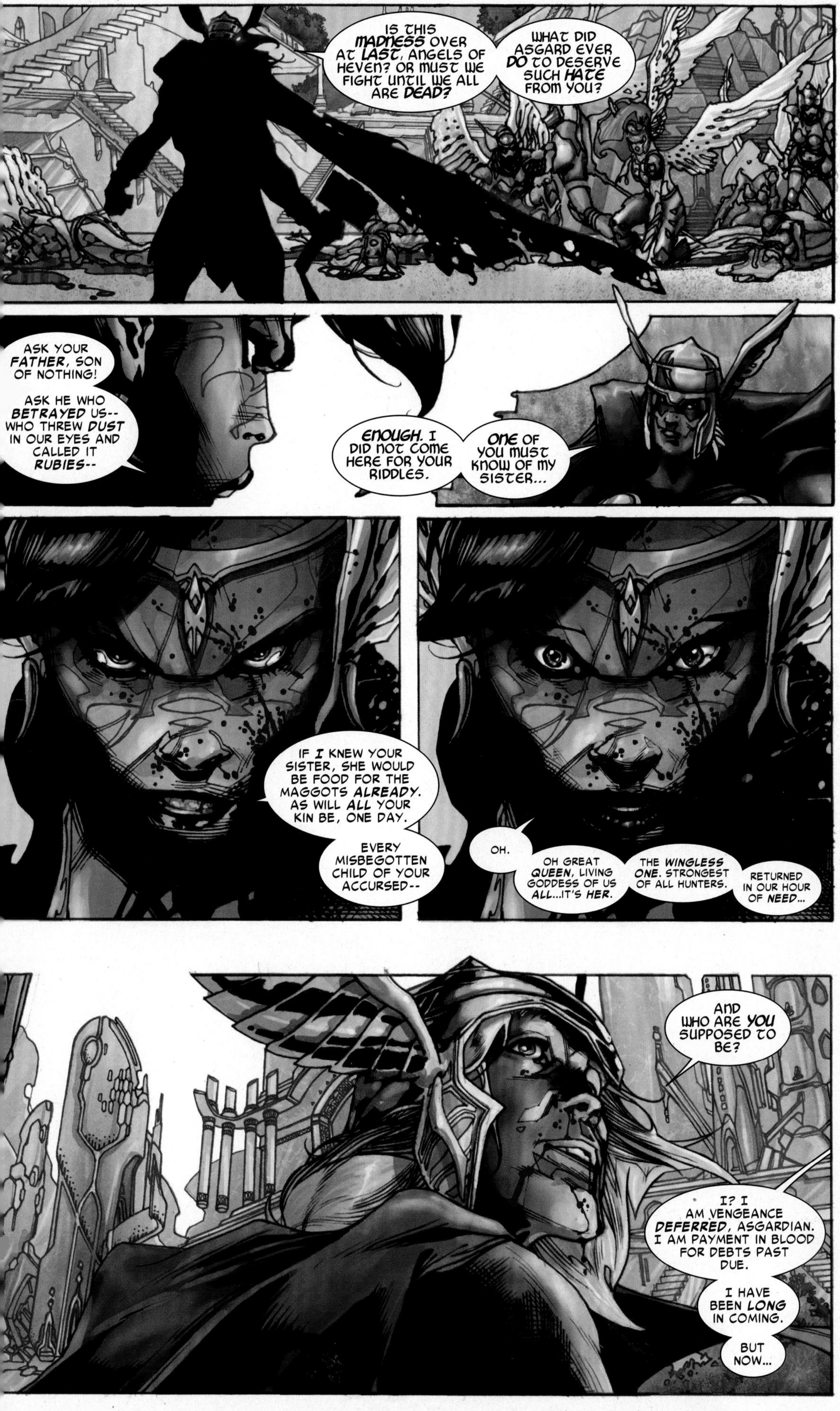
IS THIS MADNESS OVER AT LAST, ANGELS OF HEVEN? OR MUST WE FIGHT UNTIL WE ALL ARE DEAD?
WHAT DID ASGARD EVER DO TO DESERVE SUCH HATE FROM YOU?
ASK YOUR FATHER, SON OF NOTHING!
ASK HE WHO BETRAYED US-- WHO THREW DUST IN OUR EYES AND CALLED IT RUBIES--
ENOUGH. I DID NOT COME HERE FOR YOUR RIDDLES.
ONE OF YOU MUST KNOW OF MY SISTER...
IF I KNEW YOUR SISTER, SHE WOULD BE FOOD FOR THE MAGGOTS ALREADY. AS WILL ALL YOUR KIN BE, ONE DAY.
EVERY MISBEGOTTEN CHILD OF YOUR ACCURSED--
OH.
OH GREAT QUEEN, LIVING GODDESS OF US ALL...IT'S HER.
THE WINGLESS ONE. STRONGEST OF ALL HUNTERS.
RETURNED IN OUR HOUR OF NEED...
AND WHO ARE YOU SUPPOSED TO BE?
I? I AM VENGEANCE DEFERRED, ASGARDIAN. I AM PAYMENT IN BLOOD FOR DEBTS PAST DUE.
I HAVE BEEN LONG IN COMING.
BUT NOW...

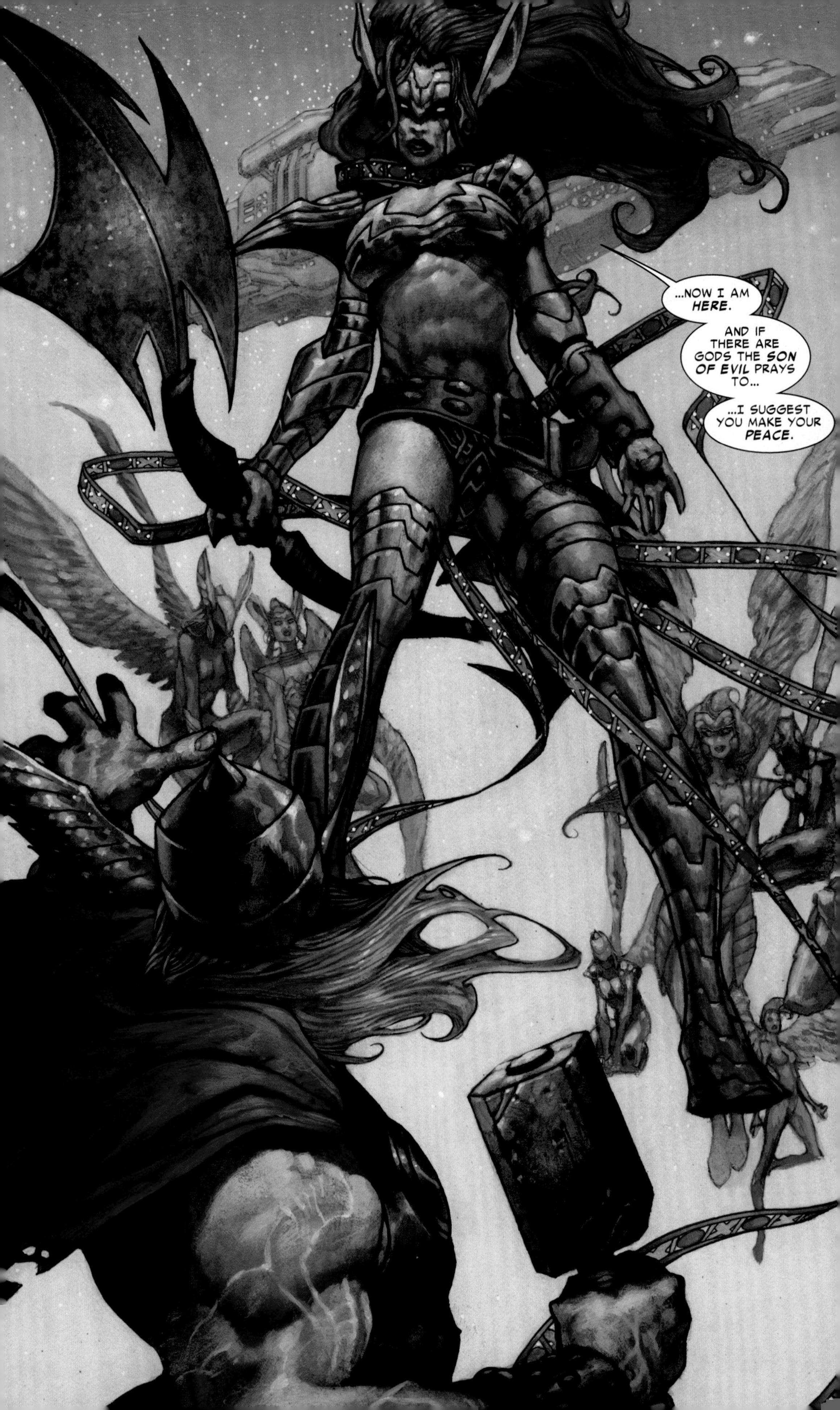
...NOW I AM HERE.
AND IF THERE ARE GODS THE SON OF EVIL PRAYS TO...
...I SUGGEST YOU MAKE YOUR PEACE.

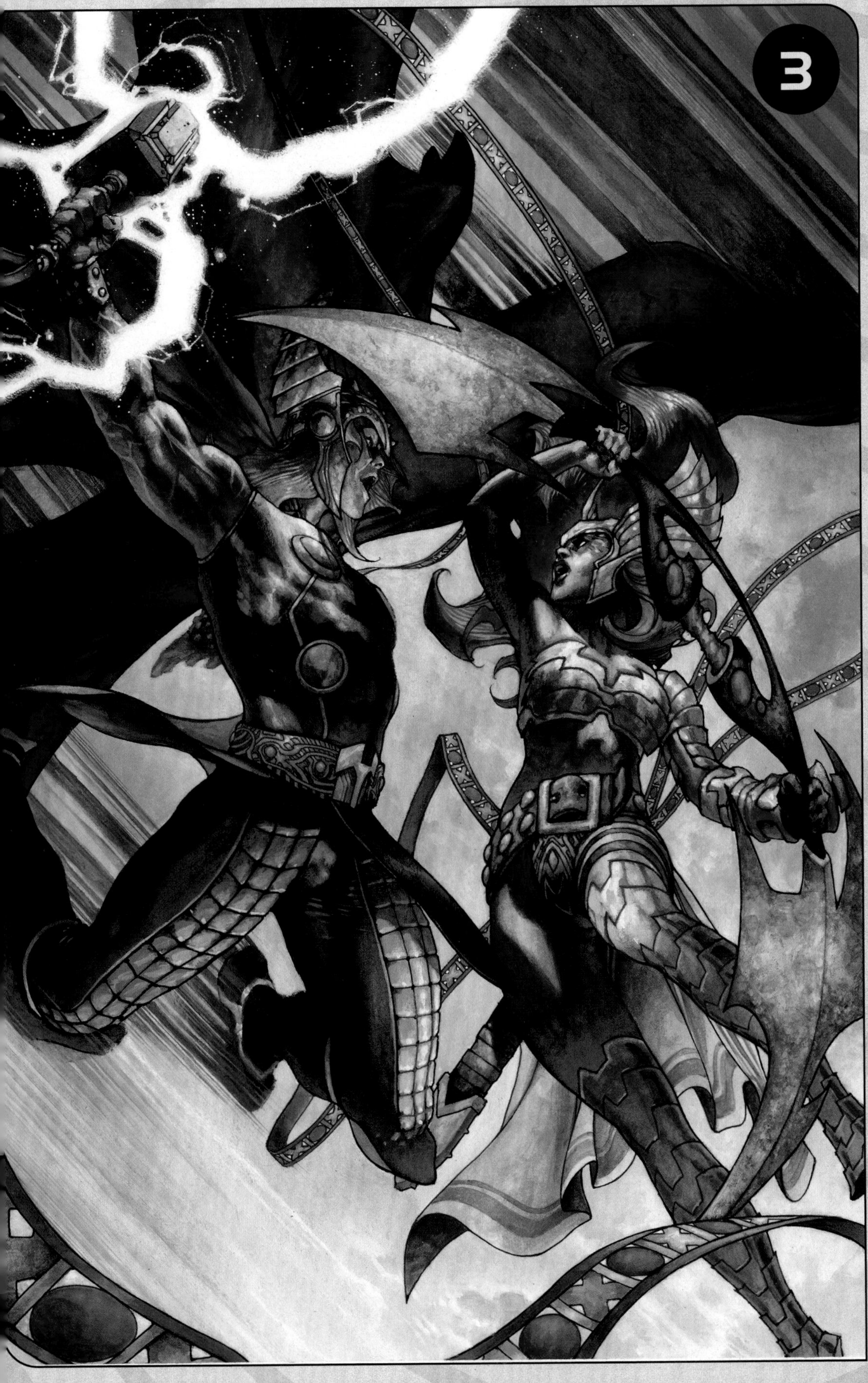
3

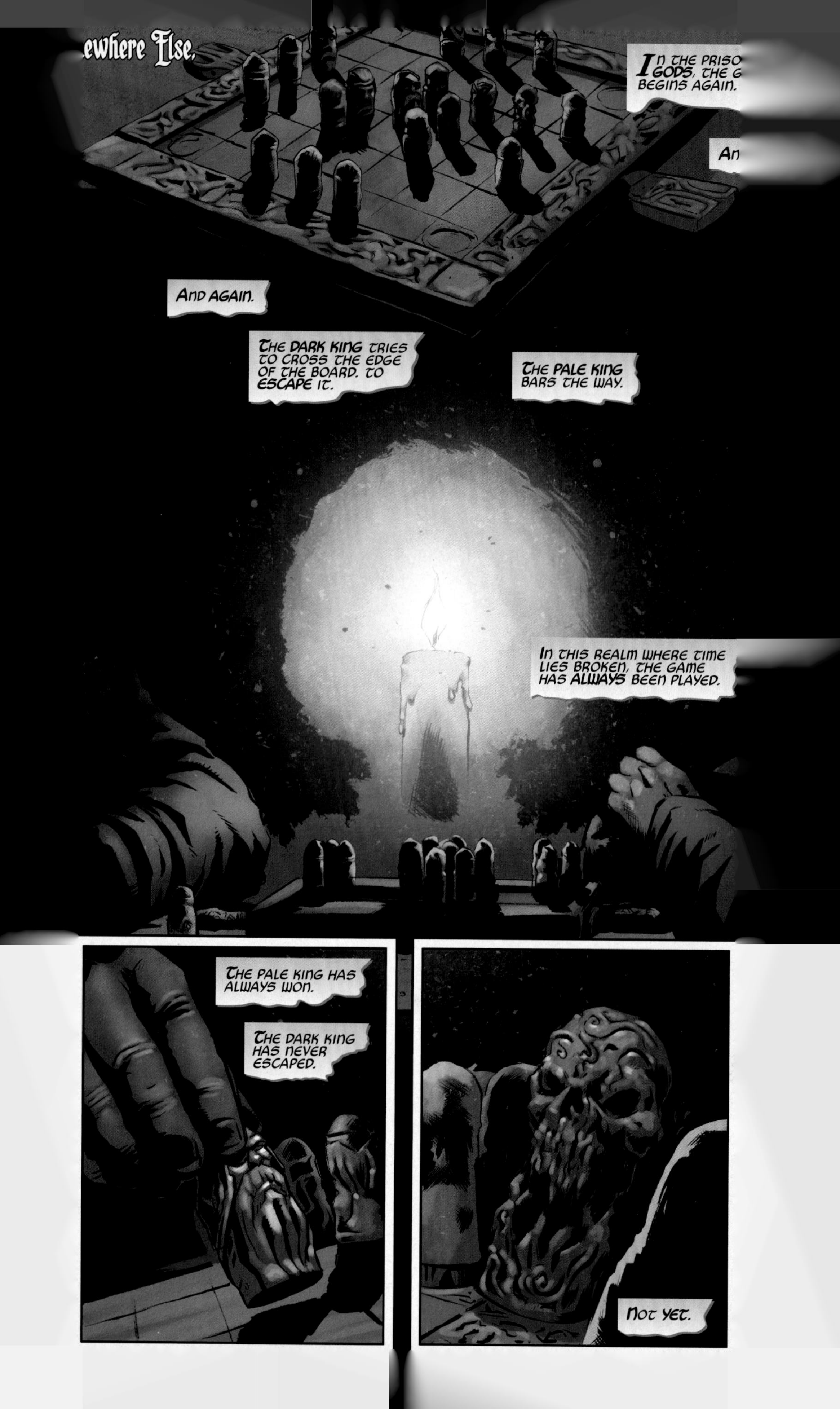

...ewhere Else,
In the priso... Gods, the g... begins again.
An...
And again.
The dark king tries to cross the edge of the board. To escape it.
The pale king bars the way.
In this realm where time lies broken, the game has always been played.
The pale king has always won.
The dark king has never escaped.
Not yet.

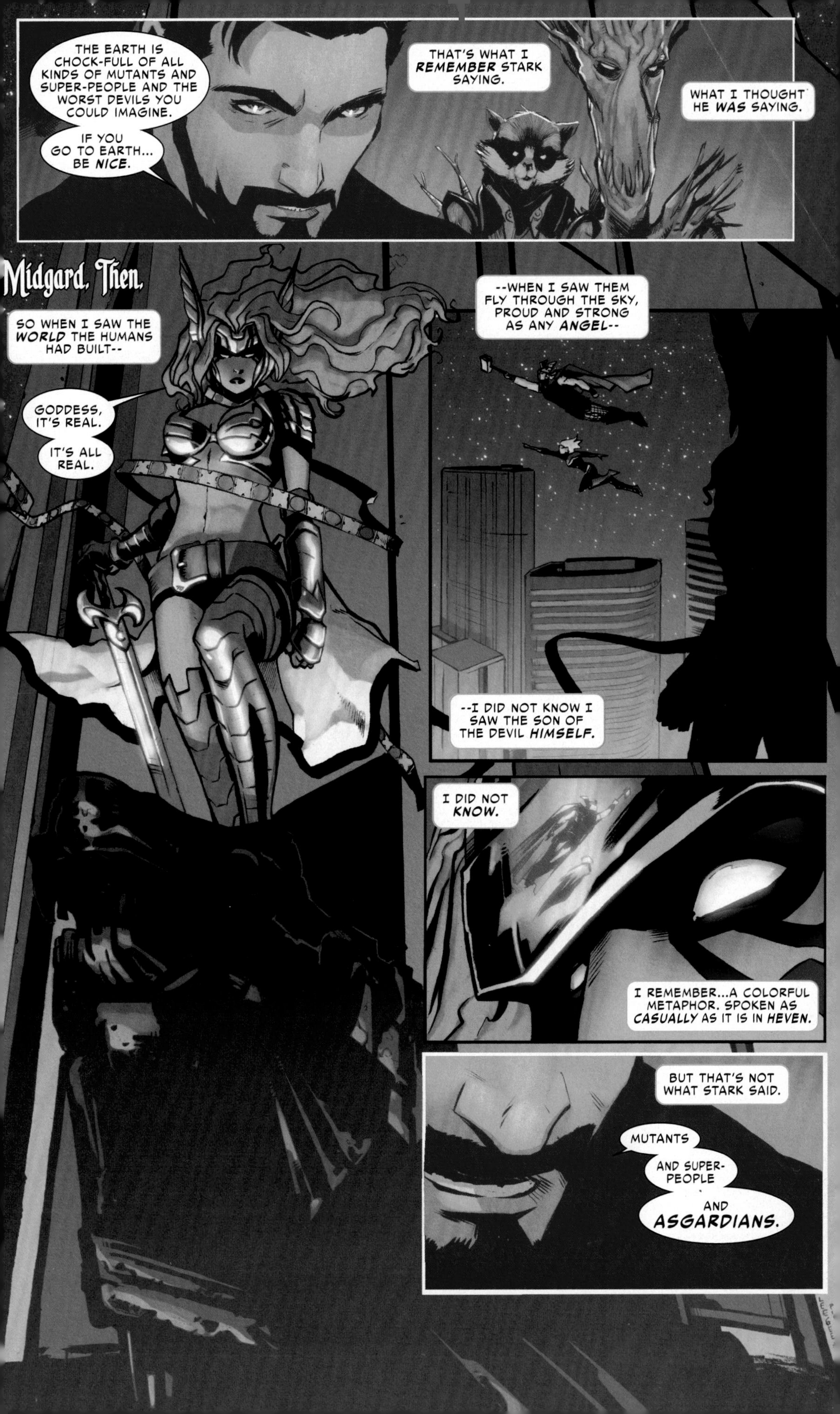
THE EARTH IS CHOCK-FULL OF ALL KINDS OF MUTANTS AND SUPER-PEOPLE AND THE WORST DEVILS YOU COULD IMAGINE.
IF YOU GO TO EARTH... BE NICE.
THAT'S WHAT I REMEMBER STARK SAYING.
WHAT I THOUGHT HE WAS SAYING.
Midgard, Then.
SO WHEN I SAW THE WORLD THE HUMANS HAD BUILT--
GODDESS, IT'S REAL.
IT'S ALL REAL.
--WHEN I SAW THEM FLY THROUGH THE SKY, PROUD AND STRONG AS ANY ANGEL--
--I DID NOT KNOW I SAW THE SON OF THE DEVIL HIMSELF.
I DID NOT KNOW.
I REMEMBER...A COLORFUL METAPHOR. SPOKEN AS CASUALLY AS IT IS IN HEVEN.
BUT THAT'S NOT WHAT STARK SAID.
MUTANTS
AND SUPER-PEOPLE
AND ASGARDIANS.

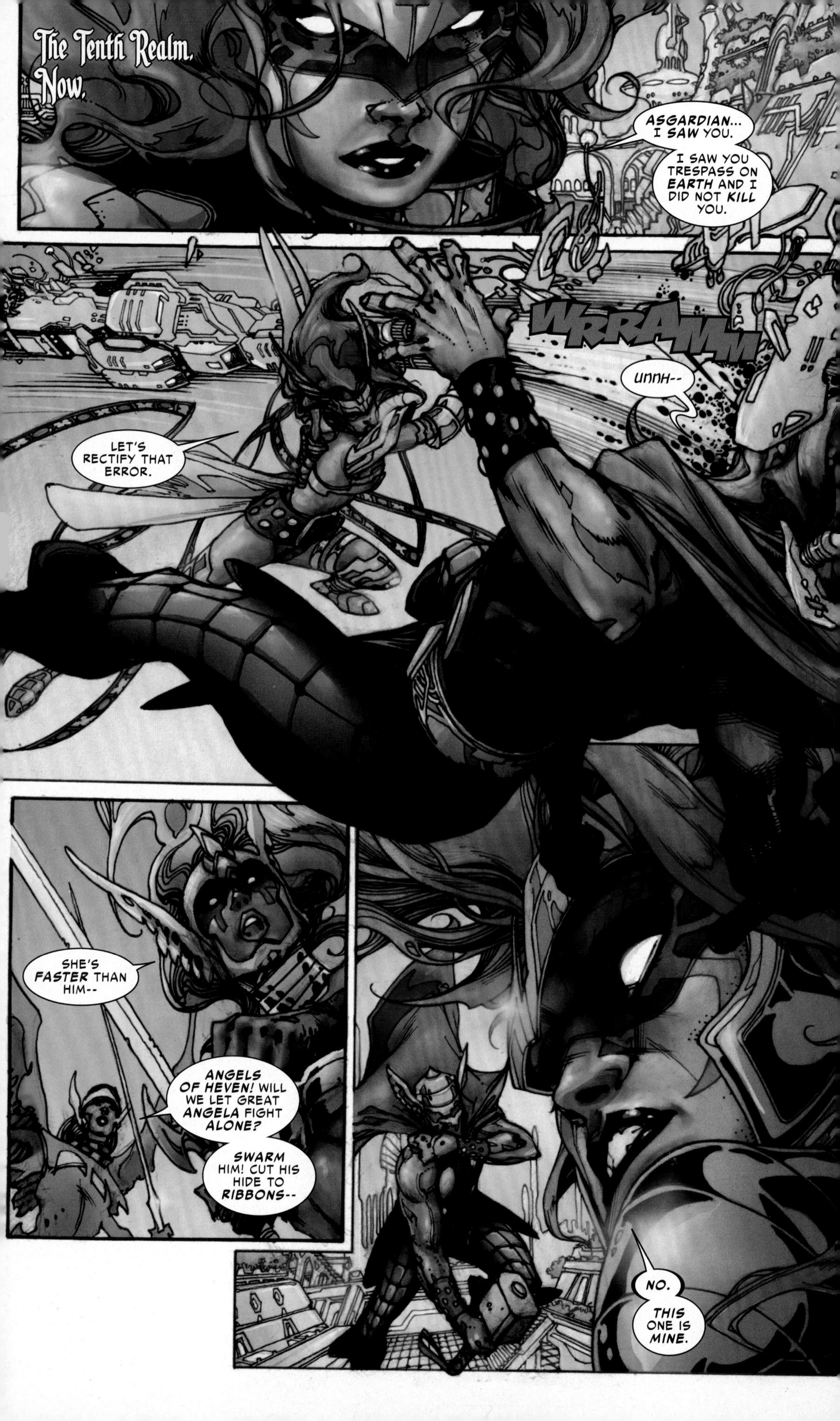
The Tenth Realm. Now.
ASGARDIAN... I SAW YOU.
I SAW YOU TRESPASS ON EARTH AND I DID NOT KILL YOU.
WRRAMM
UNNH--
LET'S RECTIFY THAT ERROR.
SHE'S FASTER THAN HIM--
ANGELS OF HEVEN! WILL WE LET GREAT ANGELA FIGHT ALONE?
SWARM HIM! CUT HIS HIDE TO RIBBONS--
NO.
THIS ONE IS MINE.

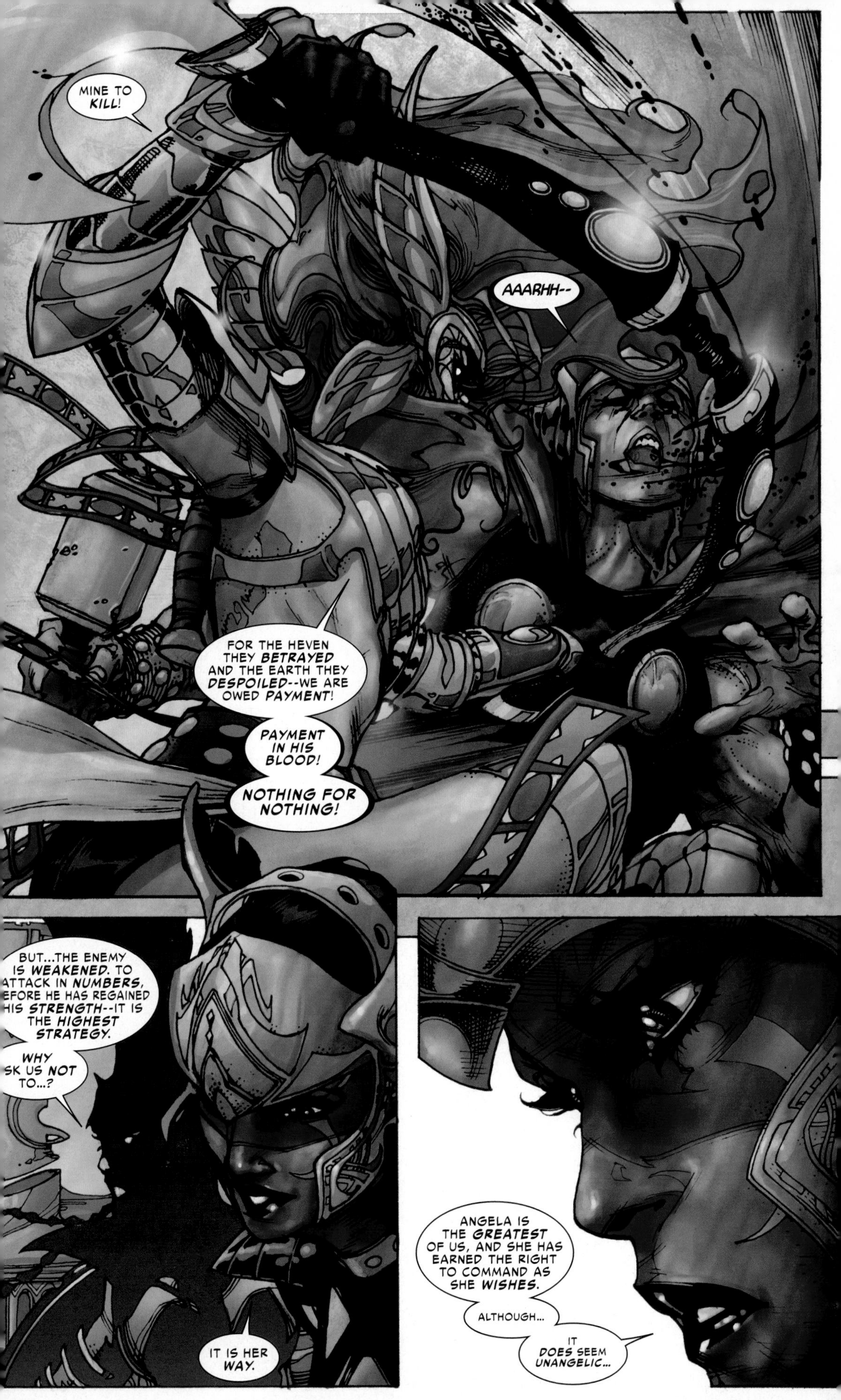

MINE TO KILL!
AAARHH--
FOR THE HEVEN THEY BETRAYED AND THE EARTH THEY DESPOILED--WE ARE OWED PAYMENT!
PAYMENT IN HIS BLOOD!
NOTHING FOR NOTHING!
BUT...THE ENEMY IS WEAKENED. TO ATTACK IN NUMBERS, EFORE HE HAS REGAINED HIS STRENGTH--IT IS THE HIGHEST STRATEGY.
WHY SK US NOT TO...?
IT IS HER WAY.
ANGELA IS THE GREATEST OF US, AND SHE HAS EARNED THE RIGHT TO COMMAND AS SHE WISHES.
ALTHOUGH...
IT DOES SEEM UNANGELIC...

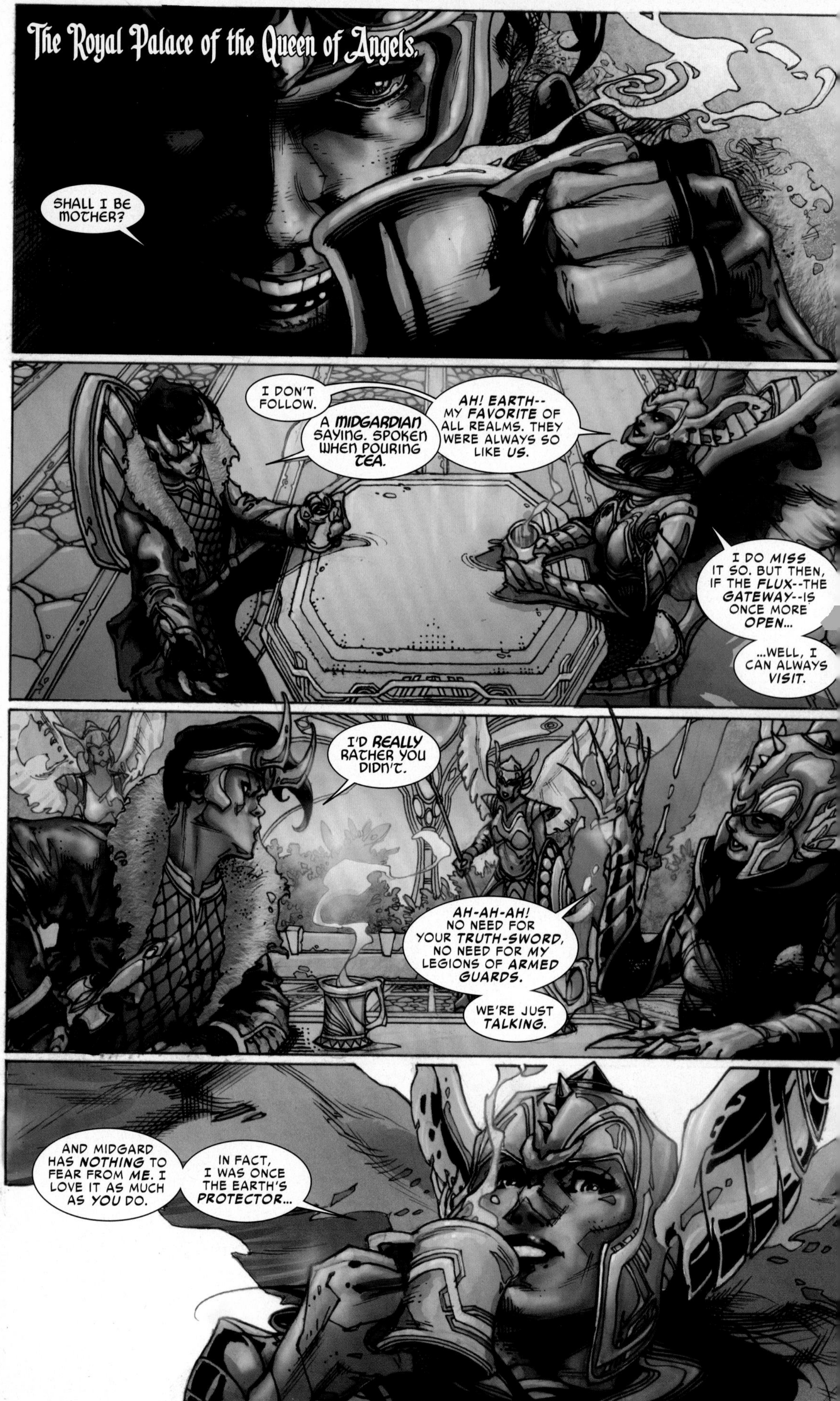
The Royal Palace of the Queen of Angels.
SHALL I BE MOTHER?
I DON'T FOLLOW.
A MIDGARDIAN SAYING. SPOKEN WHEN POURING TEA.
AH! EARTH-- MY FAVORITE OF ALL REALMS. THEY WERE ALWAYS SO LIKE US.
I DO MISS IT SO. BUT THEN, IF THE FLUX--THE GATEWAY--IS ONCE MORE OPEN...
...WELL, I CAN ALWAYS VISIT.
I'D REALLY RATHER YOU DIDN'T.
AH-AH-AH! NO NEED FOR YOUR TRUTH-SWORD, NO NEED FOR MY LEGIONS OF ARMED GUARDS.
WE'RE JUST TALKING.
AND MIDGARD HAS NOTHING TO FEAR FROM ME. I LOVE IT AS MUCH AS YOU DO.
IN FACT, I WAS ONCE THE EARTH'S PROTECTOR...

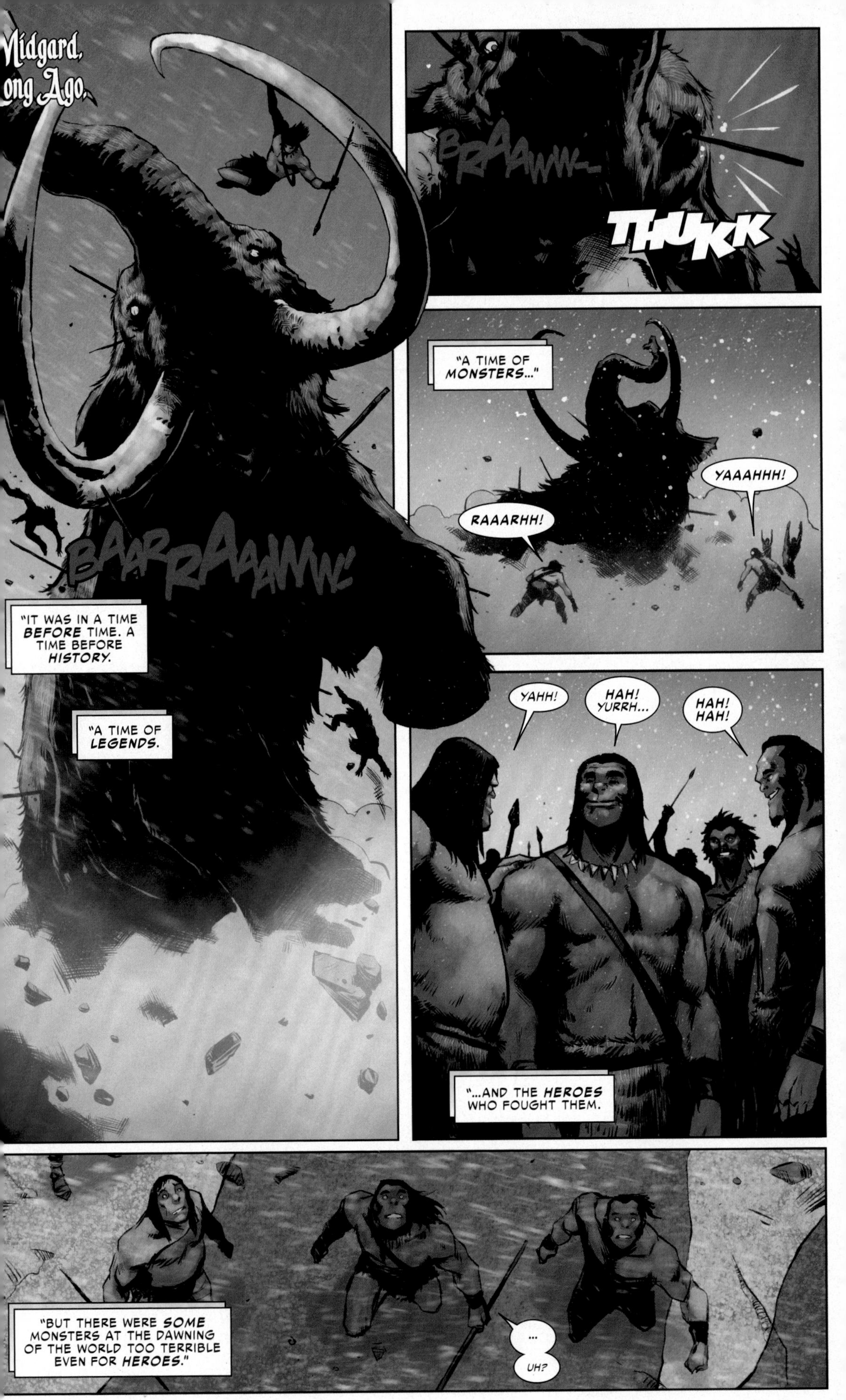
Midgard, Long Ago.
BAARRAAAWW!
"IT WAS IN A TIME BEFORE TIME. A TIME BEFORE HISTORY.
"A TIME OF LEGENDS.
BRAAWWW
THUKK
"A TIME OF MONSTERS..."
YAAAHHH!
RAAARHH!
YAHH!
HAH! YURRH...
HAH! HAH!
"...AND THE HEROES WHO FOUGHT THEM.
"BUT THERE WERE SOME MONSTERS AT THE DAWNING OF THE WORLD TOO TERRIBLE EVEN FOR HEROES."
...
UH?

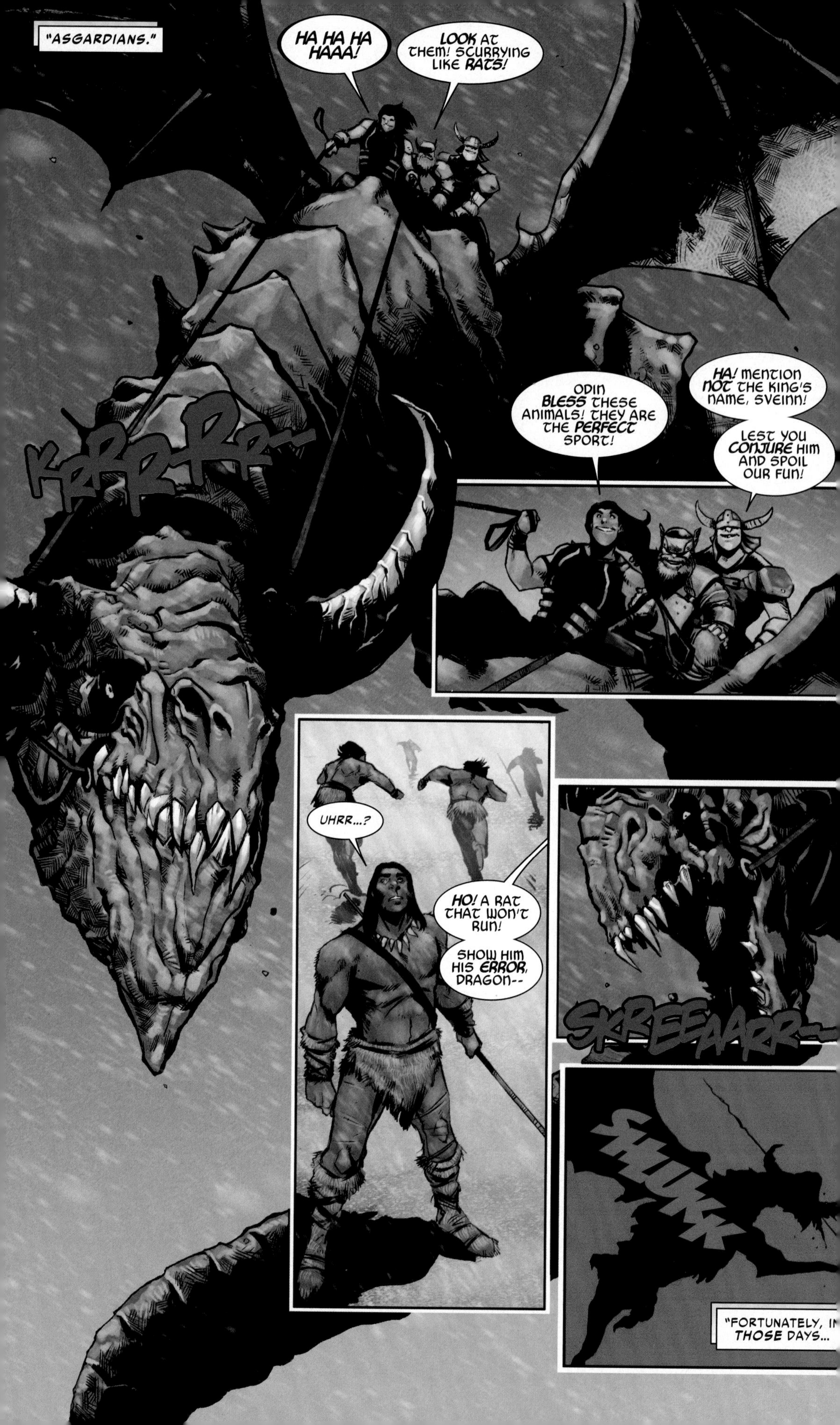
"ASGARDIANS."
HA HA HA HAAA!
LOOK AT THEM! SCURRYING LIKE RATS!
KRRR-RR--
ODIN BLESS THESE ANIMALS! THEY ARE THE PERFECT SPORT!
HA! MENTION NOT THE KING'S NAME, SVEINN!
LEST YOU CONJURE HIM AND SPOIL OUR FUN!
UHRR...?
HO! A RAT THAT WON'T RUN!
SHOW HIM HIS ERROR, DRAGON--
SKREEEAARR--
SHUNK
"FORTUNATELY, IN THOSE DAYS...

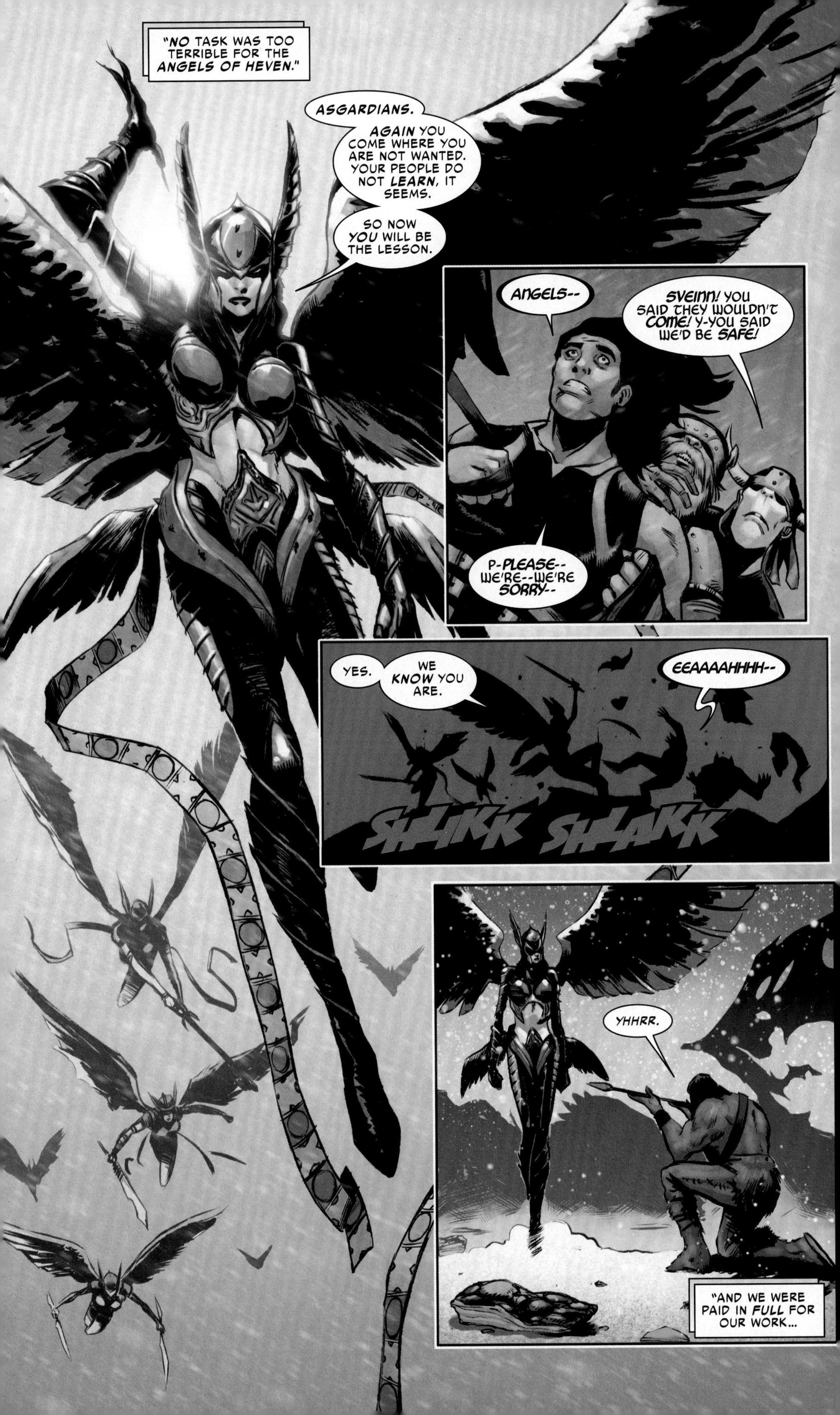
"NO TASK WAS TOO TERRIBLE FOR THE ANGELS OF HEVEN."
ASGARDIANS.
AGAIN YOU COME WHERE YOU ARE NOT WANTED. YOUR PEOPLE DO NOT LEARN, IT SEEMS.
SO NOW YOU WILL BE THE LESSON.
ANGELS--
SVEINN! YOU SAID THEY WOULDN'T COME! Y-YOU SAID WE'D BE SAFE!
P-PLEASE-- WE'RE--WE'RE SORRY--
YES.
WE KNOW YOU ARE.
EEAAAAAHHHH--
SHLIKK SHLAKK
YHHRR.
"AND WE WERE PAID IN FULL FOR OUR WORK...

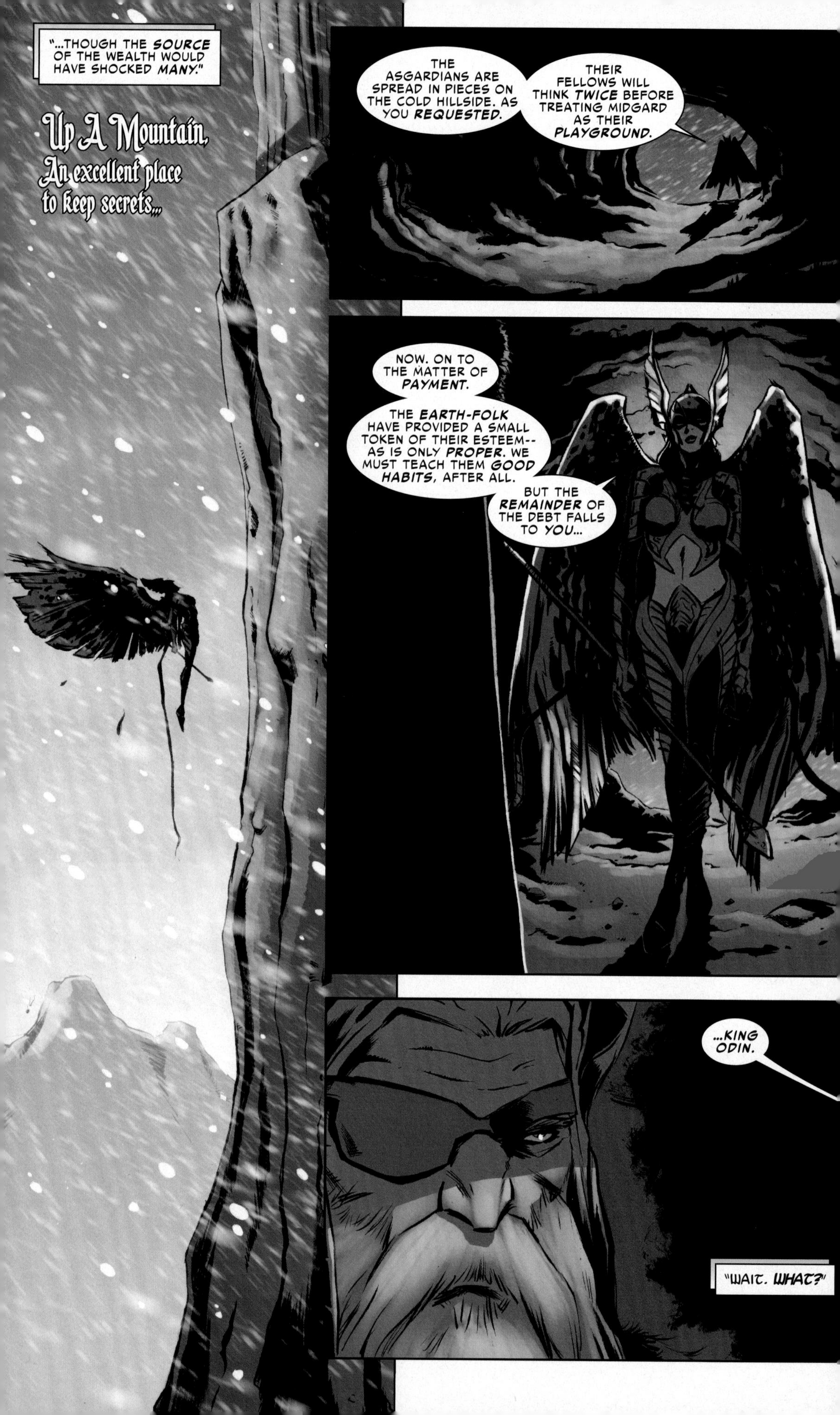
"...THOUGH THE SOURCE OF THE WEALTH WOULD HAVE SHOCKED MANY."
Up A Mountain, An excellent place to keep secrets...
THE ASGARDIANS ARE SPREAD IN PIECES ON THE COLD HILLSIDE. AS YOU REQUESTED.
THEIR FELLOWS WILL THINK TWICE BEFORE TREATING MIDGARD AS THEIR PLAYGROUND.
NOW. ON TO THE MATTER OF PAYMENT.
THE EARTH-FOLK HAVE PROVIDED A SMALL TOKEN OF THEIR ESTEEM-- AS IS ONLY PROPER. WE MUST TEACH THEM GOOD HABITS, AFTER ALL.
BUT THE REMAINDER OF THE DEBT FALLS TO YOU...
...KING ODIN.
"WAIT. WHAT?"

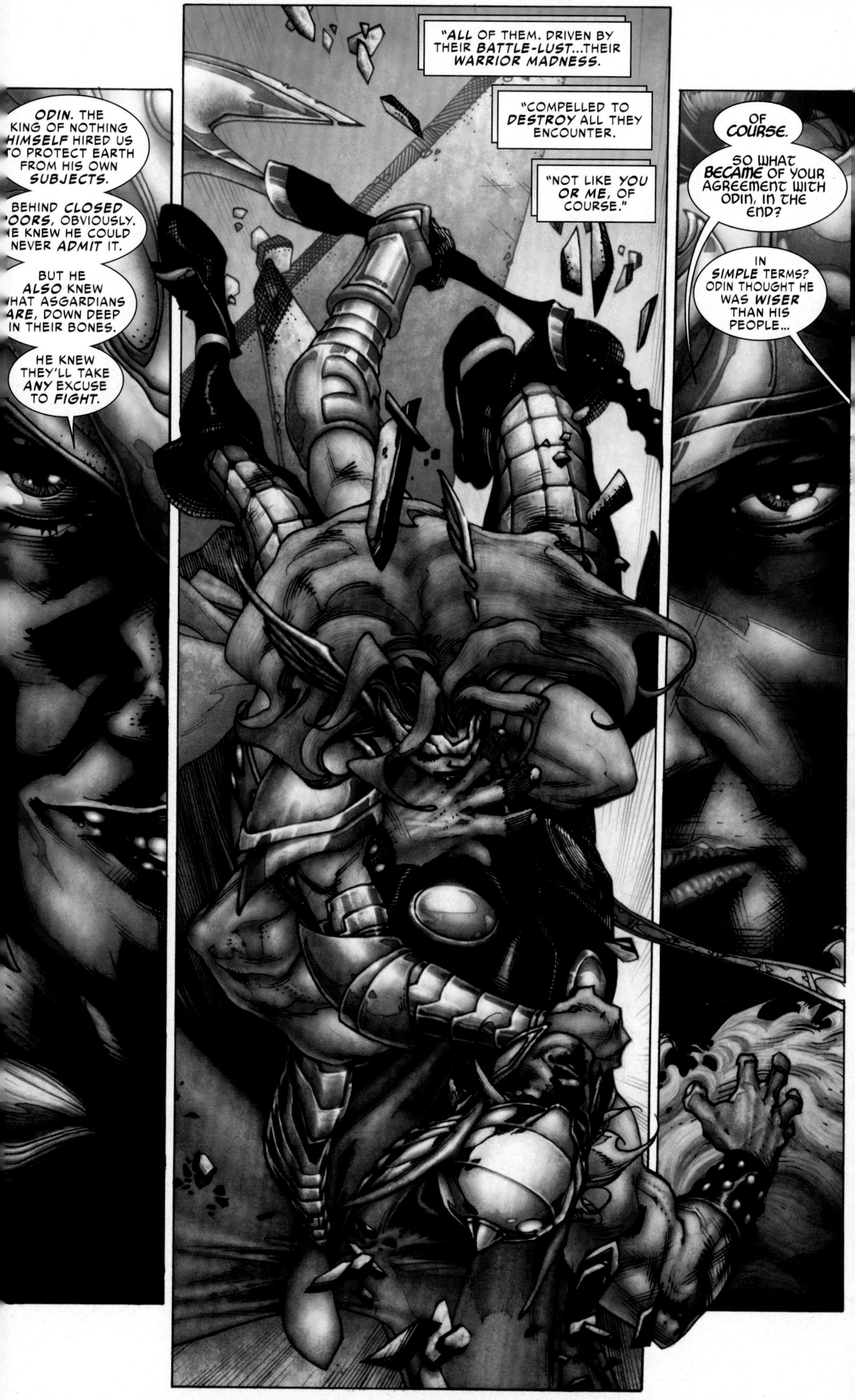
ODIN. THE KING OF NOTHING HIMSELF HIRED US TO PROTECT EARTH FROM HIS OWN SUBJECTS.
BEHIND CLOSED OORS, OBVIOUSLY. E KNEW HE COULD NEVER ADMIT IT.
BUT HE ALSO KNEW HAT ASGARDIANS ARE, DOWN DEEP IN THEIR BONES.
HE KNEW THEY'LL TAKE ANY EXCUSE TO FIGHT.
"ALL OF THEM. DRIVEN BY THEIR BATTLE-LUST...THEIR WARRIOR MADNESS.
"COMPELLED TO DESTROY ALL THEY ENCOUNTER.
"NOT LIKE YOU OR ME, OF COURSE."
OF COURSE.
SO WHAT BECAME OF YOUR AGREEMENT WITH ODIN, IN THE END?
IN SIMPLE TERMS? ODIN THOUGHT HE WAS WISER THAN HIS PEOPLE...

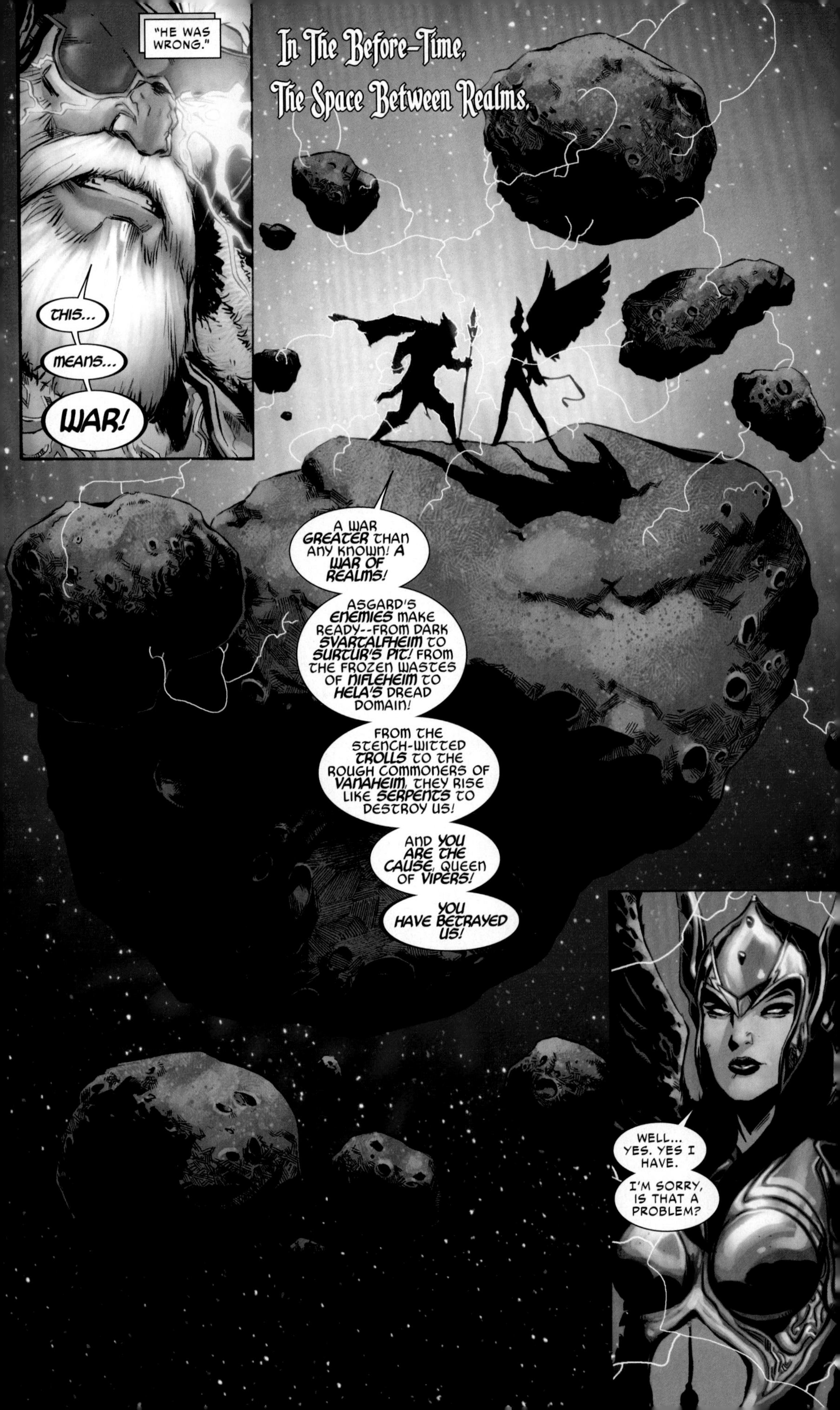
"HE WAS WRONG."
THIS...
MEANS...
WAR!
In The Before-Time, The Space Between Realms.
A WAR GREATER THAN ANY KNOWN! A WAR OF REALMS!
ASGARD'S ENEMIES MAKE READY--FROM DARK SVARTALFHEIM TO SURTUR'S PIT! FROM THE FROZEN WASTES OF NIFLEHEIM TO HELA'S DREAD DOMAIN!
FROM THE STENCH-WITTED TROLLS TO THE ROUGH COMMONERS OF VANAHEIM, THEY RISE LIKE SERPENTS TO DESTROY US!
AND YOU ARE THE CAUSE, QUEEN OF VIPERS!
YOU HAVE BETRAYED US!
WELL... YES. YES I HAVE.
I'M SORRY, IS THAT A PROBLEM?

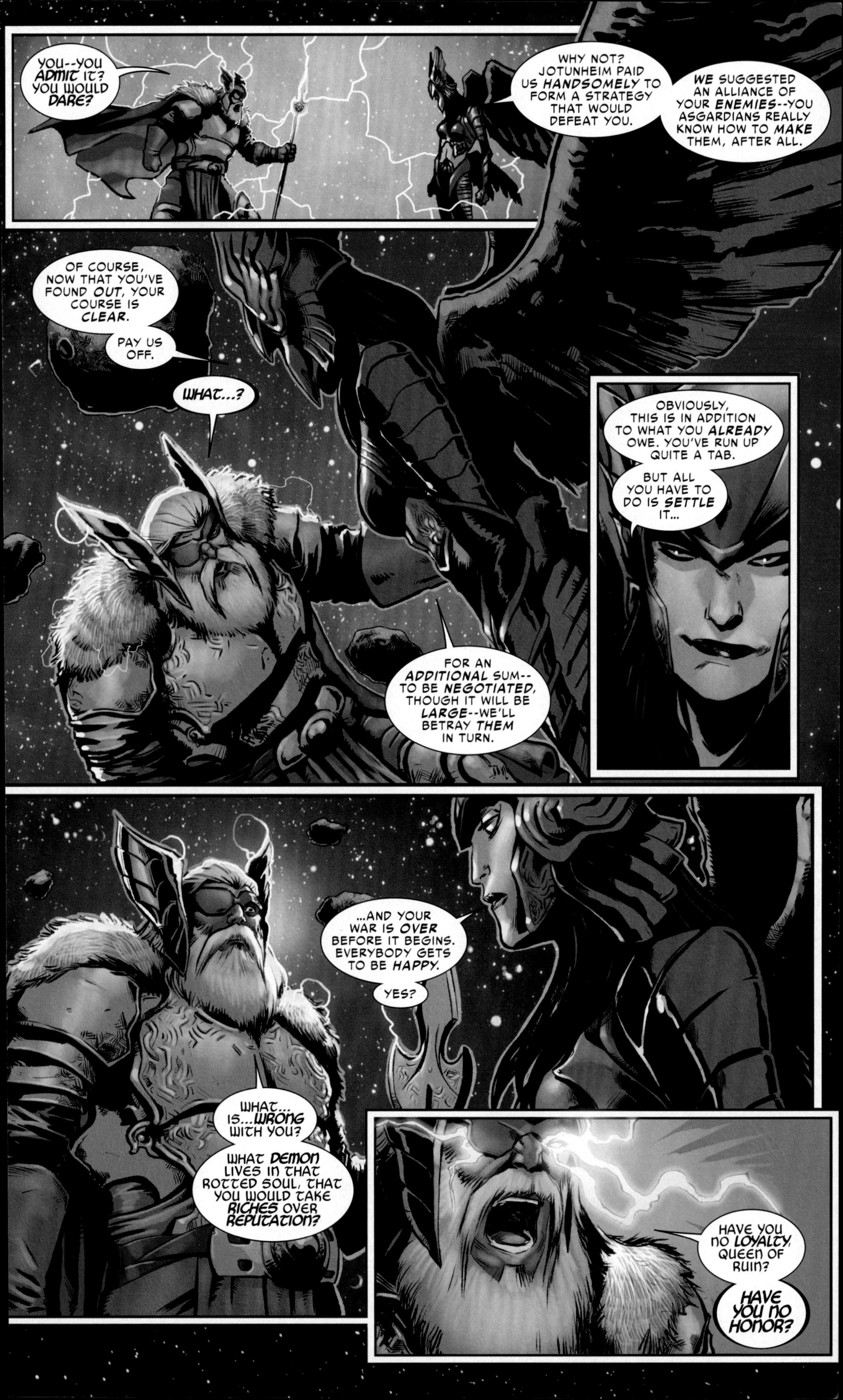

YOU--YOU ADMIT IT? YOU WOULD DARE?
WHY NOT? JOTUNHEIM PAID US HANDSOMELY TO FORM A STRATEGY THAT WOULD DEFEAT YOU.
WE SUGGESTED AN ALLIANCE OF YOUR ENEMIES--YOU ASGARDIANS REALLY KNOW HOW TO MAKE THEM, AFTER ALL.
OF COURSE, NOW THAT YOU'VE FOUND OUT, YOUR COURSE IS CLEAR.
PAY US OFF.
WHAT...?
OBVIOUSLY, THIS IS IN ADDITION TO WHAT YOU ALREADY OWE. YOU'VE RUN UP QUITE A TAB.
BUT ALL YOU HAVE TO DO IS SETTLE IT...
FOR AN ADDITIONAL SUM--TO BE NEGOTIATED, THOUGH IT WILL BE LARGE--WE'LL BETRAY THEM IN TURN.
...AND YOUR WAR IS OVER BEFORE IT BEGINS. EVERYBODY GETS TO BE HAPPY.
YES?
WHAT... IS...WRONG WITH YOU?
WHAT DEMON LIVES IN THAT ROTTED SOUL, THAT YOU WOULD TAKE RICHES OVER REPUTATION?
HAVE YOU NO LOYALTY, QUEEN OF RUIN?
HAVE YOU NO HONOR?

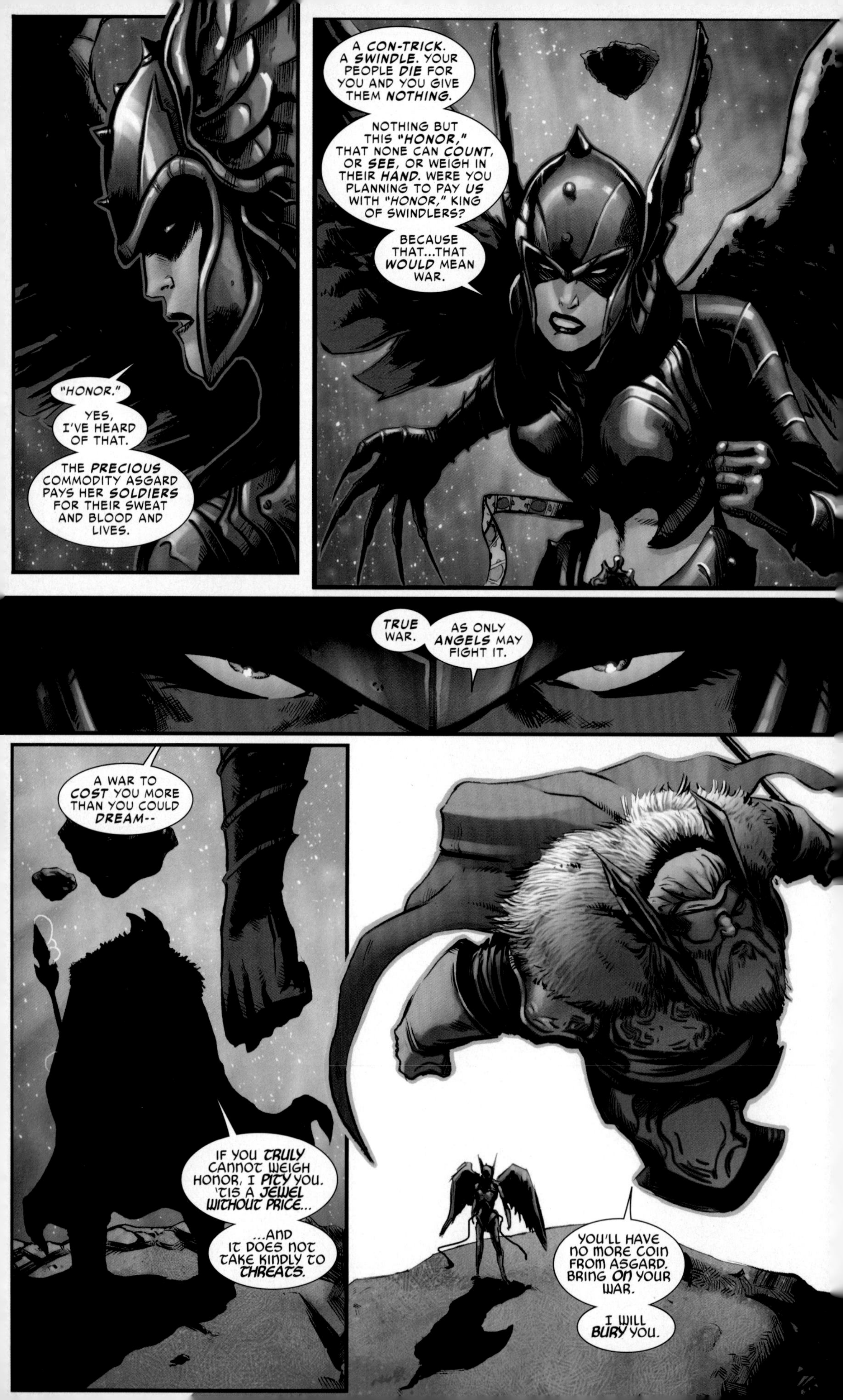

"HONOR."
YES, I'VE HEARD OF THAT.
THE PRECIOUS COMMODITY ASGARD PAYS HER SOLDIERS FOR THEIR SWEAT AND BLOOD AND LIVES.
A CON-TRICK. A SWINDLE. YOUR PEOPLE DIE FOR YOU AND YOU GIVE THEM NOTHING.
NOTHING BUT THIS "HONOR," THAT NONE CAN COUNT, OR SEE, OR WEIGH IN THEIR HAND. WERE YOU PLANNING TO PAY US WITH "HONOR," KING OF SWINDLERS?
BECAUSE THAT...THAT WOULD MEAN WAR.
TRUE WAR.
AS ONLY ANGELS MAY FIGHT IT.
A WAR TO COST YOU MORE THAN YOU COULD DREAM--
IF YOU TRULY CANNOT WEIGH HONOR, I PITY YOU. 'TIS A JEWEL WITHOUT PRICE...
...AND IT DOES NOT TAKE KINDLY TO THREATS.
YOU'LL HAVE NO MORE COIN FROM ASGARD. BRING ON YOUR WAR.
I WILL BURY YOU.

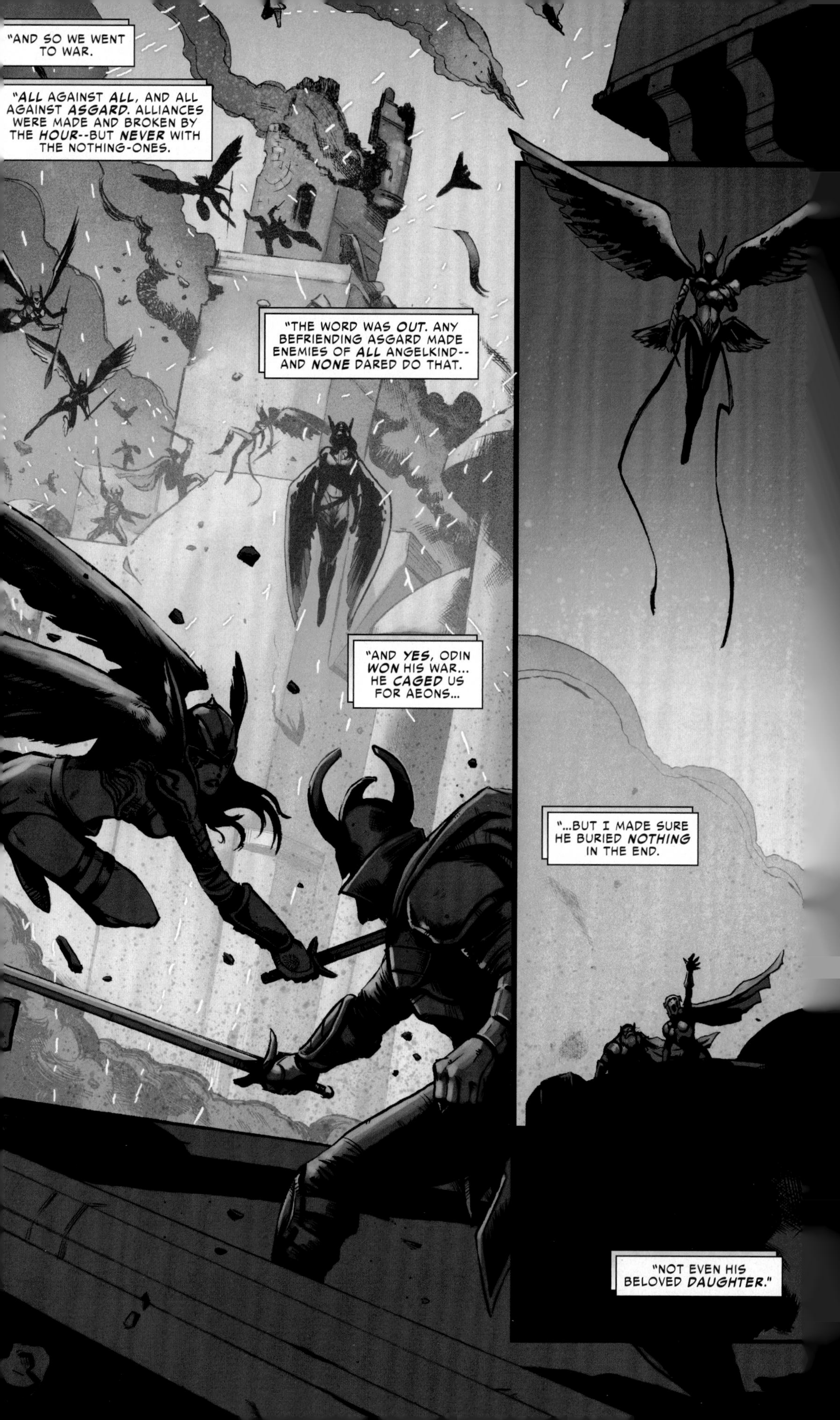
"AND SO WE WENT TO WAR.
"ALL AGAINST ALL, AND ALL AGAINST ASGARD. ALLIANCES WERE MADE AND BROKEN BY THE HOUR--BUT NEVER WITH THE NOTHING-ONES.
"THE WORD WAS OUT. ANY BEFRIENDING ASGARD MADE ENEMIES OF ALL ANGELKIND--AND NONE DARED DO THAT.
"AND YES, ODIN WON HIS WAR... HE CAGED US FOR AEONS...
"...BUT I MADE SURE HE BURIED NOTHING IN THE END.
"NOT EVEN HIS BELOVED DAUGHTER."

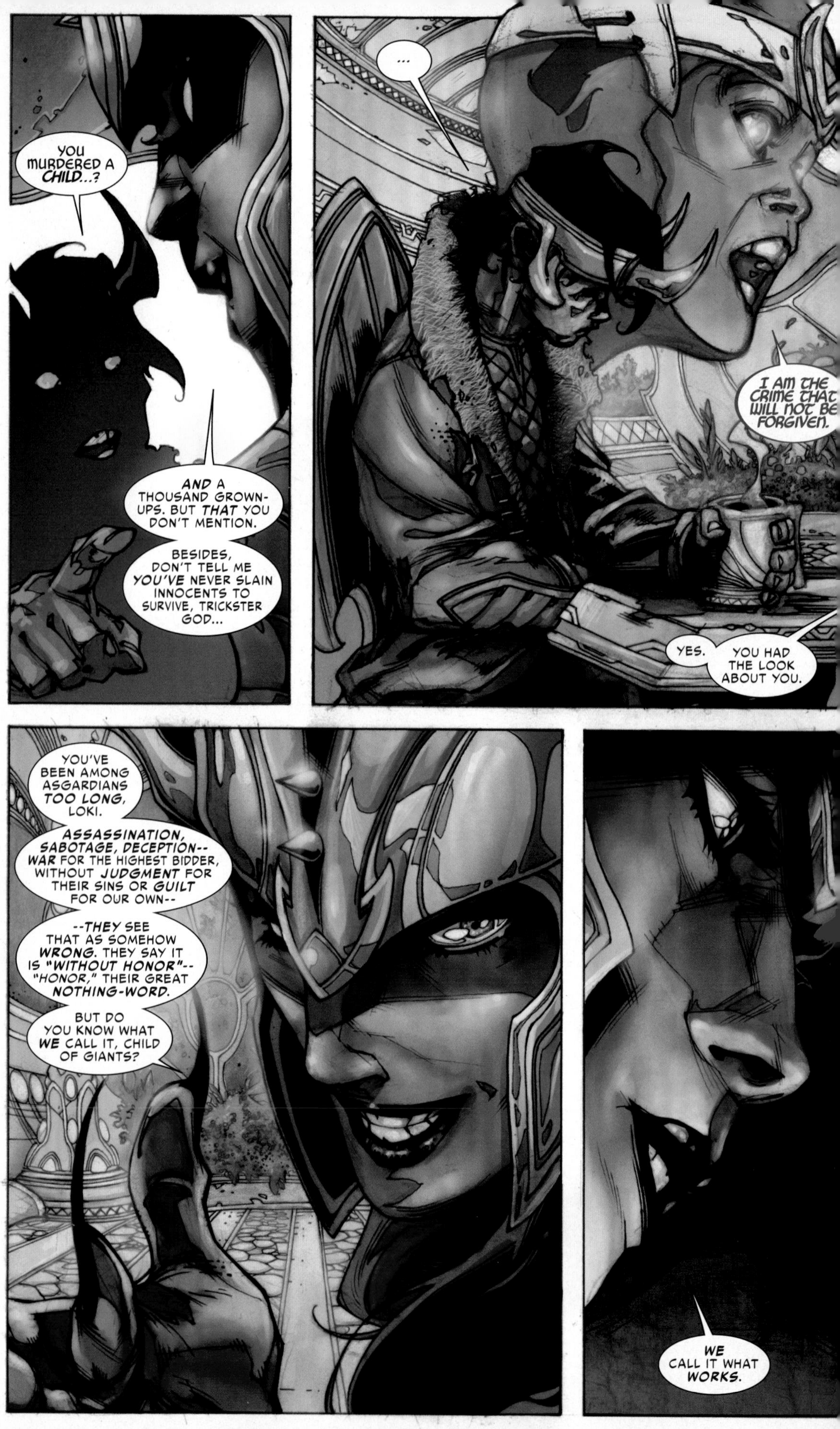
YOU MURDERED A CHILD...?
...
AND A THOUSAND GROWN-UPS. BUT THAT YOU DON'T MENTION.
BESIDES, DON'T TELL ME YOU'VE NEVER SLAIN INNOCENTS TO SURVIVE, TRICKSTER GOD...
I AM THE CRIME THAT WILL NOT BE FORGIVEN.
YES.
YOU HAD THE LOOK ABOUT YOU.
YOU'VE BEEN AMONG ASGARDIANS TOO LONG, LOKI.
ASSASSINATION, SABOTAGE, DECEPTION-- WAR FOR THE HIGHEST BIDDER, WITHOUT JUDGMENT FOR THEIR SINS OR GUILT FOR OUR OWN--
--THEY SEE THAT AS SOMEHOW WRONG. THEY SAY IT IS "WITHOUT HONOR"-- "HONOR," THEIR GREAT NOTHING-WORD.
BUT DO YOU KNOW WHAT WE CALL IT, CHILD OF GIANTS?
WE CALL IT WHAT WORKS.

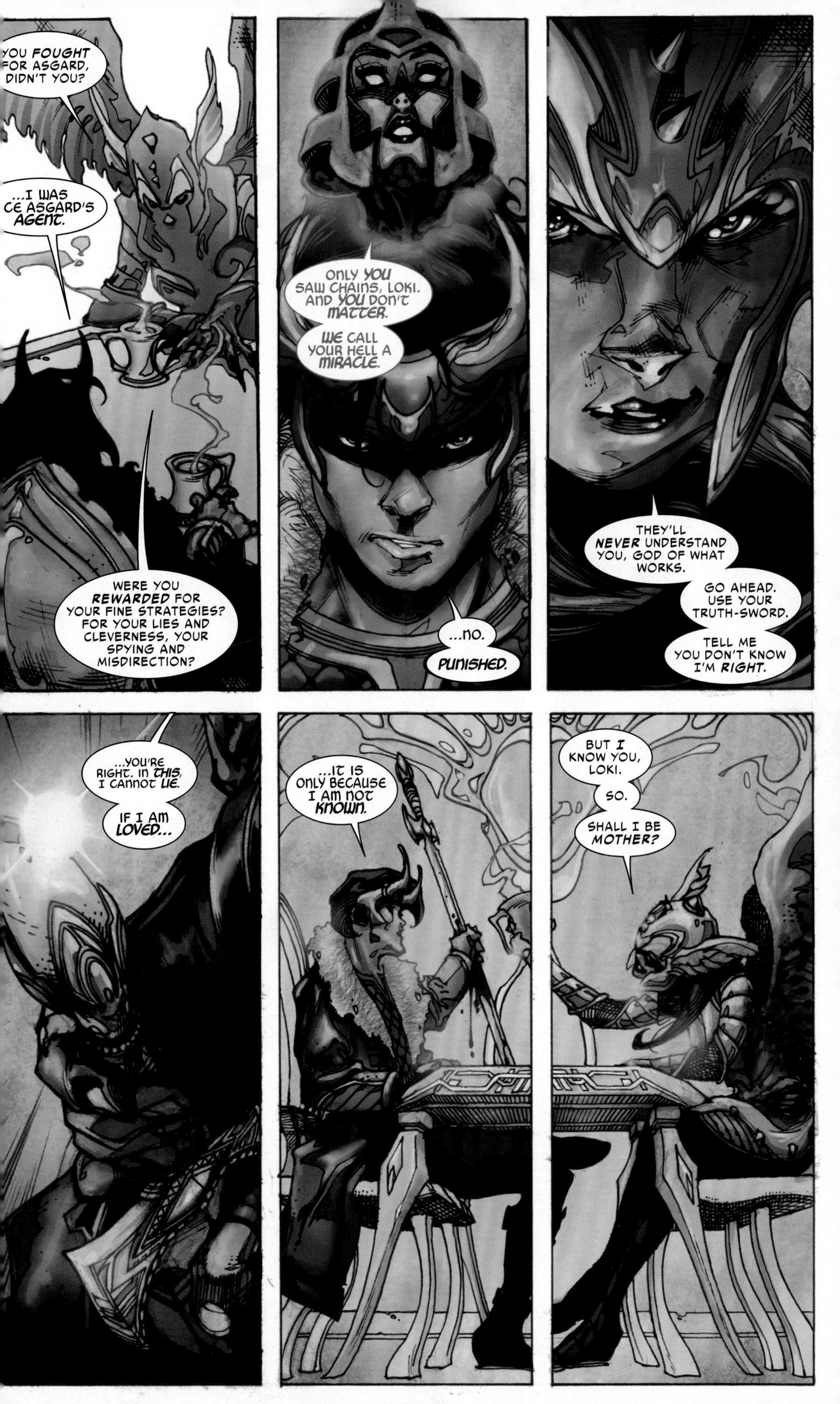
YOU FOUGHT FOR ASGARD, DIDN'T YOU?
...I WAS CE ASGARD'S AGENT.
WERE YOU REWARDED FOR YOUR FINE STRATEGIES? FOR YOUR LIES AND CLEVERNESS, YOUR SPYING AND MISDIRECTION?
ONLY YOU SAW CHAINS, LOKI. AND YOU DON'T MATTER.
WE CALL YOUR HELL A MIRACLE.
...NO.
PUNISHED.
THEY'LL NEVER UNDERSTAND YOU, GOD OF WHAT WORKS.
GO AHEAD. USE YOUR TRUTH-SWORD.
TELL ME YOU DON'T KNOW I'M RIGHT.
...YOU'RE RIGHT. IN THIS, I CANNOT LIE.
IF I AM LOVED...
...IT IS ONLY BECAUSE I AM NOT KNOWN.
BUT I KNOW YOU, LOKI.
SO.
SHALL I BE MOTHER?

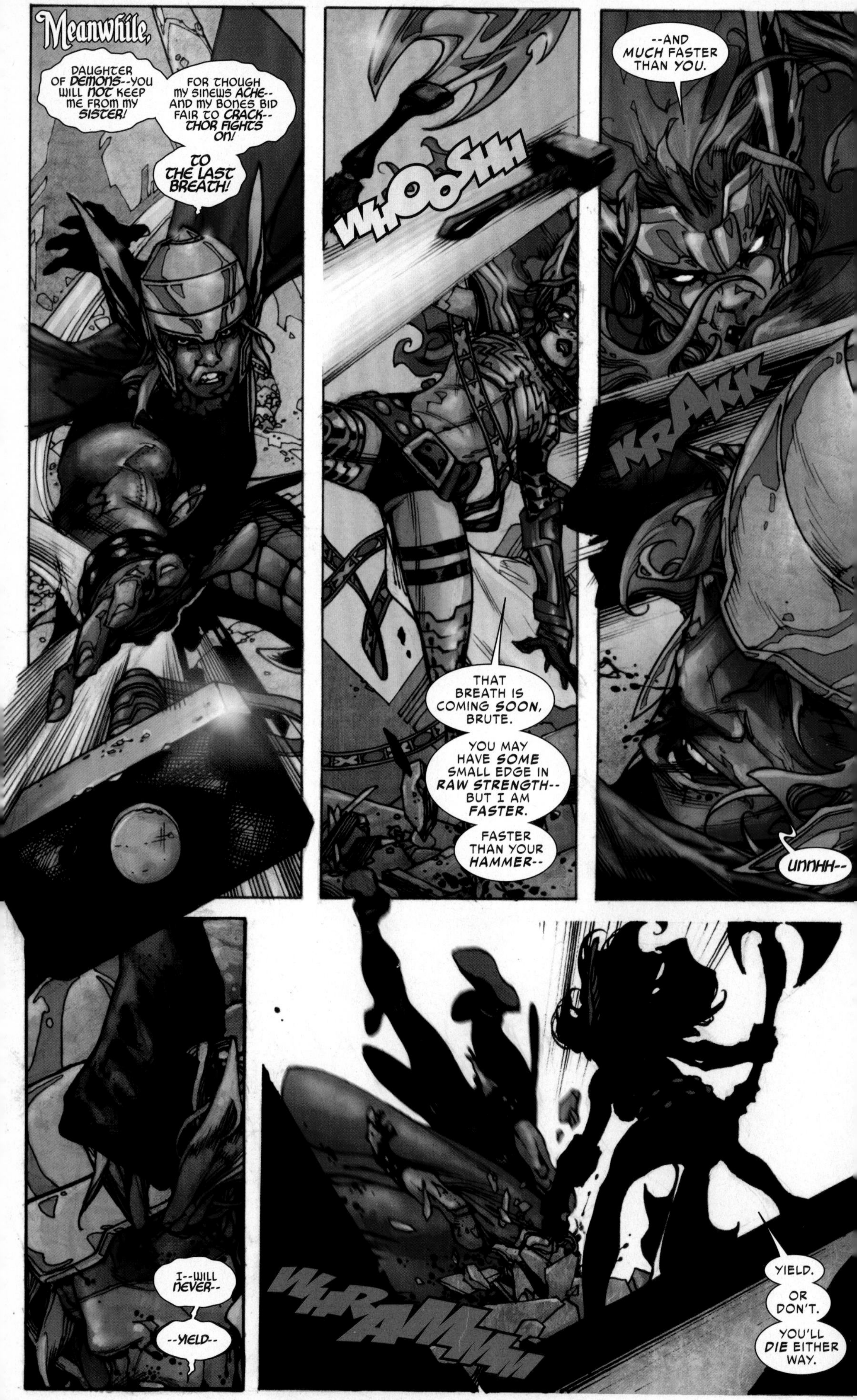
Meanwhile,
DAUGHTER OF DEMONS--YOU WILL NOT KEEP ME FROM MY SISTER!
FOR THOUGH MY SINEWS ACHE--AND MY BONES BID FAIR TO CRACK--THOR FIGHTS ON!
TO THE LAST BREATH!
WHOOSHH
THAT BREATH IS COMING SOON, BRUTE.
YOU MAY HAVE SOME SMALL EDGE IN RAW STRENGTH--BUT I AM FASTER.
FASTER THAN YOUR HAMMER--
--AND MUCH FASTER THAN YOU.
KRAKK
UNNHH--
I--WILL NEVER--
--YIELD--
WHRAMMM
YIELD.
OR DON'T.
YOU'LL DIE EITHER WAY.

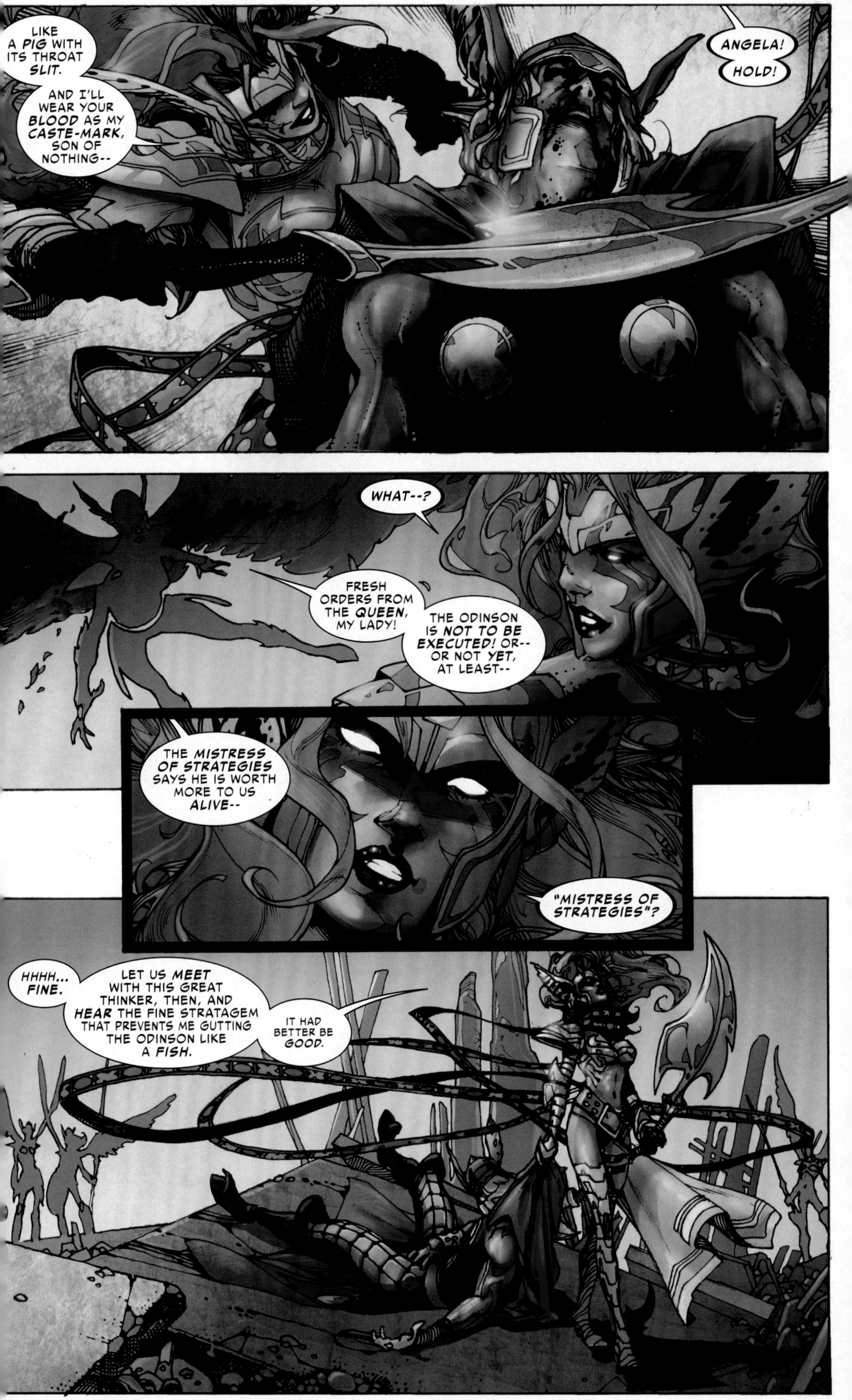
LIKE A *PIG* WITH ITS THROAT *SLIT*.
AND I'LL WEAR YOUR *BLOOD* AS MY *CASTE-MARK*, SON OF NOTHING--
ANGELA!
HOLD!
WHAT--?
FRESH ORDERS FROM THE *QUEEN*, MY LADY!
THE ODINSON IS *NOT TO BE EXECUTED!* OR-- OR NOT *YET*, AT LEAST--
THE *MISTRESS OF STRATEGIES* SAYS HE IS WORTH MORE TO US *ALIVE*--
"MISTRESS OF STRATEGIES"?
HHHH... *FINE*.
LET US *MEET* WITH THIS GREAT THINKER, THEN, AND *HEAR* THE FINE STRATAGEM THAT PREVENTS ME GUTTING THE ODINSON LIKE A *FISH*.
IT HAD BETTER BE *GOOD*.

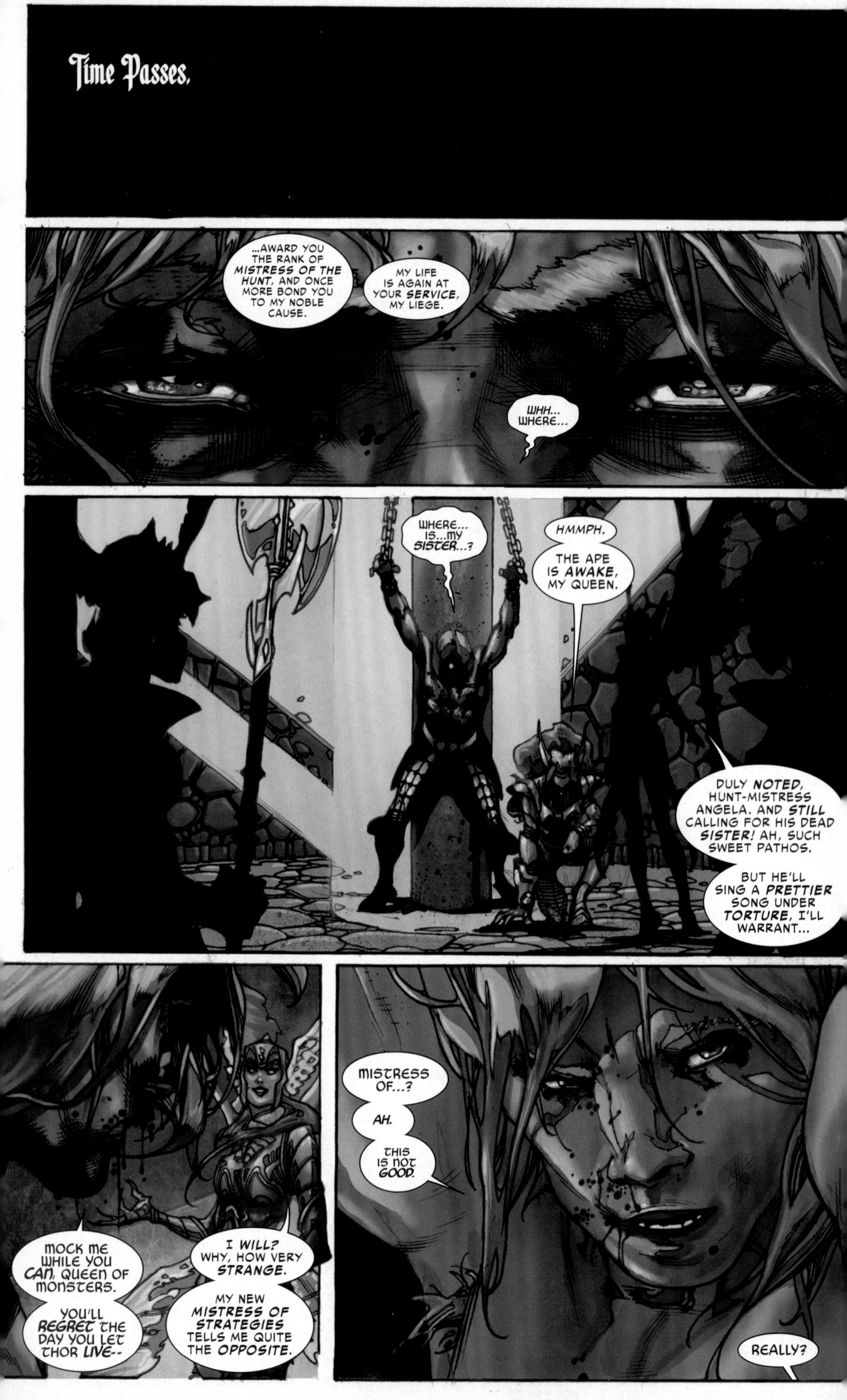
Time Passes.
...AWARD YOU THE RANK OF MISTRESS OF THE HUNT, AND ONCE MORE BOND YOU TO MY NOBLE CAUSE.
MY LIFE IS AGAIN AT YOUR SERVICE, MY LIEGE.
WHH... WHERE...
WHERE... IS...MY SISTER...?
HMMPH.
THE APE IS AWAKE, MY QUEEN.
DULY NOTED, HUNT-MISTRESS ANGELA. AND STILL CALLING FOR HIS DEAD SISTER! AH, SUCH SWEET PATHOS.
BUT HE'LL SING A PRETTIER SONG UNDER TORTURE, I'LL WARRANT...
MOCK ME WHILE YOU CAN, QUEEN OF MONSTERS.
YOU'LL REGRET THE DAY YOU LET THOR LIVE--
I WILL? WHY, HOW VERY STRANGE.
MY NEW MISTRESS OF STRATEGIES TELLS ME QUITE THE OPPOSITE.
MISTRESS OF...?
AH.
THIS IS NOT GOOD.
REALLY?

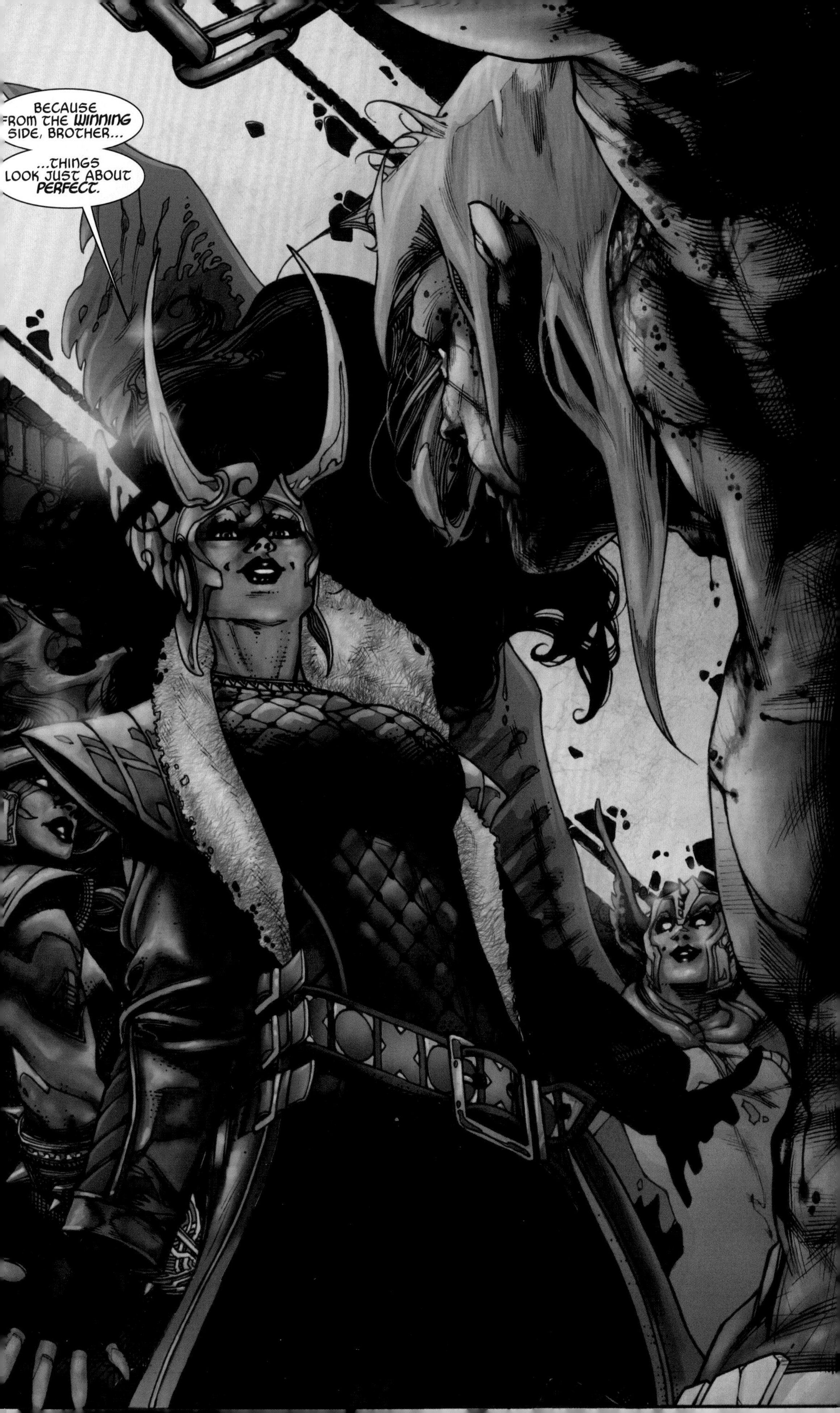
BECAUSE FROM THE WINNING SIDE, BROTHER...
...THINGS LOOK JUST ABOUT PERFECT.

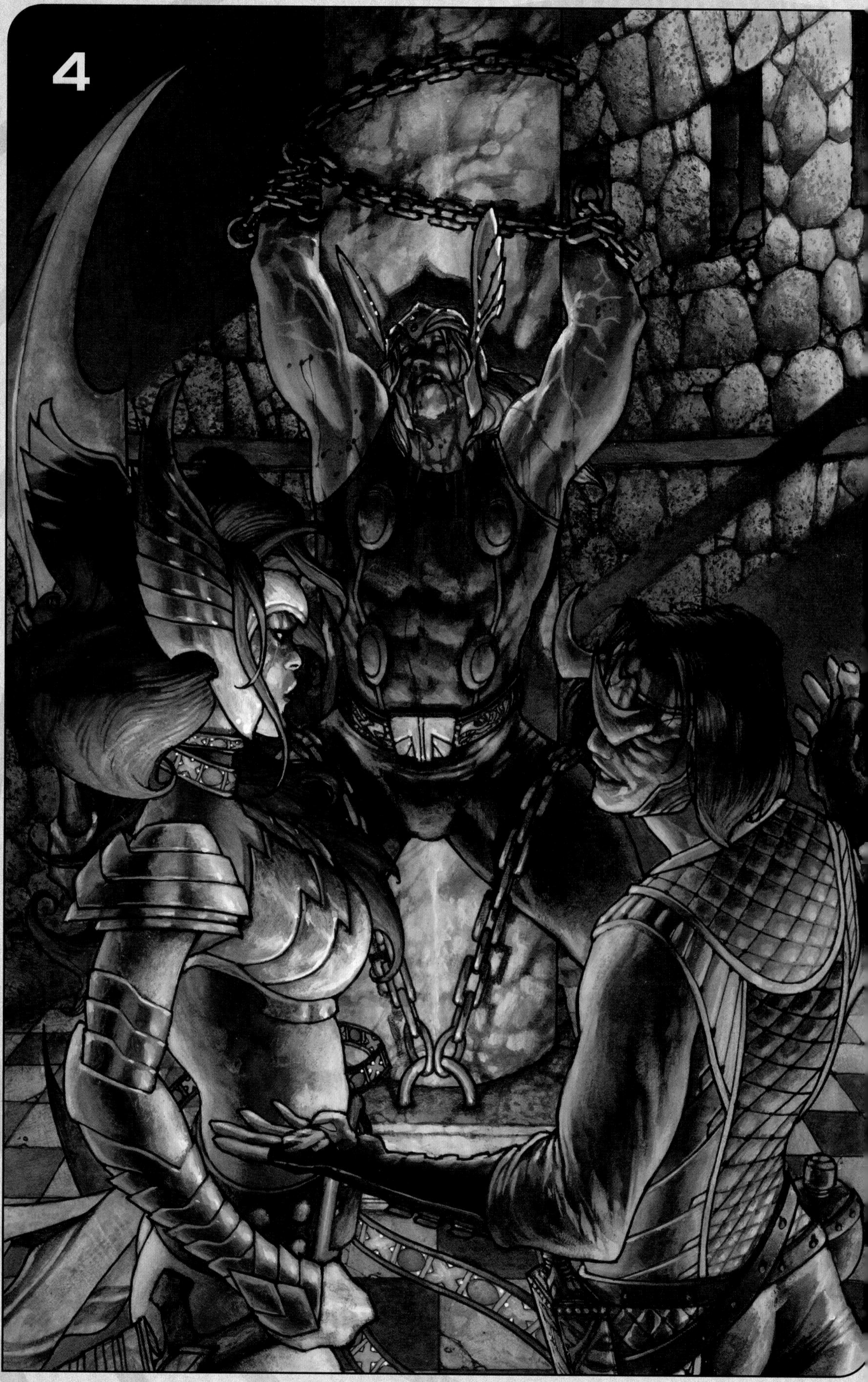
4

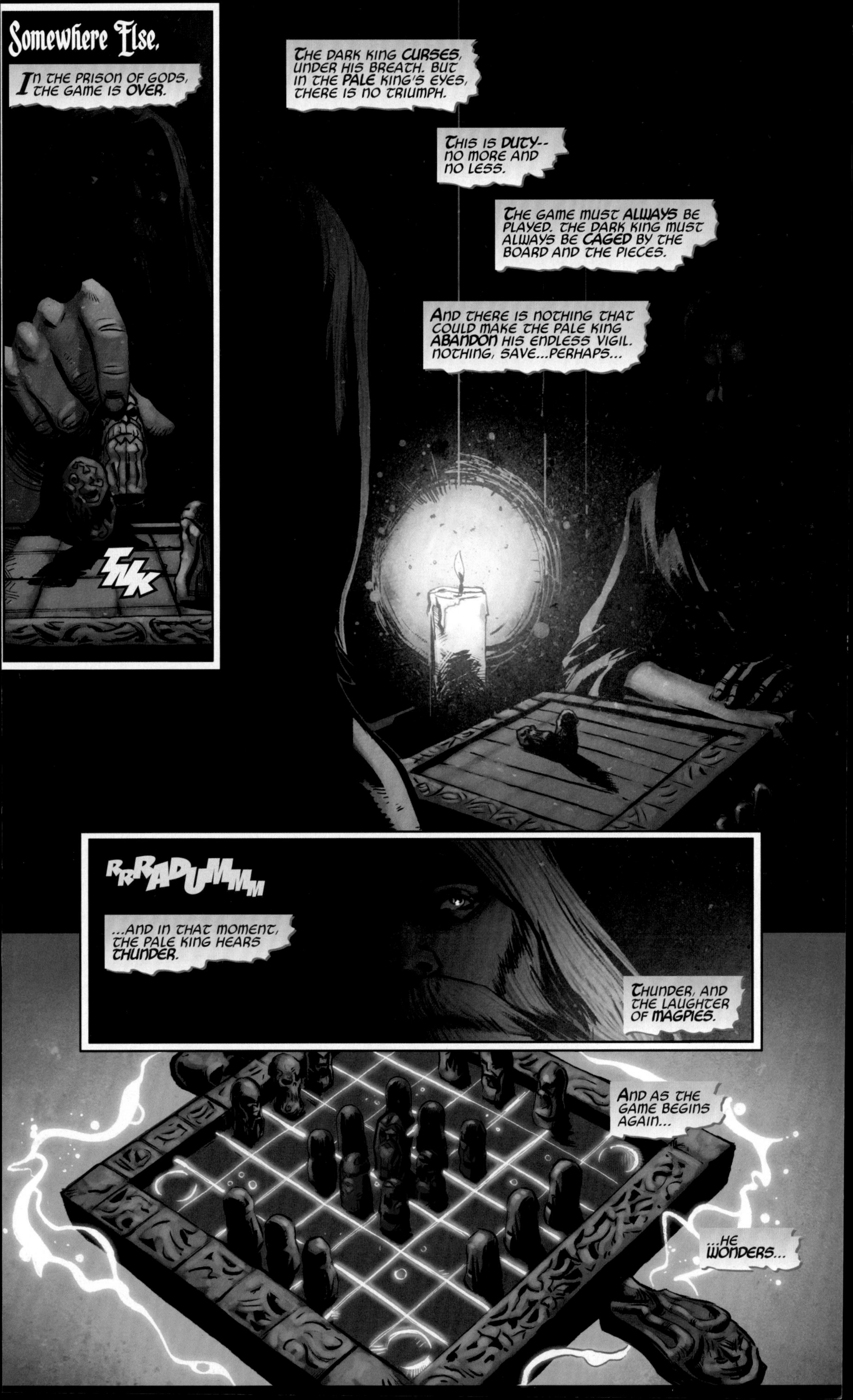
Somewhere Else.
In the prison of gods, the game is OVER.
TNK
The dark king CURSES, under his breath. But in the PALE king's eyes, there is no triumph.
This is DUTY-- no more and no less.
The game must ALWAYS be played. The dark king must always be CAGED by the board and the pieces.
And there is nothing that could make the pale king ABANDON his endless vigil. Nothing, save...perhaps...
RRRADUMMM
...and in that moment, the pale king hears THUNDER.
Thunder, and the laughter of MAGPIES.
And as the game begins again...
...he WONDERS...

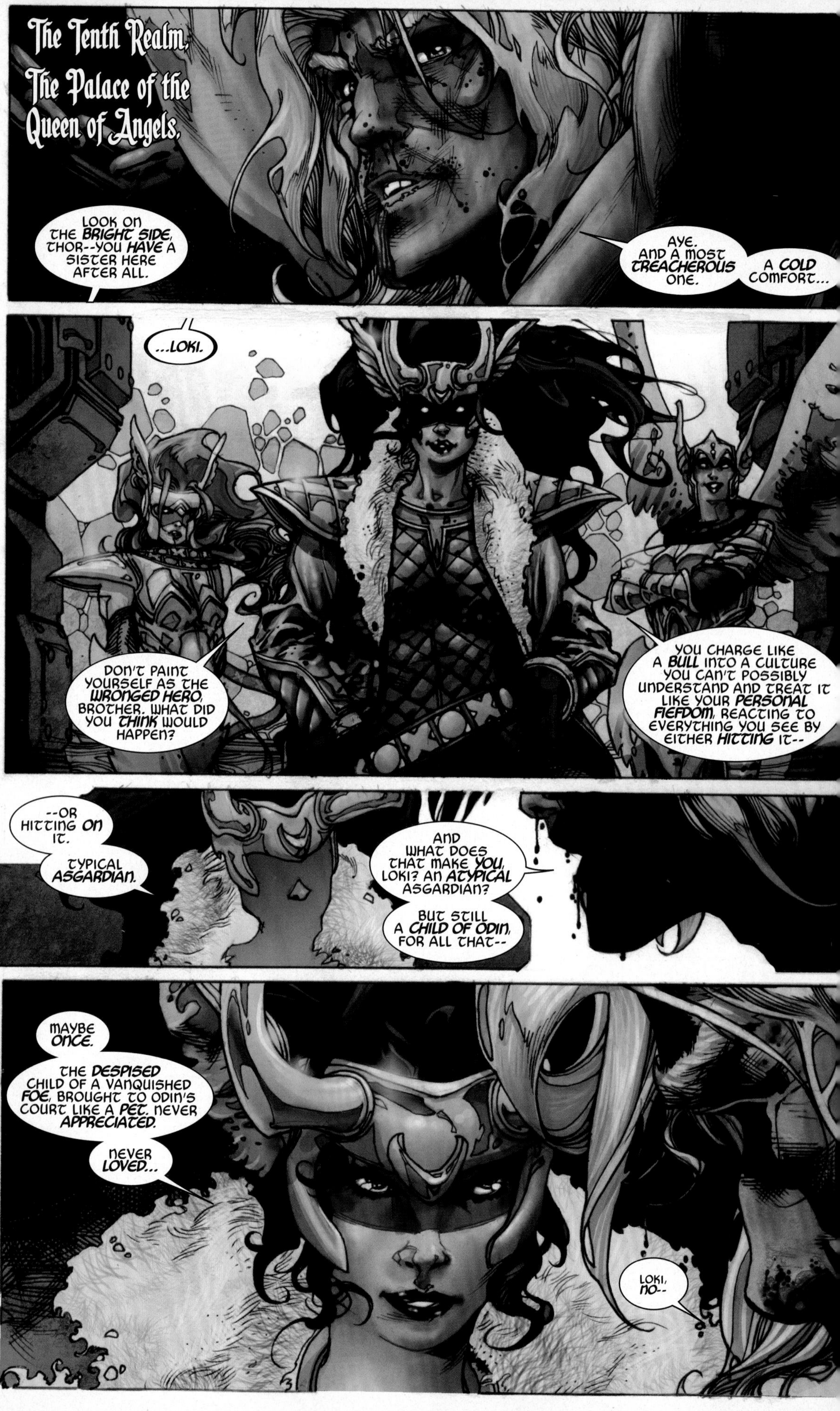

The Tenth Realm. The Palace of the Queen of Angels.
LOOK ON THE BRIGHT SIDE, THOR--YOU HAVE A SISTER HERE AFTER ALL.
AYE. AND A MOST TREACHEROUS ONE.
A COLD COMFORT...
...LOKI.
DON'T PAINT YOURSELF AS THE WRONGED HERO, BROTHER. WHAT DID YOU THINK WOULD HAPPEN?
YOU CHARGE LIKE A BULL INTO A CULTURE YOU CAN'T POSSIBLY UNDERSTAND AND TREAT IT LIKE YOUR PERSONAL FIEFDOM, REACTING TO EVERYTHING YOU SEE BY EITHER HITTING IT--
--OR HITTING ON IT.
TYPICAL ASGARDIAN.
AND WHAT DOES THAT MAKE YOU, LOKI? AN ATYPICAL ASGARDIAN?
BUT STILL A CHILD OF ODIN, FOR ALL THAT--
MAYBE ONCE.
THE DESPISED CHILD OF A VANQUISHED FOE, BROUGHT TO ODIN'S COURT LIKE A PET. NEVER APPRECIATED.
NEVER LOVED...
LOKI, NO--

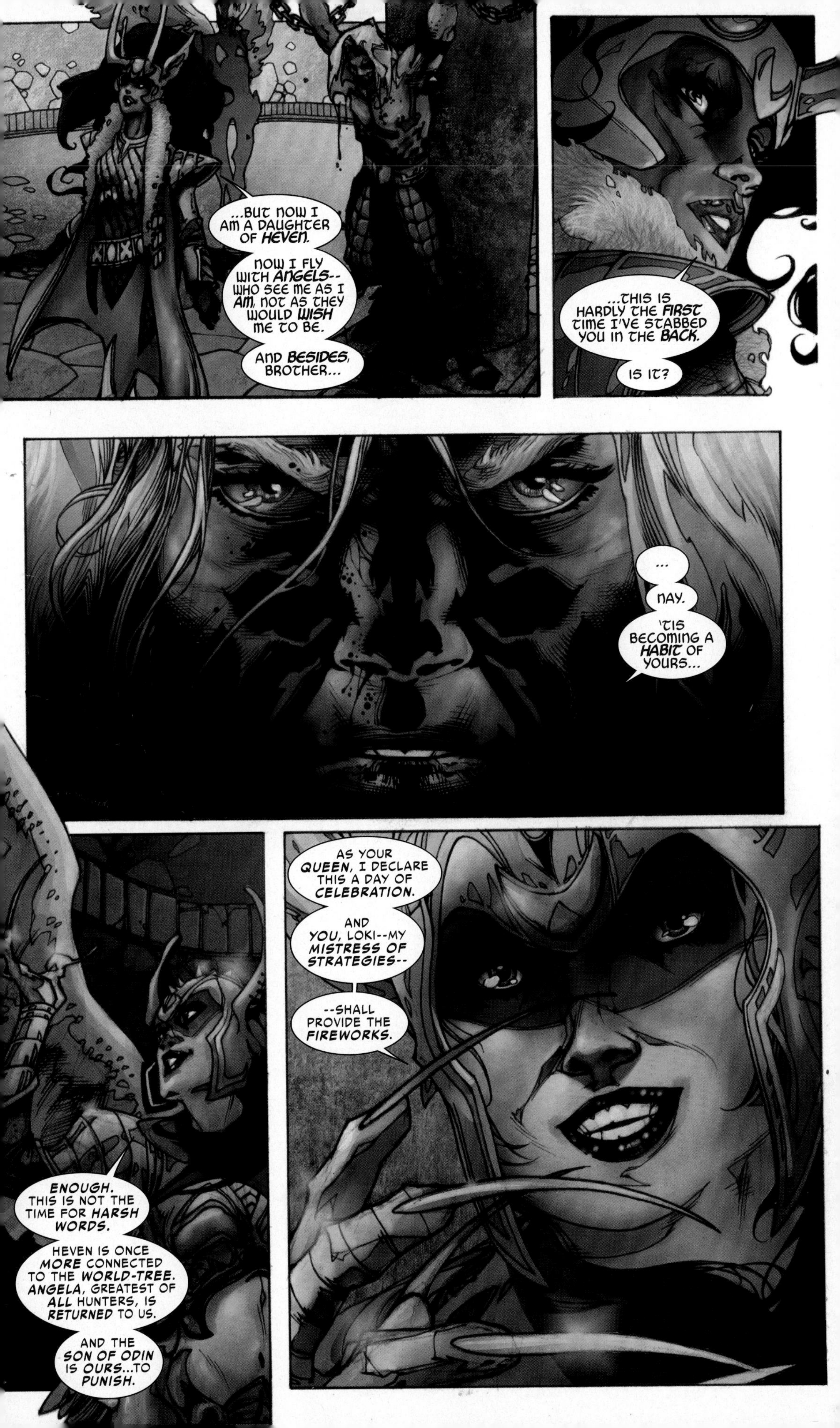
...BUT NOW I AM A DAUGHTER OF HEVEN.
NOW I FLY WITH ANGELS--WHO SEE ME AS I AM, NOT AS THEY WOULD WISH ME TO BE.
AND BESIDES, BROTHER...
...THIS IS HARDLY THE FIRST TIME I'VE STABBED YOU IN THE BACK.
IS IT?
...
NAY.
'TIS BECOMING A HABIT OF YOURS...
ENOUGH. THIS IS NOT THE TIME FOR HARSH WORDS.
HEVEN IS ONCE MORE CONNECTED TO THE WORLD-TREE. ANGELA, GREATEST OF ALL HUNTERS, IS RETURNED TO US.
AND THE SON OF ODIN IS OURS...TO PUNISH.
AS YOUR QUEEN, I DECLARE THIS A DAY OF CELEBRATION.
AND YOU, LOKI--MY MISTRESS OF STRATEGIES--
--SHALL PROVIDE THE FIREWORKS.

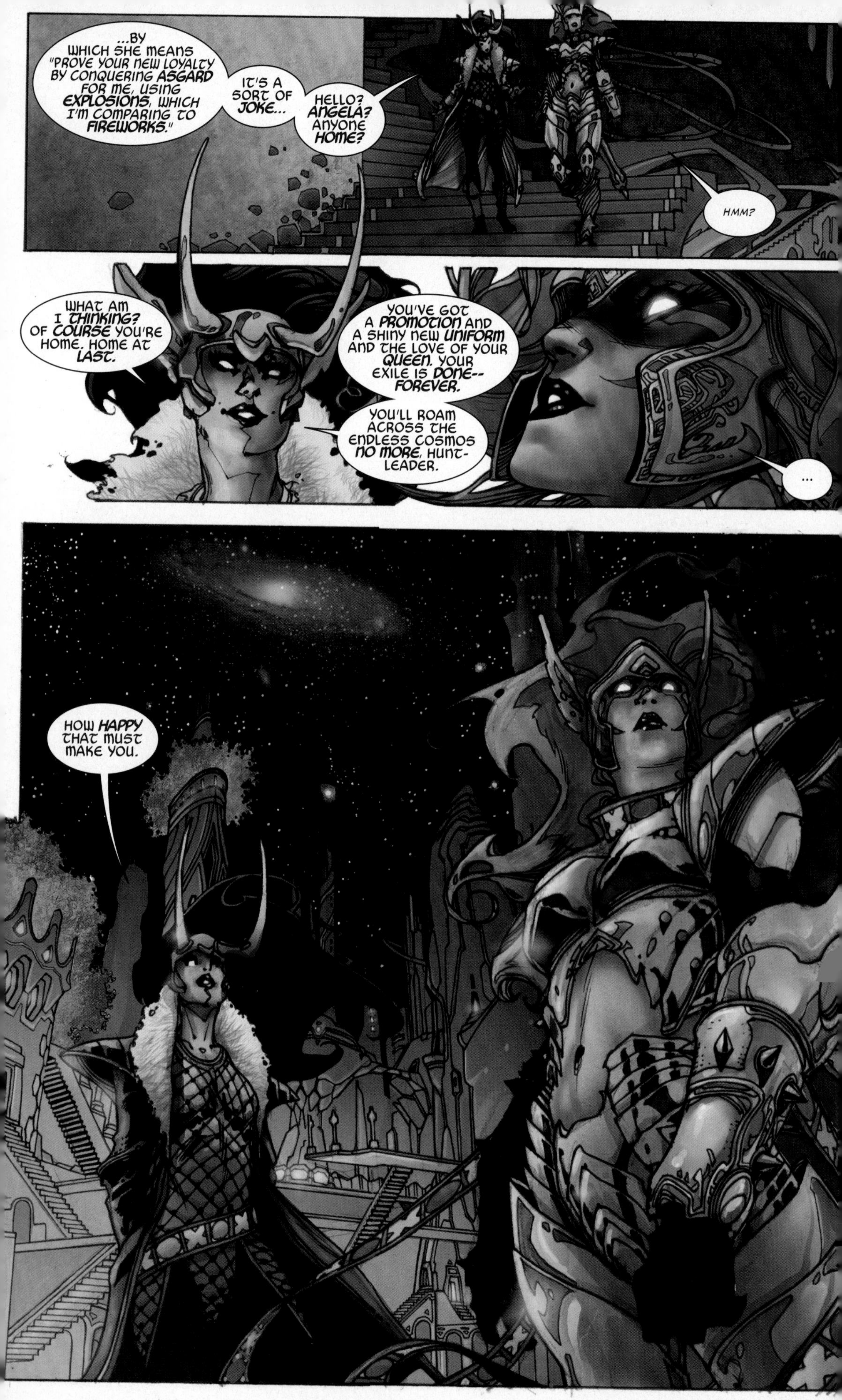
...BY WHICH SHE MEANS "PROVE YOUR NEW LOYALTY BY CONQUERING ASGARD FOR ME, USING EXPLOSIONS, WHICH I'M COMPARING TO FIREWORKS."
IT'S A SORT OF JOKE...
HELLO? ANGELA? ANYONE HOME?
HMM?
WHAT AM I THINKING? OF COURSE YOU'RE HOME. HOME AT LAST.
YOU'VE GOT A PROMOTION AND A SHINY NEW UNIFORM AND THE LOVE OF YOUR QUEEN. YOUR EXILE IS DONE-- FOREVER.
YOU'LL ROAM ACROSS THE ENDLESS COSMOS NO MORE, HUNT-LEADER.
...
HOW HAPPY THAT MUST MAKE YOU.

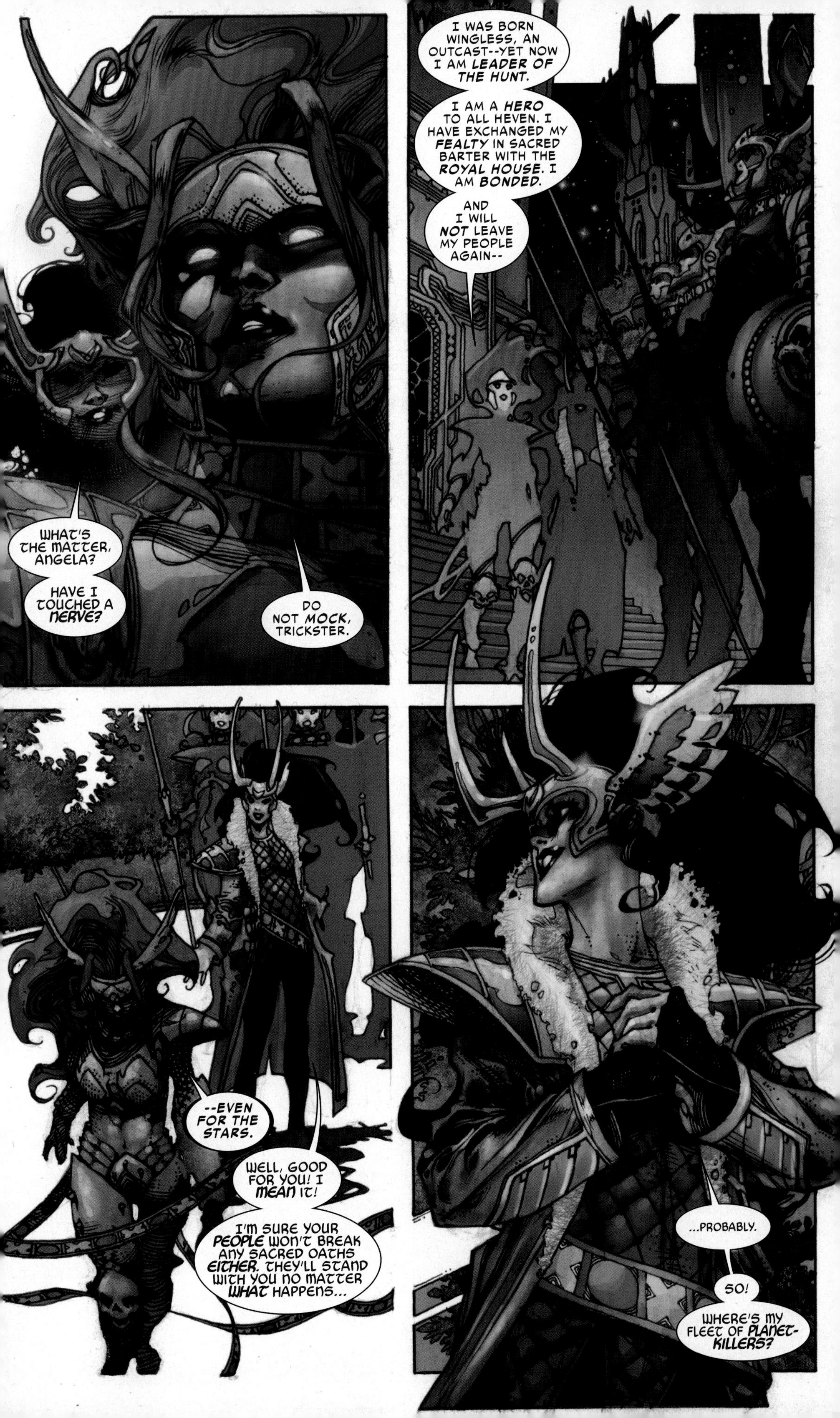
WHAT'S THE MATTER, ANGELA?
HAVE I TOUCHED A NERVE?
DO NOT MOCK, TRICKSTER.
I WAS BORN WINGLESS, AN OUTCAST--YET NOW I AM LEADER OF THE HUNT.
I AM A HERO TO ALL HEVEN. I HAVE EXCHANGED MY FEALTY IN SACRED BARTER WITH THE ROYAL HOUSE. I AM BONDED.
AND I WILL NOT LEAVE MY PEOPLE AGAIN--
--EVEN FOR THE STARS.
WELL, GOOD FOR YOU! I MEAN IT!
I'M SURE YOUR PEOPLE WON'T BREAK ANY SACRED OATHS EITHER. THEY'LL STAND WITH YOU NO MATTER WHAT HAPPENS...
...PROBABLY.
SO!
WHERE'S MY FLEET OF PLANET-KILLERS?

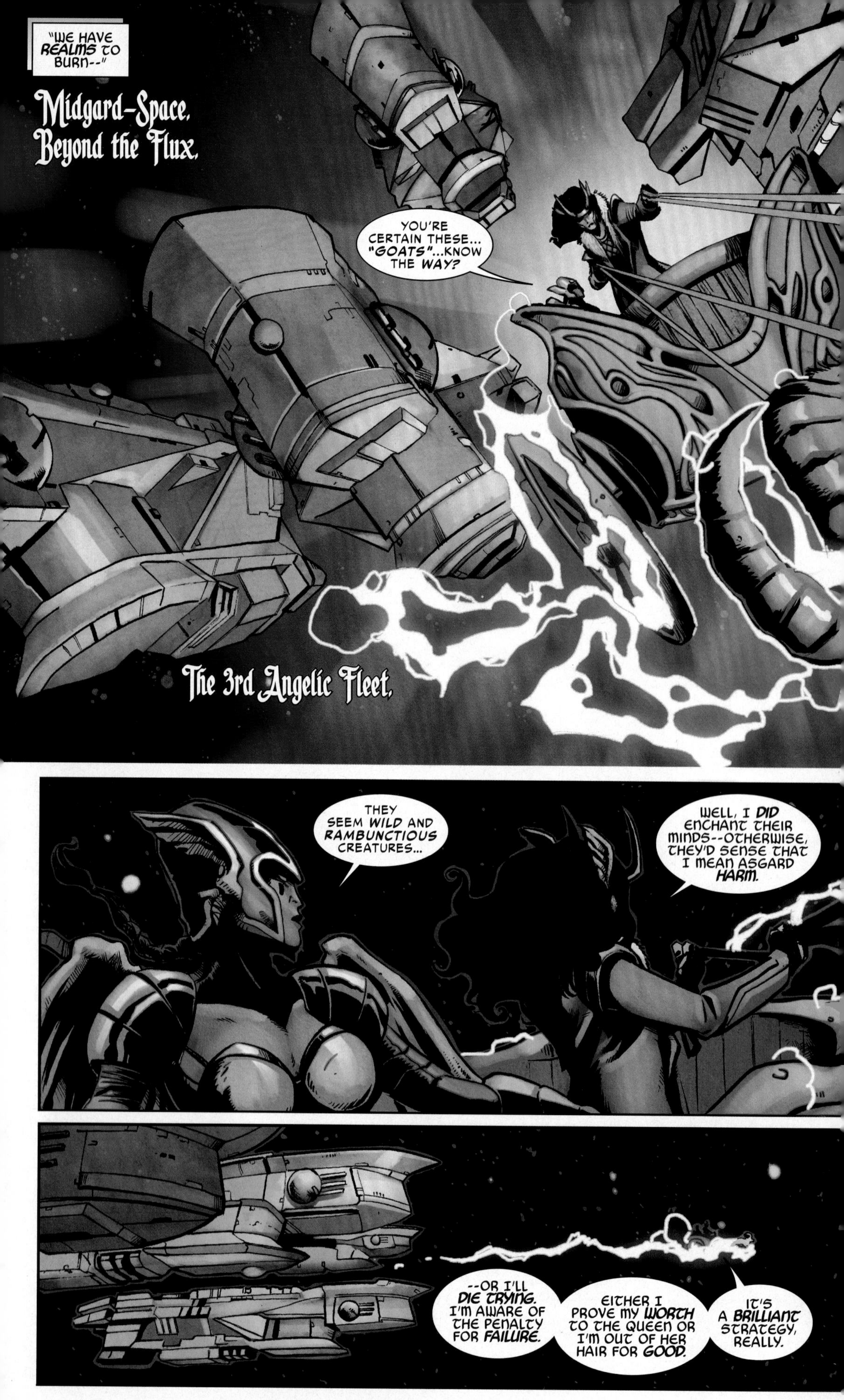
"WE HAVE REALMS TO BURN--"
Midgard-Space, Beyond the Flux,
YOU'RE CERTAIN THESE... "GOATS"...KNOW THE WAY?
The 3rd Angelic Fleet,
THEY SEEM WILD AND RAMBUNCTIOUS CREATURES...
WELL, I DID ENCHANT THEIR MINDS--OTHERWISE, THEY'D SENSE THAT I MEAN ASGARD HARM.
IT'S A BRILLIANT STRATEGY, REALLY.
EITHER I PROVE MY WORTH TO THE QUEEN OR I'M OUT OF HER HAIR FOR GOOD.
--OR I'LL DIE TRYING. I'M AWARE OF THE PENALTY FOR FAILURE.

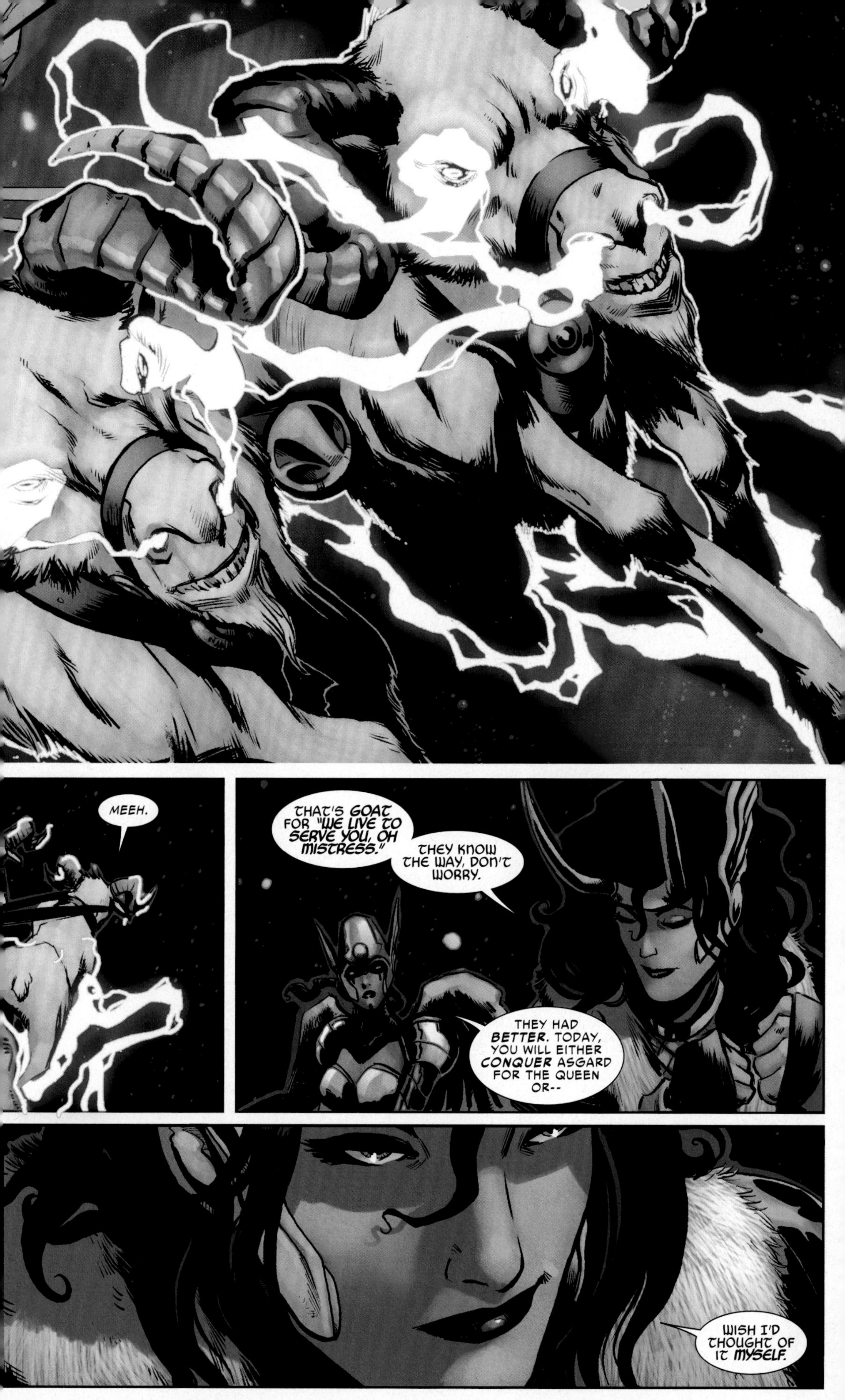
MEEH.
THAT'S GOAT FOR "WE LIVE TO SERVE YOU, OH MISTRESS."
THEY KNOW THE WAY, DON'T WORRY.
THEY HAD BETTER. TODAY, YOU WILL EITHER CONQUER ASGARD FOR THE QUEEN OR--
WISH I'D THOUGHT OF IT MYSELF.

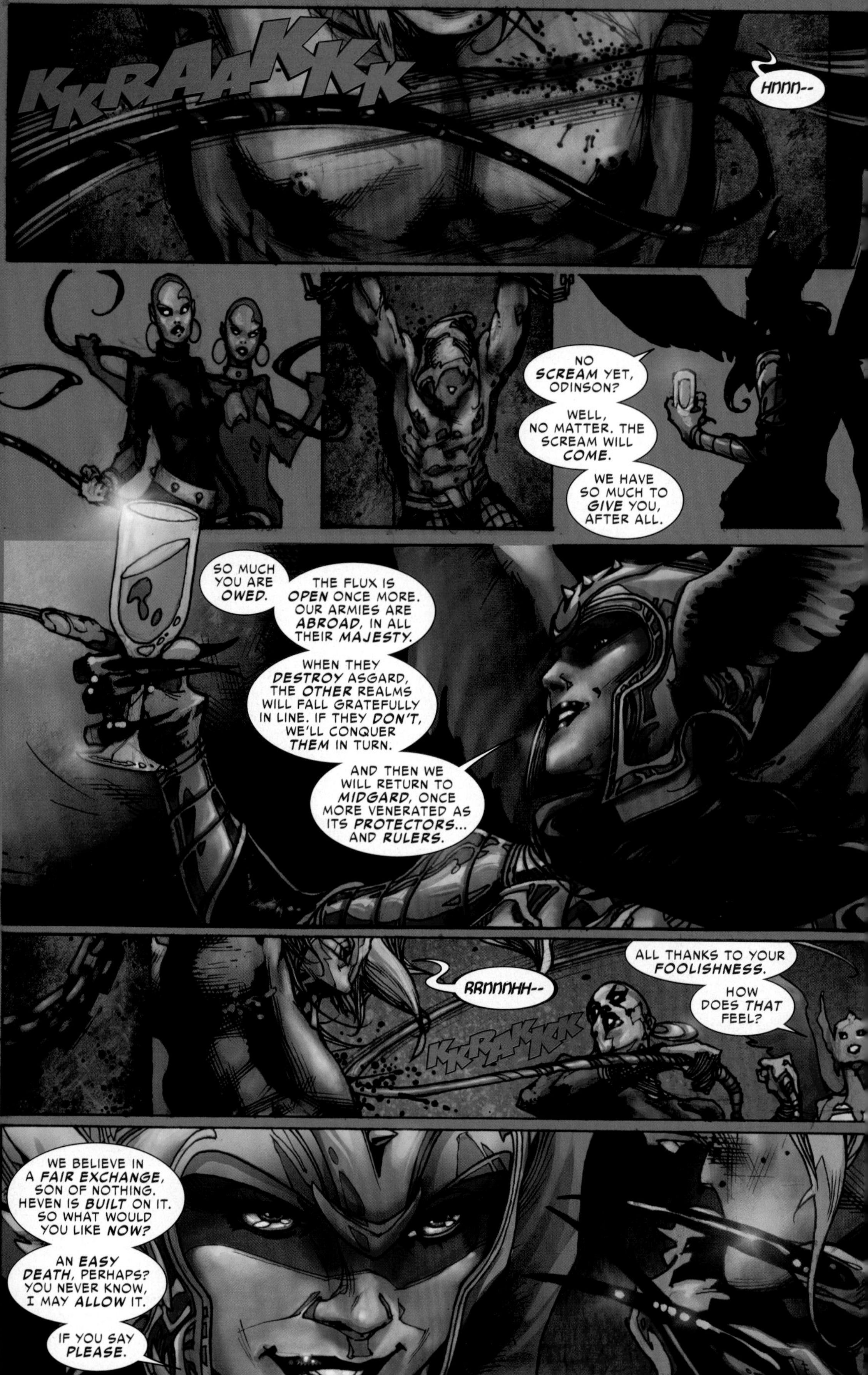
KKRAAKKKK
HNNN--
NO SCREAM YET, ODINSON?
WELL, NO MATTER. THE SCREAM WILL COME.
WE HAVE SO MUCH TO GIVE YOU, AFTER ALL.
SO MUCH YOU ARE OWED.
THE FLUX IS OPEN ONCE MORE. OUR ARMIES ARE ABROAD, IN ALL THEIR MAJESTY.
WHEN THEY DESTROY ASGARD, THE OTHER REALMS WILL FALL GRATEFULLY IN LINE. IF THEY DON'T, WE'LL CONQUER THEM IN TURN.
AND THEN WE WILL RETURN TO MIDGARD, ONCE MORE VENERATED AS ITS PROTECTORS... AND RULERS.
BRNNNHH--
KKRAKKK
ALL THANKS TO YOUR FOOLISHNESS.
HOW DOES THAT FEEL?
WE BELIEVE IN A FAIR EXCHANGE, SON OF NOTHING. HEVEN IS BUILT ON IT. SO WHAT WOULD YOU LIKE NOW?
AN EASY DEATH, PERHAPS? YOU NEVER KNOW, I MAY ALLOW IT.
IF YOU SAY PLEASE.

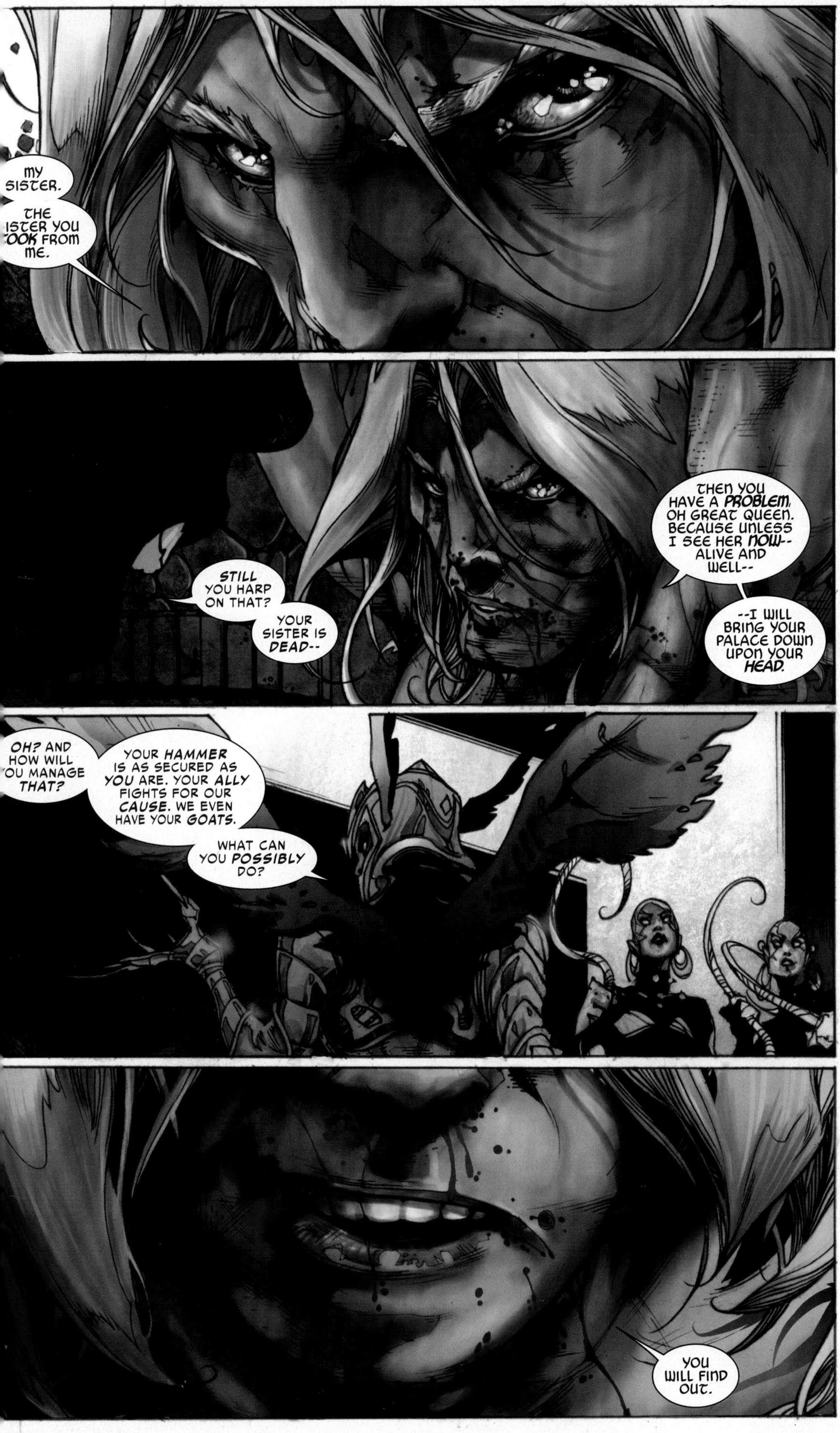
MY SISTER.
THE ISTER YOU OOK FROM ME.
STILL YOU HARP ON THAT?
YOUR SISTER IS DEAD--
THEN YOU HAVE A PROBLEM, OH GREAT QUEEN. BECAUSE UNLESS I SEE HER NOW-- ALIVE AND WELL--
--I WILL BRING YOUR PALACE DOWN UPON YOUR HEAD.
OH? AND HOW WILL OU MANAGE THAT?
YOUR HAMMER IS AS SECURED AS YOU ARE. YOUR ALLY FIGHTS FOR OUR CAUSE. WE EVEN HAVE YOUR GOATS.
WHAT CAN YOU POSSIBLY DO?
YOU WILL FIND OUT.

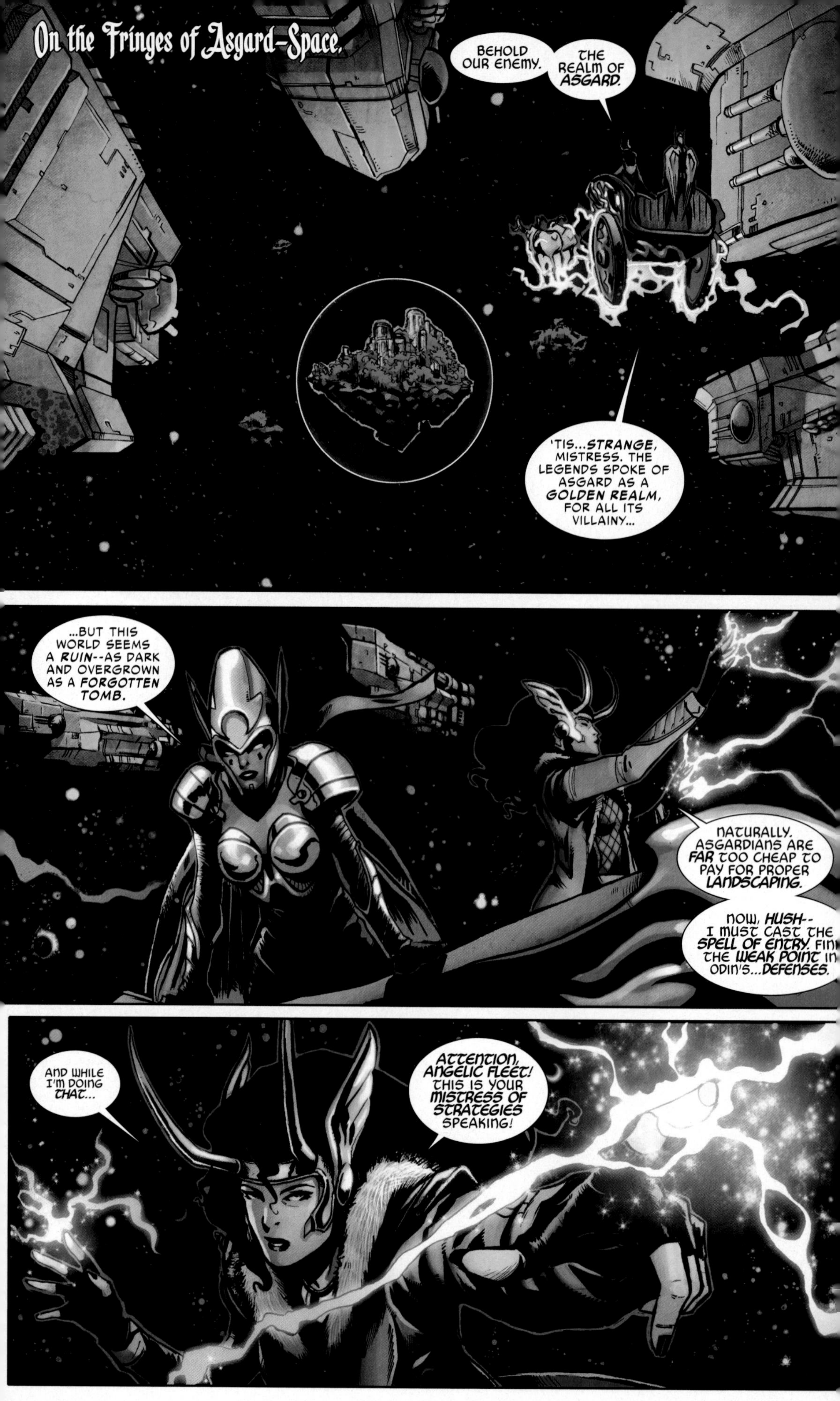
On the Fringes of Asgard-Space.
BEHOLD OUR ENEMY.
THE REALM OF ASGARD.
'TIS...STRANGE, MISTRESS. THE LEGENDS SPOKE OF ASGARD AS A GOLDEN REALM, FOR ALL ITS VILLAINY...
...BUT THIS WORLD SEEMS A RUIN--AS DARK AND OVERGROWN AS A FORGOTTEN TOMB.
NATURALLY. ASGARDIANS ARE FAR TOO CHEAP TO PAY FOR PROPER LANDSCAPING.
NOW, HUSH-- I MUST CAST THE SPELL OF ENTRY. FIN THE WEAK POINT IN ODIN'S...DEFENSES.
AND WHILE I'M DOING THAT...
ATTENTION, ANGELIC FLEET! THIS IS YOUR MISTRESS OF STRATEGIES SPEAKING!

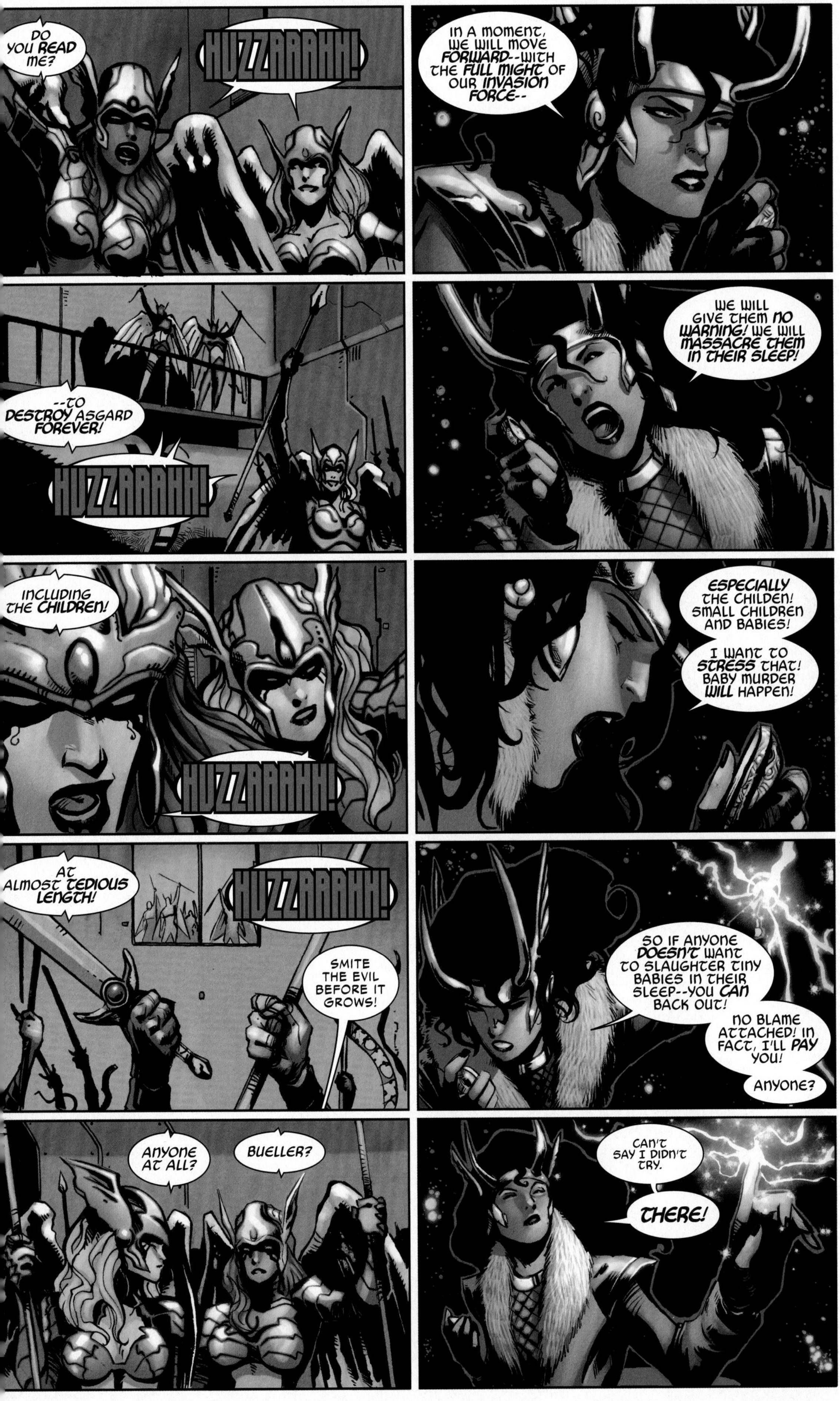

DO YOU READ ME?
HUZZAAAHH!
IN A MOMENT, WE WILL MOVE FORWARD--WITH THE FULL MIGHT OF OUR INVASION FORCE--
--TO DESTROY ASGARD FOREVER!
HUZZAAAHH!
WE WILL GIVE THEM NO WARNING! WE WILL MASSACRE THEM IN THEIR SLEEP!
INCLUDING THE CHILDREN!
HUZZAAAHH!
ESPECIALLY THE CHILDEN! SMALL CHILDREN AND BABIES!
I WANT TO STRESS THAT! BABY MURDER WILL HAPPEN!
AT ALMOST TEDIOUS LENGTH!
HUZZAAAHH!
SMITE THE EVIL BEFORE IT GROWS!
SO IF ANYONE DOESN'T WANT TO SLAUGHTER TINY BABIES IN THEIR SLEEP--YOU CAN BACK OUT!
NO BLAME ATTACHED! IN FACT, I'LL PAY YOU!
ANYONE?
ANYONE AT ALL?
BUELLER?
CAN'T SAY I DIDN'T TRY.
THERE!

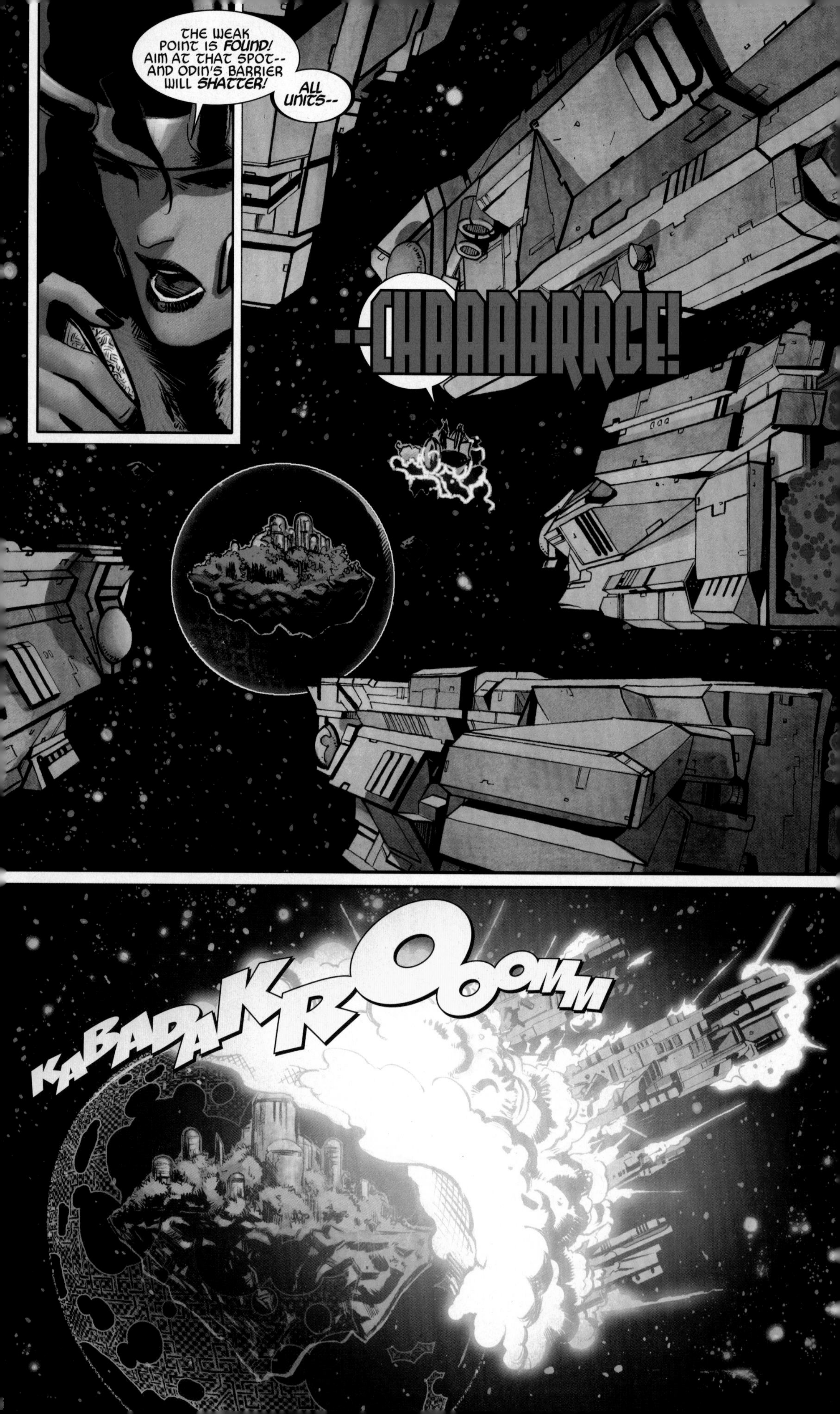

THE WEAK POINT IS FOUND! AIM AT THAT SPOT-- AND ODIN'S BARRIER WILL SHATTER!
ALL UNITS--
--CHAAAARRGE!
KABADAKROOOOMM

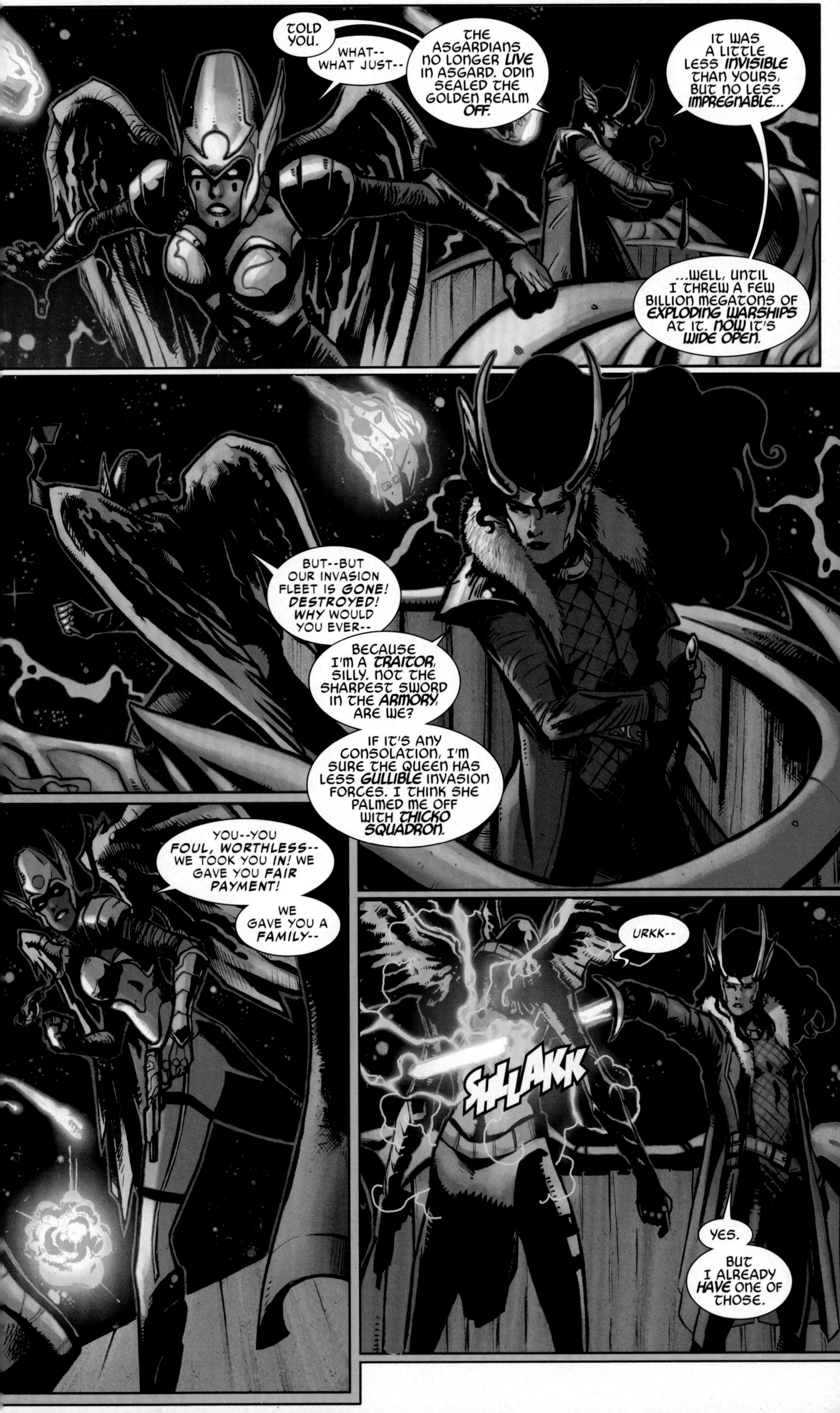
TOLD YOU.
WHAT-- WHAT JUST--
THE ASGARDIANS NO LONGER LIVE IN ASGARD. ODIN SEALED THE GOLDEN REALM OFF.
IT WAS A LITTLE LESS INVISIBLE THAN YOURS, BUT NO LESS IMPREGNABLE...
...WELL, UNTIL I THREW A FEW BILLION MEGATONS OF EXPLODING WARSHIPS AT IT. NOW IT'S WIDE OPEN.
BUT--BUT OUR INVASION FLEET IS GONE! DESTROYED! WHY WOULD YOU EVER--
BECAUSE I'M A TRAITOR, SILLY. NOT THE SHARPEST SWORD IN THE ARMORY, ARE WE?
IF IT'S ANY CONSOLATION, I'M SURE THE QUEEN HAS LESS GULLIBLE INVASION FORCES. I THINK SHE PALMED ME OFF WITH THICKO SQUADRON.
YOU--YOU FOUL, WORTHLESS-- WE TOOK YOU IN! WE GAVE YOU FAIR PAYMENT!
WE GAVE YOU A FAMILY--
URKK--
SHHLAKK
YES.
BUT I ALREADY HAVE ONE OF THOSE.

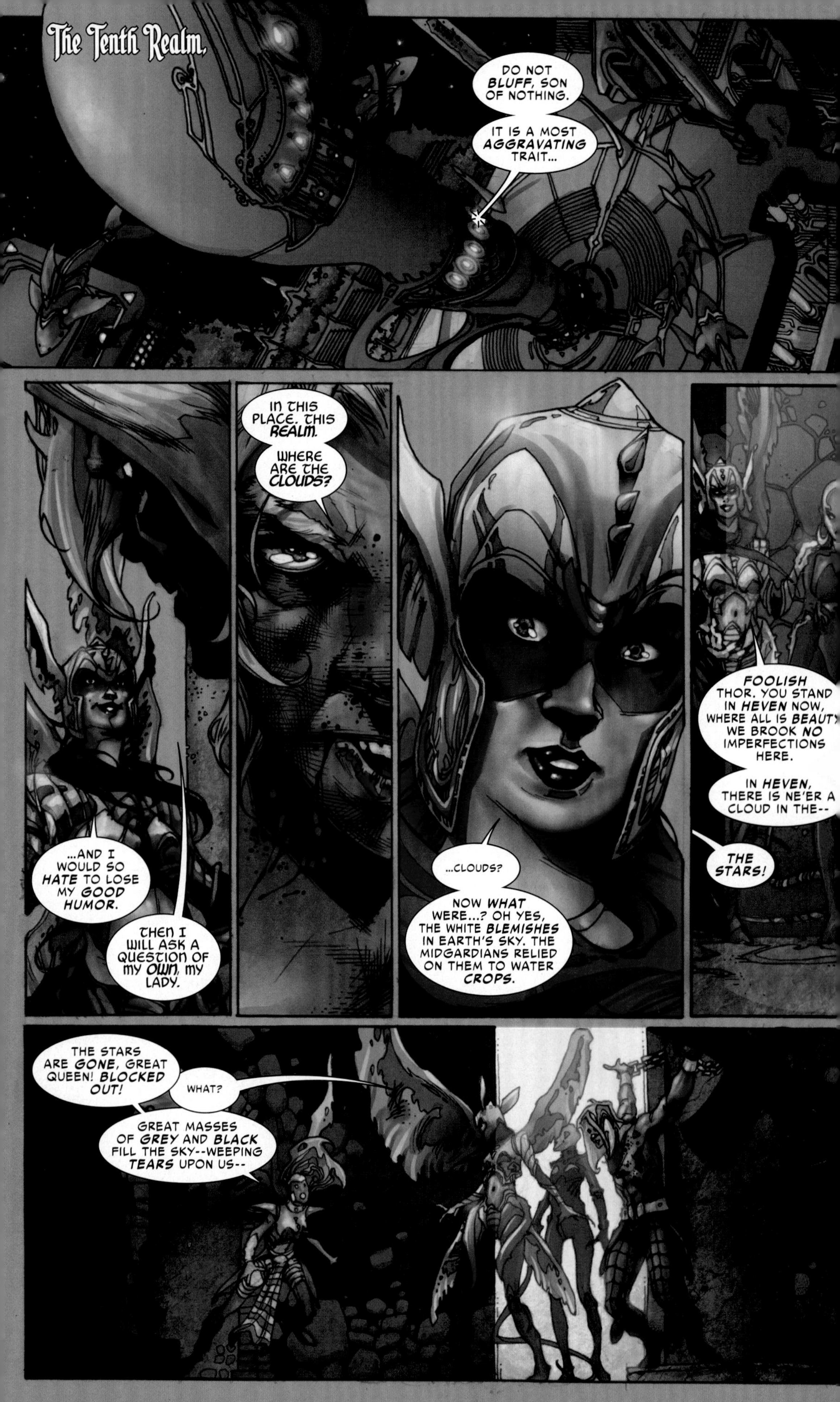

The Tenth Realm,
DO NOT BLUFF, SON OF NOTHING.
IT IS A MOST AGGRAVATING TRAIT...
...AND I WOULD SO HATE TO LOSE MY GOOD HUMOR.
THEN I WILL ASK A QUESTION OF MY OWN, MY LADY.
IN THIS PLACE. THIS REALM.
WHERE ARE THE CLOUDS?
...CLOUDS?
NOW WHAT WERE...? OH YES, THE WHITE BLEMISHES IN EARTH'S SKY. THE MIDGARDIANS RELIED ON THEM TO WATER CROPS.
FOOLISH THOR. YOU STAND IN HEVEN NOW, WHERE ALL IS BEAUTY. WE BROOK NO IMPERFECTIONS HERE.
IN HEVEN, THERE IS NE'ER A CLOUD IN THE--
THE STARS!
THE STARS ARE GONE, GREAT QUEEN! BLOCKED OUT!
WHAT?
GREAT MASSES OF GREY AND BLACK FILL THE SKY--WEEPING TEARS UPON US--

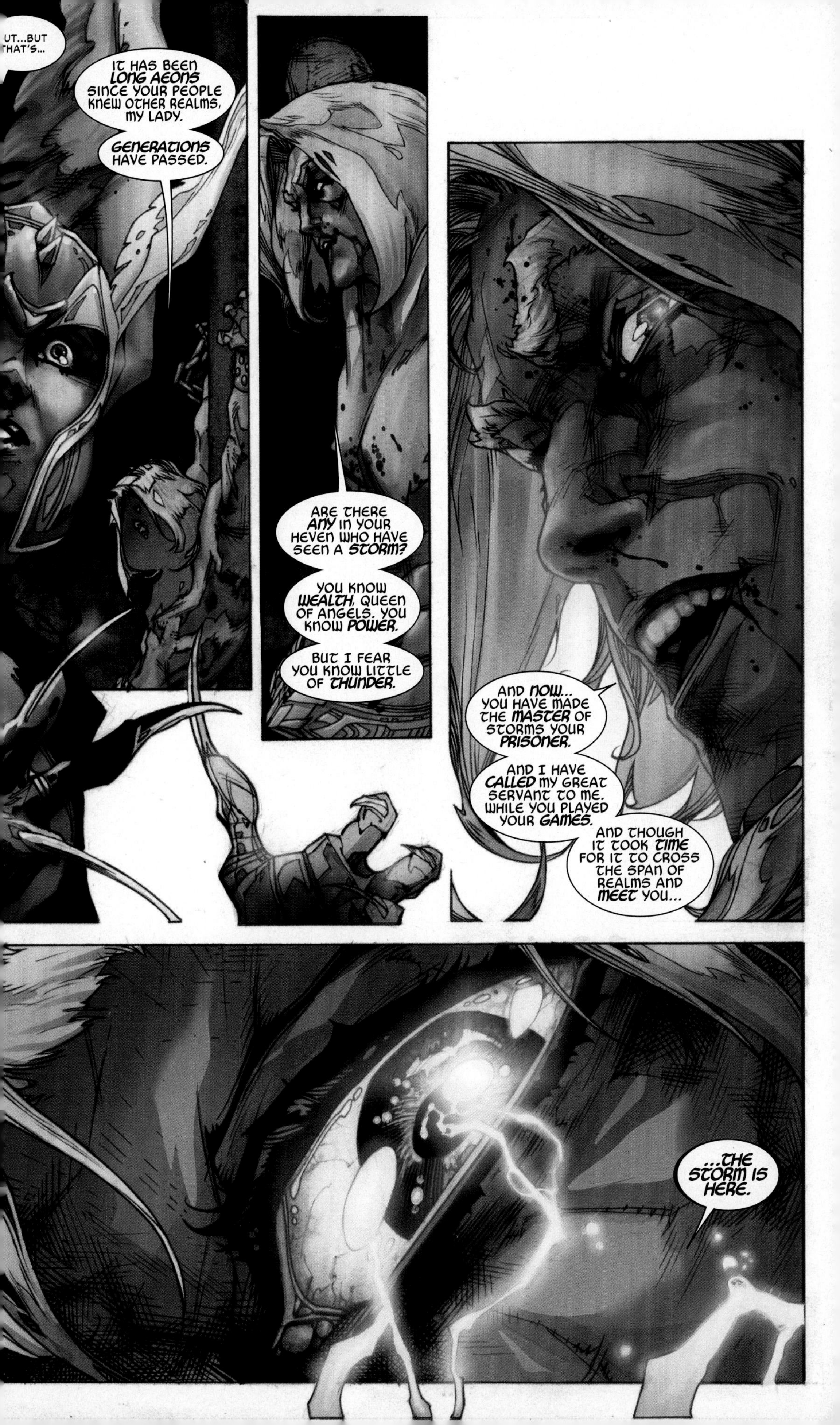

UT...BUT THAT'S...
IT HAS BEEN LONG AEONS SINCE YOUR PEOPLE KNEW OTHER REALMS, MY LADY.
GENERATIONS HAVE PASSED.
ARE THERE ANY IN YOUR HEVEN WHO HAVE SEEN A STORM?
YOU KNOW WEALTH, QUEEN OF ANGELS. YOU KNOW POWER.
BUT I FEAR YOU KNOW LITTLE OF THUNDER.
AND NOW... YOU HAVE MADE THE MASTER OF STORMS YOUR PRISONER.
AND I HAVE CALLED MY GREAT SERVANT TO ME. WHILE YOU PLAYED YOUR GAMES.
AND THOUGH IT TOOK TIME FOR IT TO CROSS THE SPAN OF REALMS AND MEET YOU...
...THE STORM IS HERE.

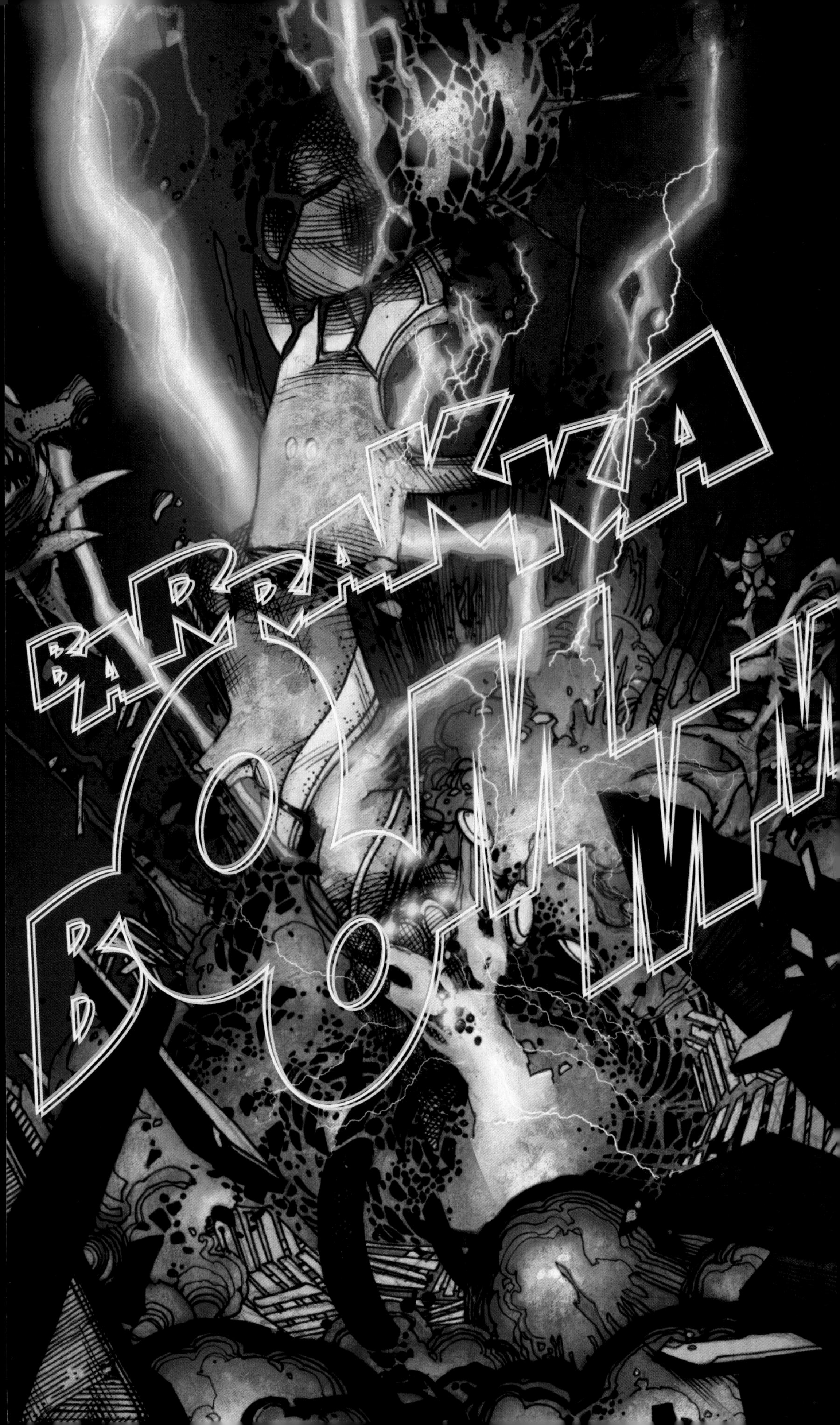

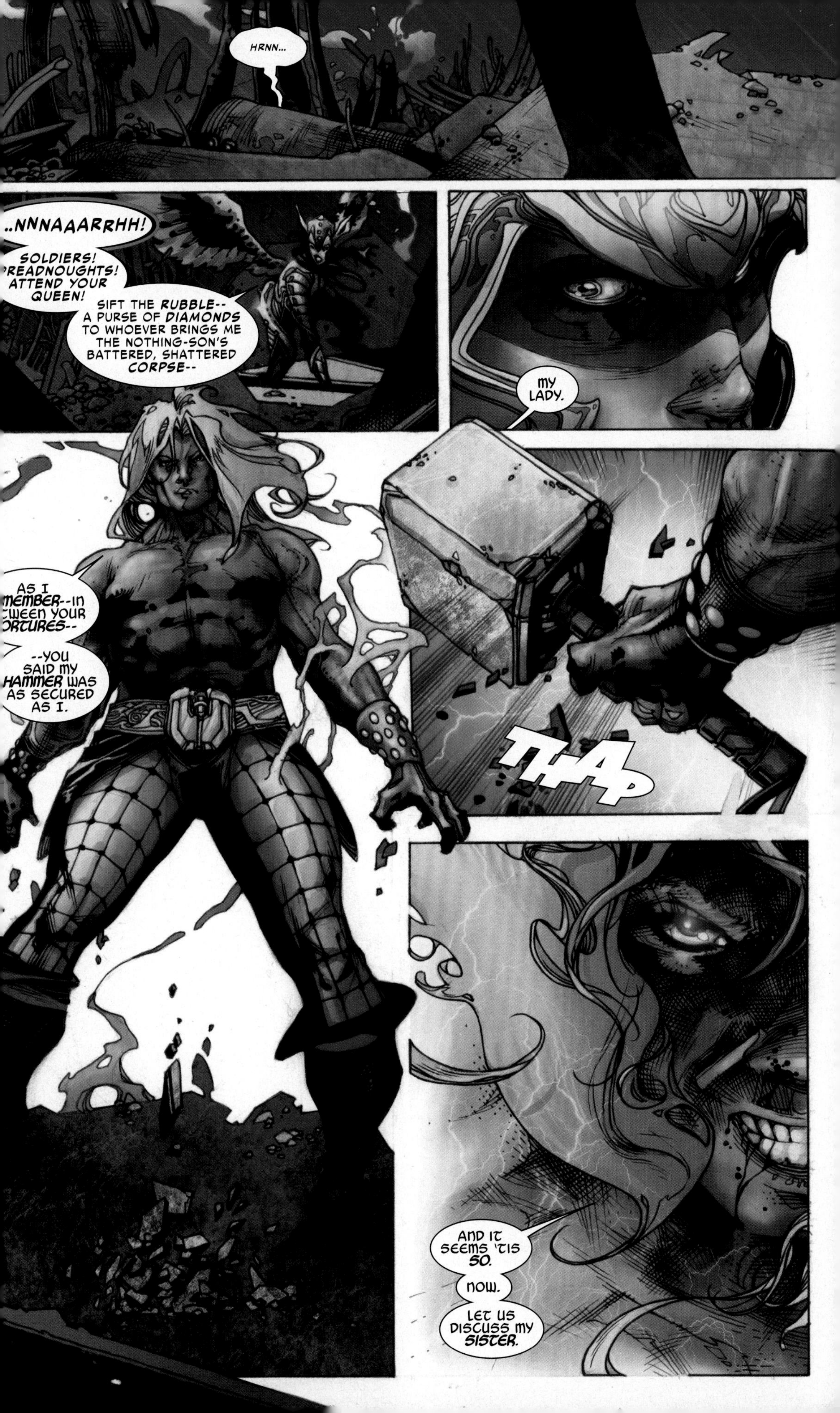
HRNN...
..NNNAAARRHH!
SOLDIERS! DREADNOUGHTS! ATTEND YOUR QUEEN!
SIFT THE RUBBLE-- A PURSE OF DIAMONDS TO WHOEVER BRINGS ME THE NOTHING-SON'S BATTERED, SHATTERED CORPSE--
MY LADY.
AS I MEMBER--IN TWEEN YOUR ORTURES--
--YOU SAID MY HAMMER WAS AS SECURED AS I.
THAP
AND IT SEEMS 'TIS SO.
NOW.
LET US DISCUSS MY SISTER.

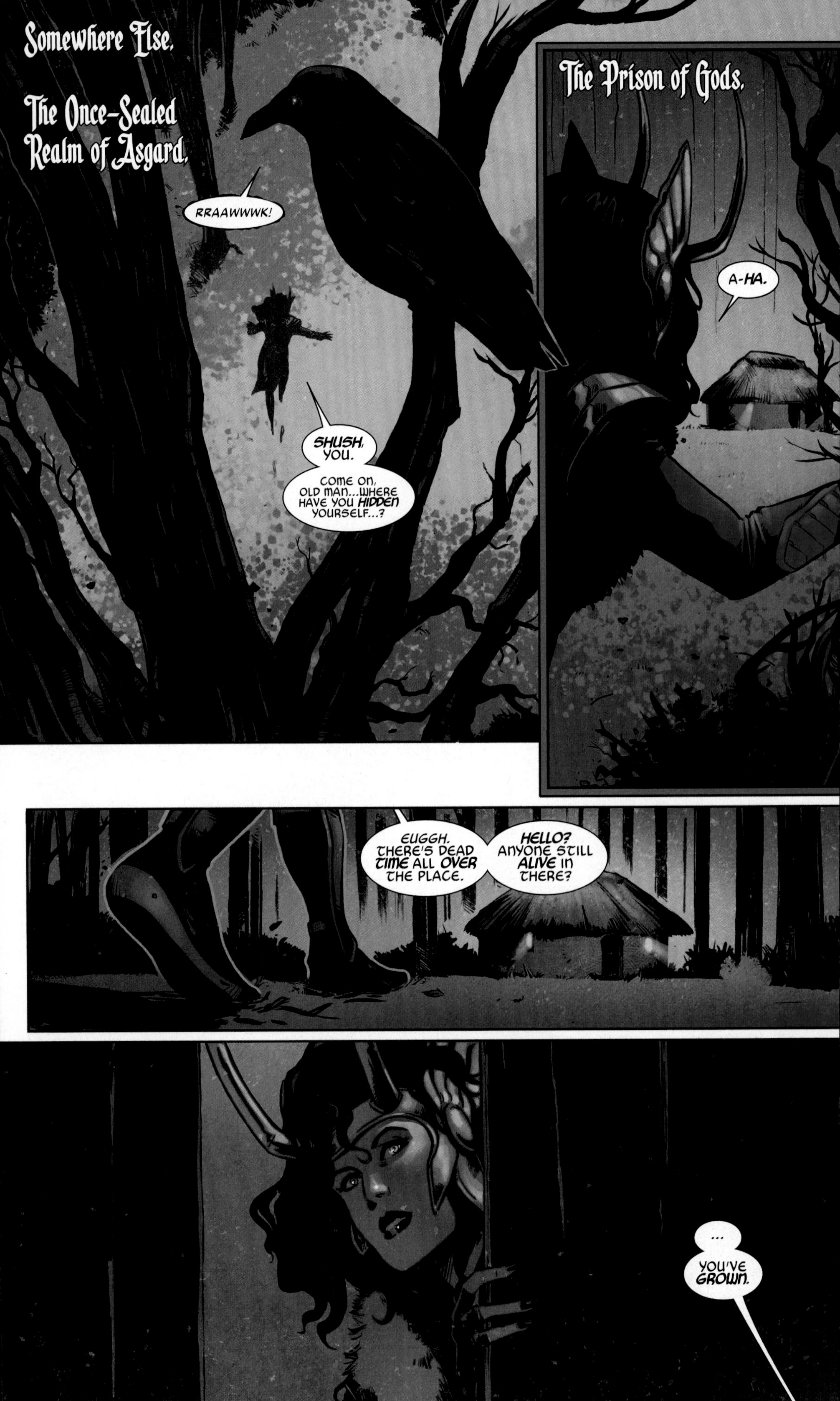
Somewhere Else.
The Once-Sealed Realm of Asgard.
RRAAWWWK!
SHUSH, YOU.
COME ON, OLD MAN...WHERE HAVE YOU HIDDEN YOURSELF...?
The Prison of Gods.
A-HA.
EUGGH. THERE'S DEAD TIME ALL OVER THE PLACE.
HELLO? ANYONE STILL ALIVE IN THERE?
...
YOU'VE GROWN.

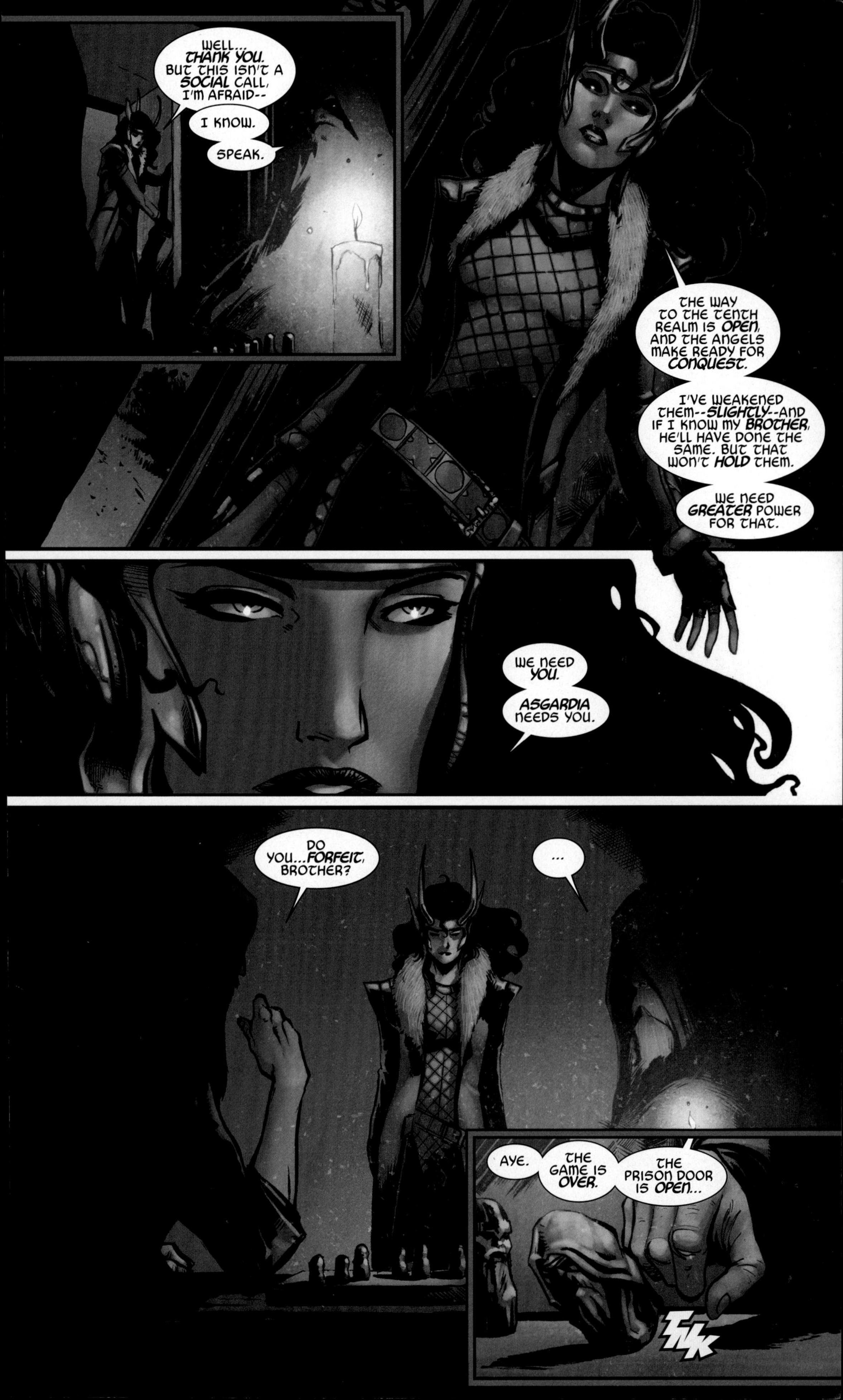
WELL... THANK YOU. BUT THIS ISN'T A SOCIAL CALL, I'M AFRAID--
I KNOW.
SPEAK.
THE WAY TO THE TENTH REALM IS OPEN, AND THE ANGELS MAKE READY FOR CONQUEST.
I'VE WEAKENED THEM--SLIGHTLY--AND IF I KNOW MY BROTHER, HE'LL HAVE DONE THE SAME. BUT THAT WON'T HOLD THEM.
WE NEED GREATER POWER FOR THAT.
WE NEED YOU.
ASGARDIA NEEDS YOU.
DO YOU...FORFEIT, BROTHER?
...
AYE.
THE GAME IS OVER.
THE PRISON DOOR IS OPEN...
TIK

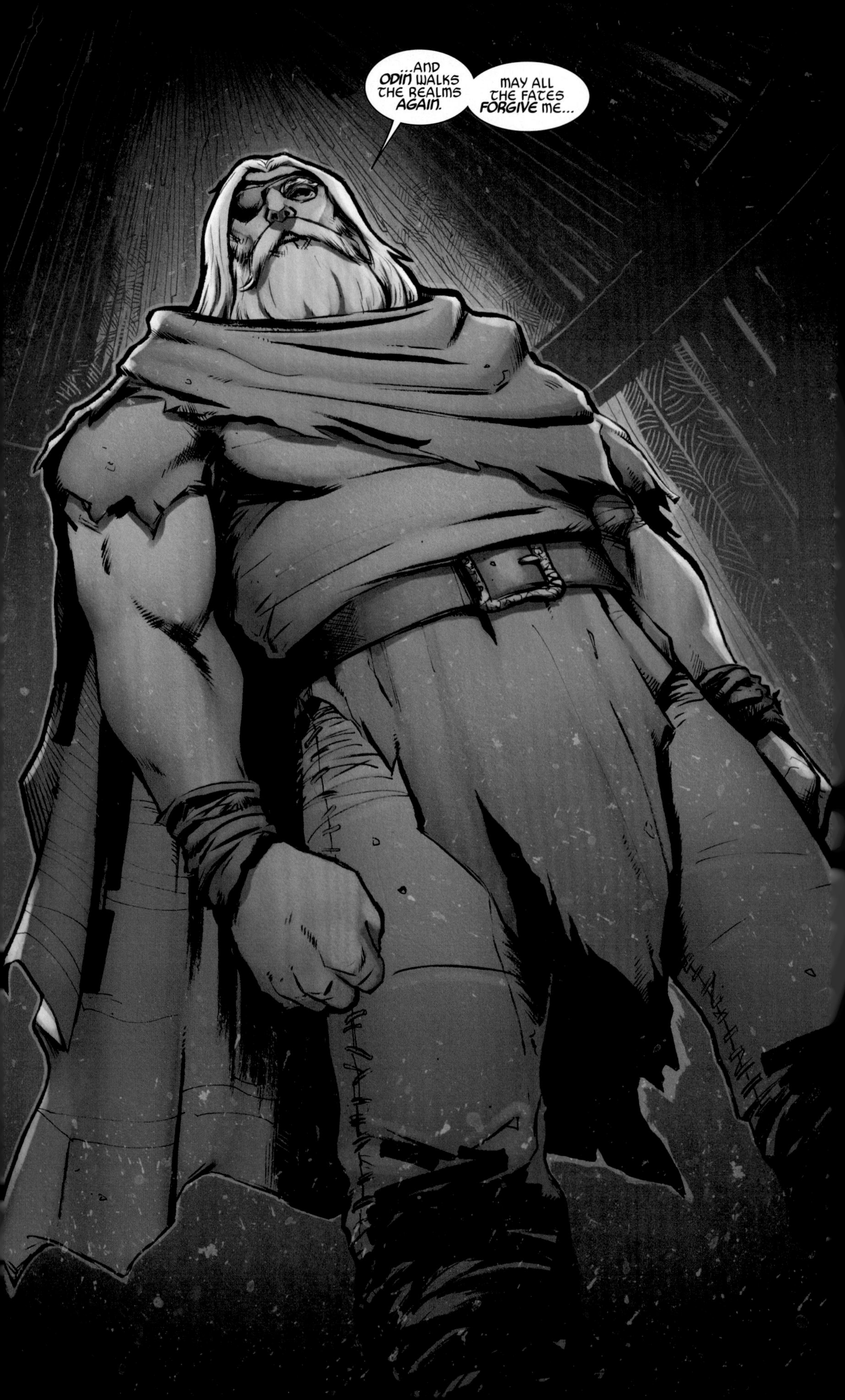
...AND ODIN WALKS THE REALMS AGAIN.
MAY ALL THE FATES FORGIVE ME...

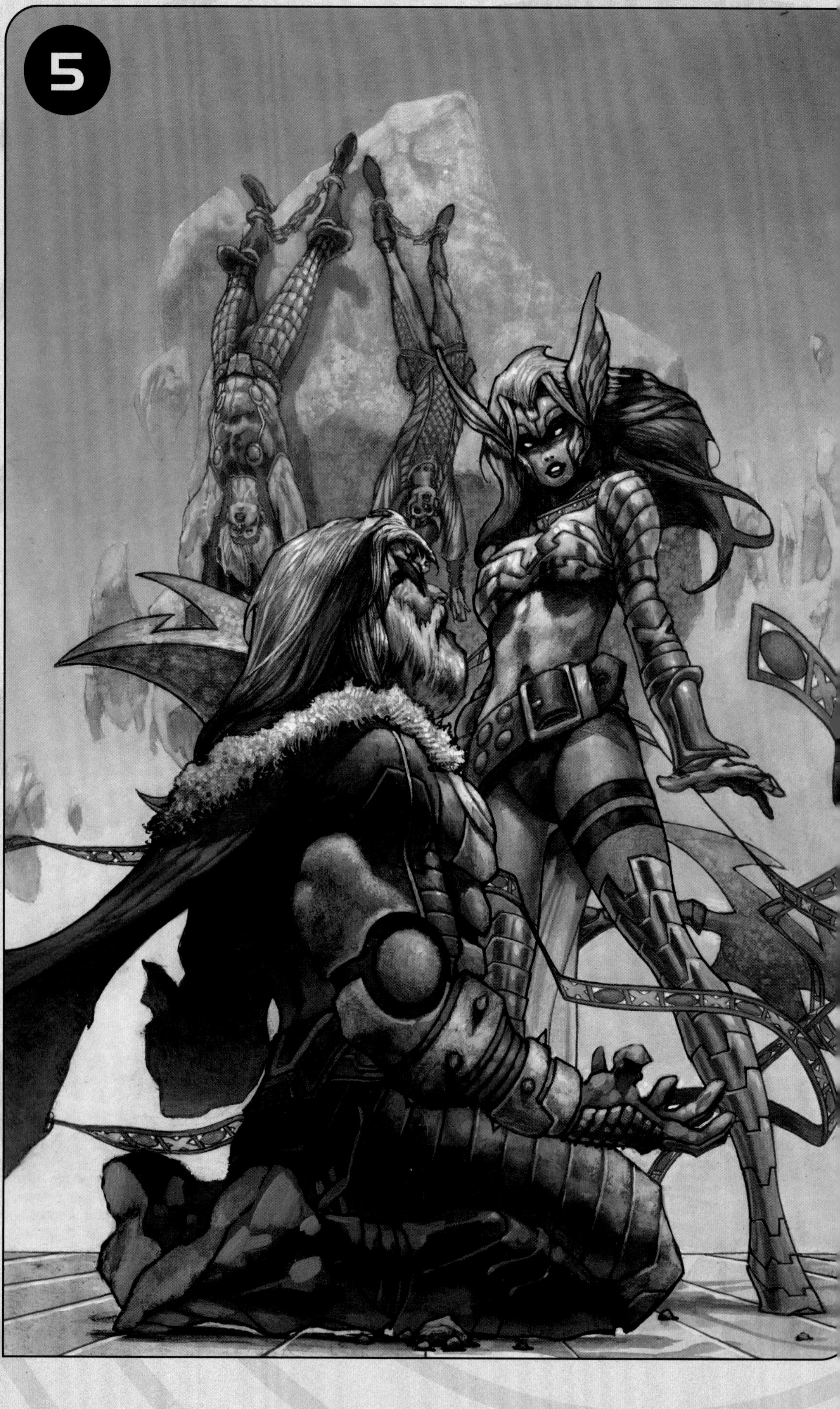
5

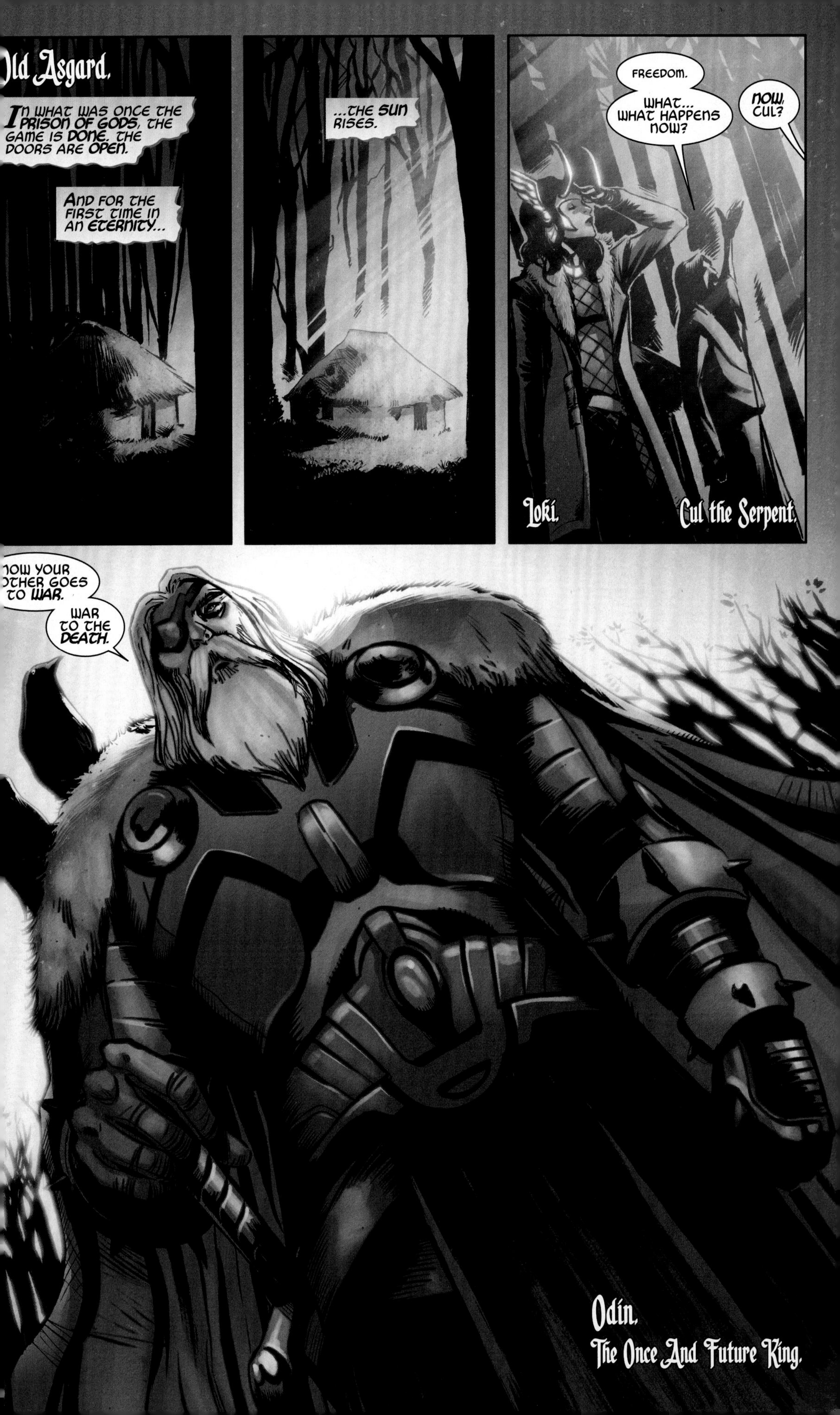
Old Asgard.
In what was once the prison of gods, the game is done. The doors are open.
And for the first time in an eternity...
...the sun rises.
Freedom.
What... what happens now?
Now, Cul?
Loki.
Cul the Serpent.
Now your other goes to war.
War to the death.
Odin.
The Once And Future King.

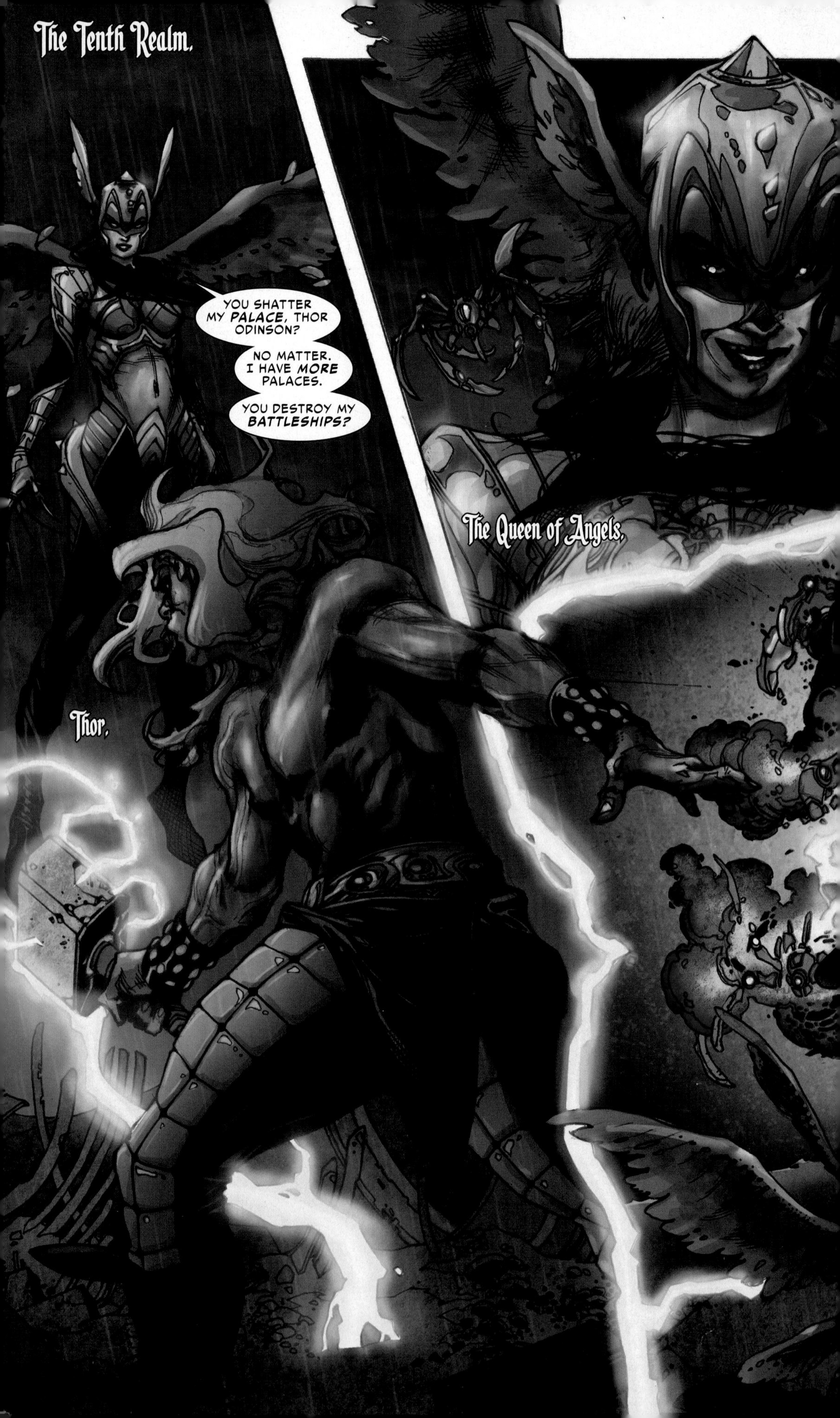
The Tenth Realm.
YOU SHATTER MY PALACE, THOR ODINSON?
NO MATTER. I HAVE MORE PALACES.
YOU DESTROY MY BATTLESHIPS?
The Queen of Angels.
Thor.

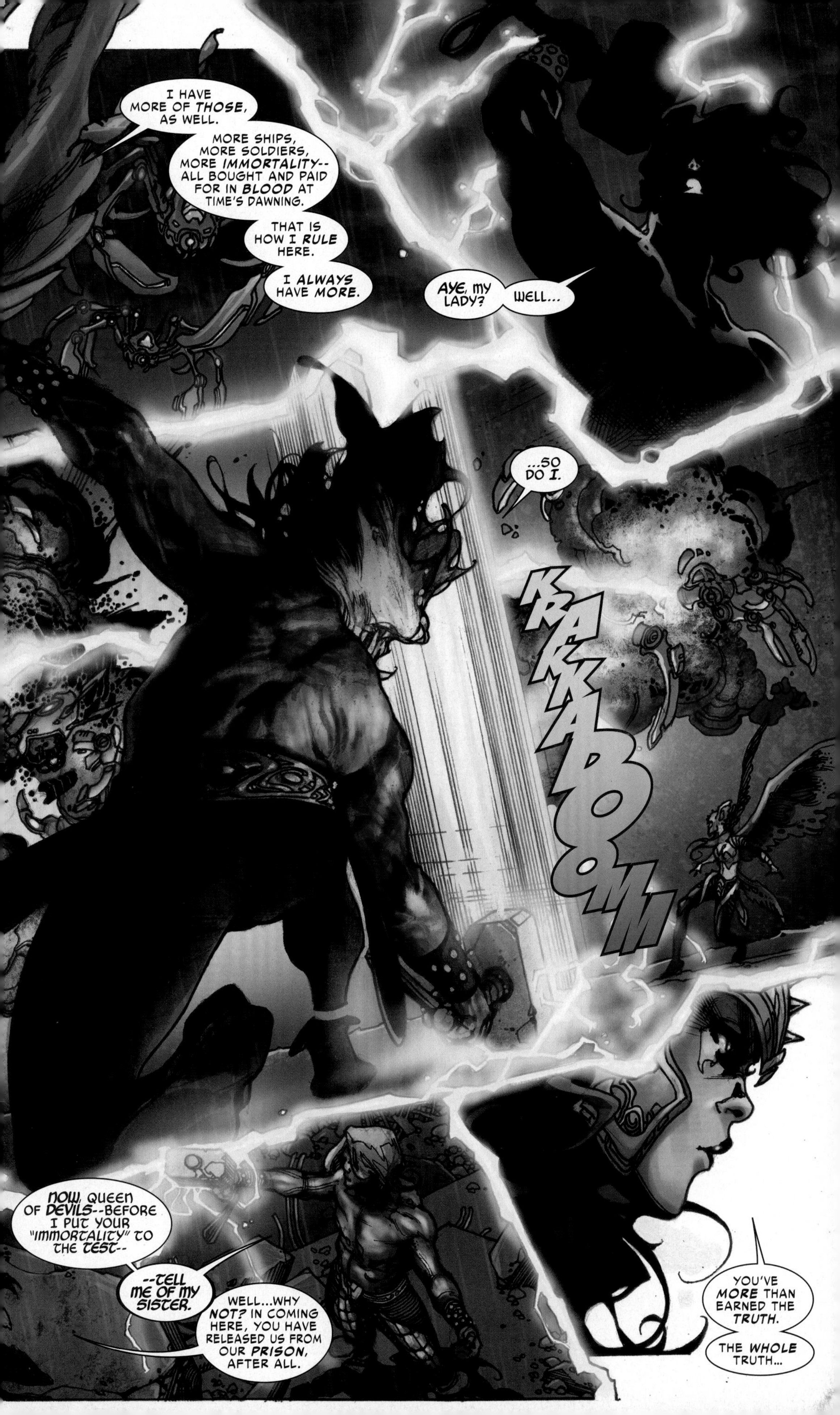

I HAVE MORE OF THOSE, AS WELL.
MORE SHIPS, MORE SOLDIERS, MORE IMMORTALITY-- ALL BOUGHT AND PAID FOR IN BLOOD AT TIME'S DAWNING.
THAT IS HOW I RULE HERE.
I ALWAYS HAVE MORE.
AYE, MY LADY?
WELL...
...SO DO I.
KRAKKABOOMM
NOW, QUEEN OF DEVILS--BEFORE I PUT YOUR "IMMORTALITY" TO THE TEST--
--TELL ME OF MY SISTER.
WELL...WHY NOT? IN COMING HERE, YOU HAVE RELEASED US FROM OUR PRISON, AFTER ALL.
YOU'VE MORE THAN EARNED THE TRUTH.
THE WHOLE TRUTH...

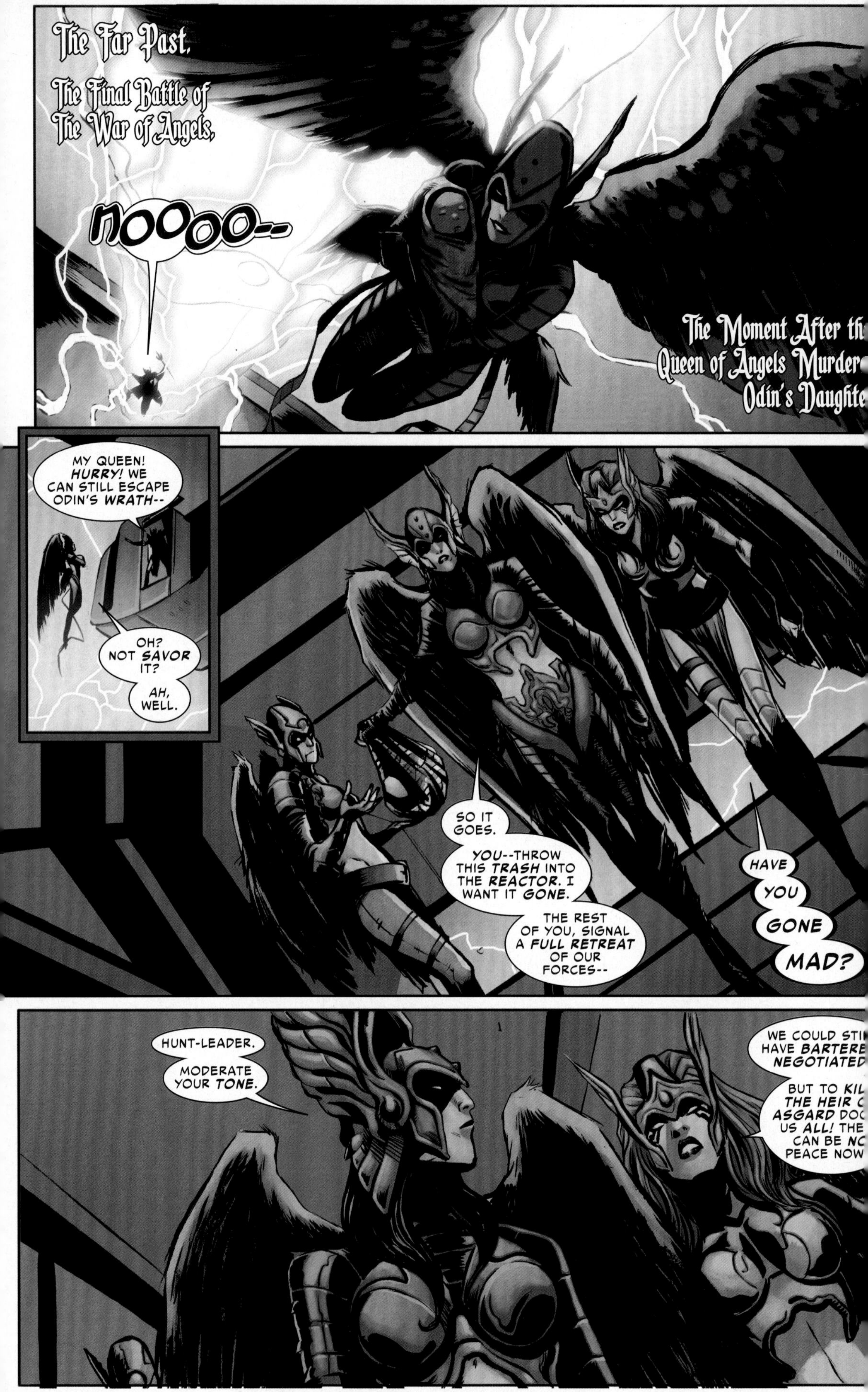
The Far Past.
The Final Battle of The War of Angels.
NOOOO--
The Moment After th
Queen of Angels Murder
Odin's Daughte
MY QUEEN! HURRY! WE CAN STILL ESCAPE ODIN'S WRATH--
OH? NOT SAVOR IT?
AH, WELL.
SO IT GOES.
YOU--THROW THIS TRASH INTO THE REACTOR. I WANT IT GONE.
THE REST OF YOU, SIGNAL A FULL RETREAT OF OUR FORCES--
HAVE YOU GONE MAD?
HUNT-LEADER.
MODERATE YOUR TONE.
WE COULD STI
HAVE BARTERE
NEGOTIATED
BUT TO KIL
THE HEIR
ASGARD DOO
US ALL! THE
CAN BE NO
PEACE NOW

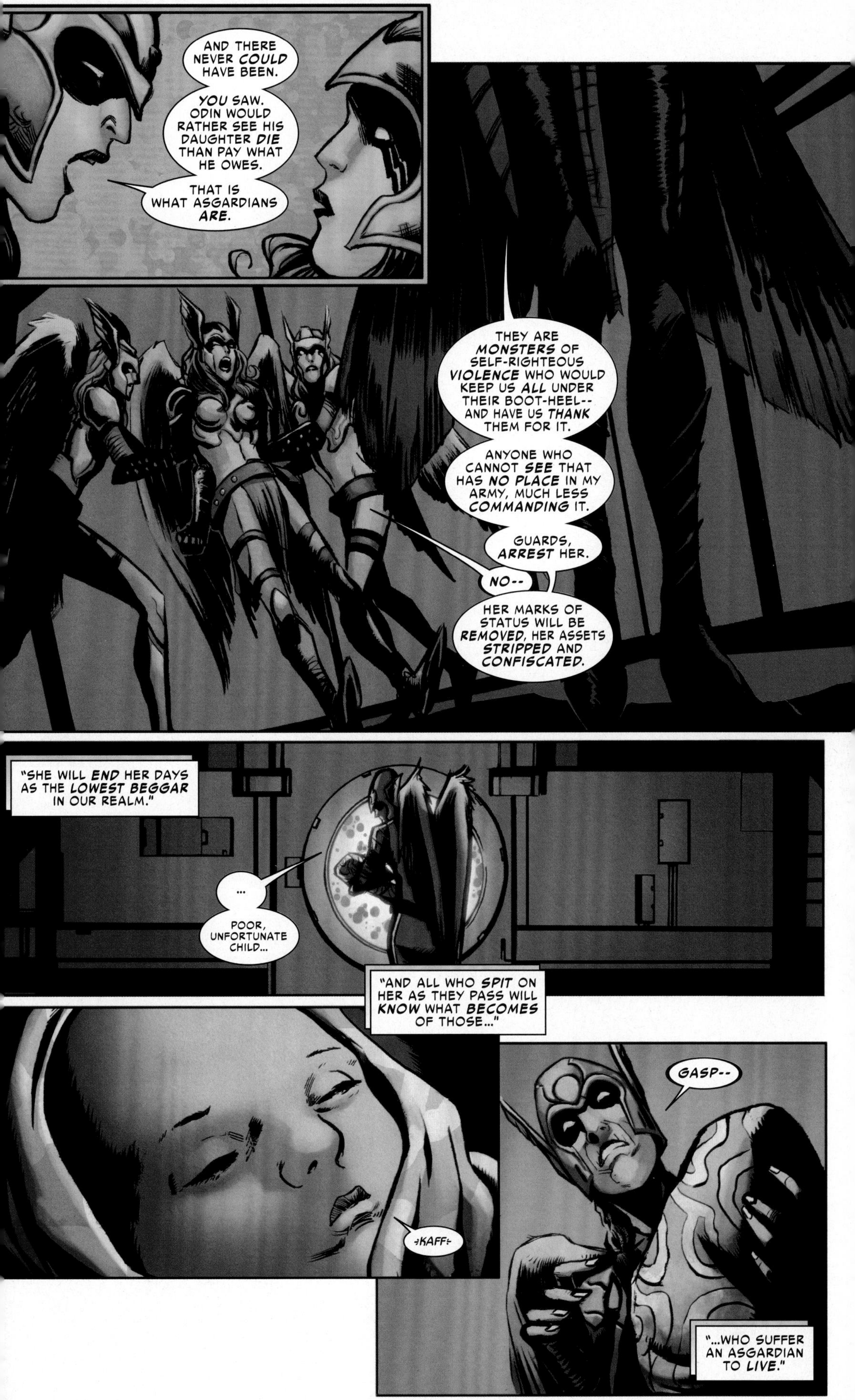
AND THERE NEVER COULD HAVE BEEN.
YOU SAW. ODIN WOULD RATHER SEE HIS DAUGHTER DIE THAN PAY WHAT HE OWES.
THAT IS WHAT ASGARDIANS ARE.
THEY ARE MONSTERS OF SELF-RIGHTEOUS VIOLENCE WHO WOULD KEEP US ALL UNDER THEIR BOOT-HEEL-- AND HAVE US THANK THEM FOR IT.
ANYONE WHO CANNOT SEE THAT HAS NO PLACE IN MY ARMY, MUCH LESS COMMANDING IT.
GUARDS, ARREST HER.
NO--
HER MARKS OF STATUS WILL BE REMOVED, HER ASSETS STRIPPED AND CONFISCATED.
"SHE WILL END HER DAYS AS THE LOWEST BEGGAR IN OUR REALM."
...
POOR, UNFORTUNATE CHILD...
"AND ALL WHO SPIT ON HER AS THEY PASS WILL KNOW WHAT BECOMES OF THOSE..."
=KAFF=
GASP--
"...WHO SUFFER AN ASGARDIAN TO LIVE."

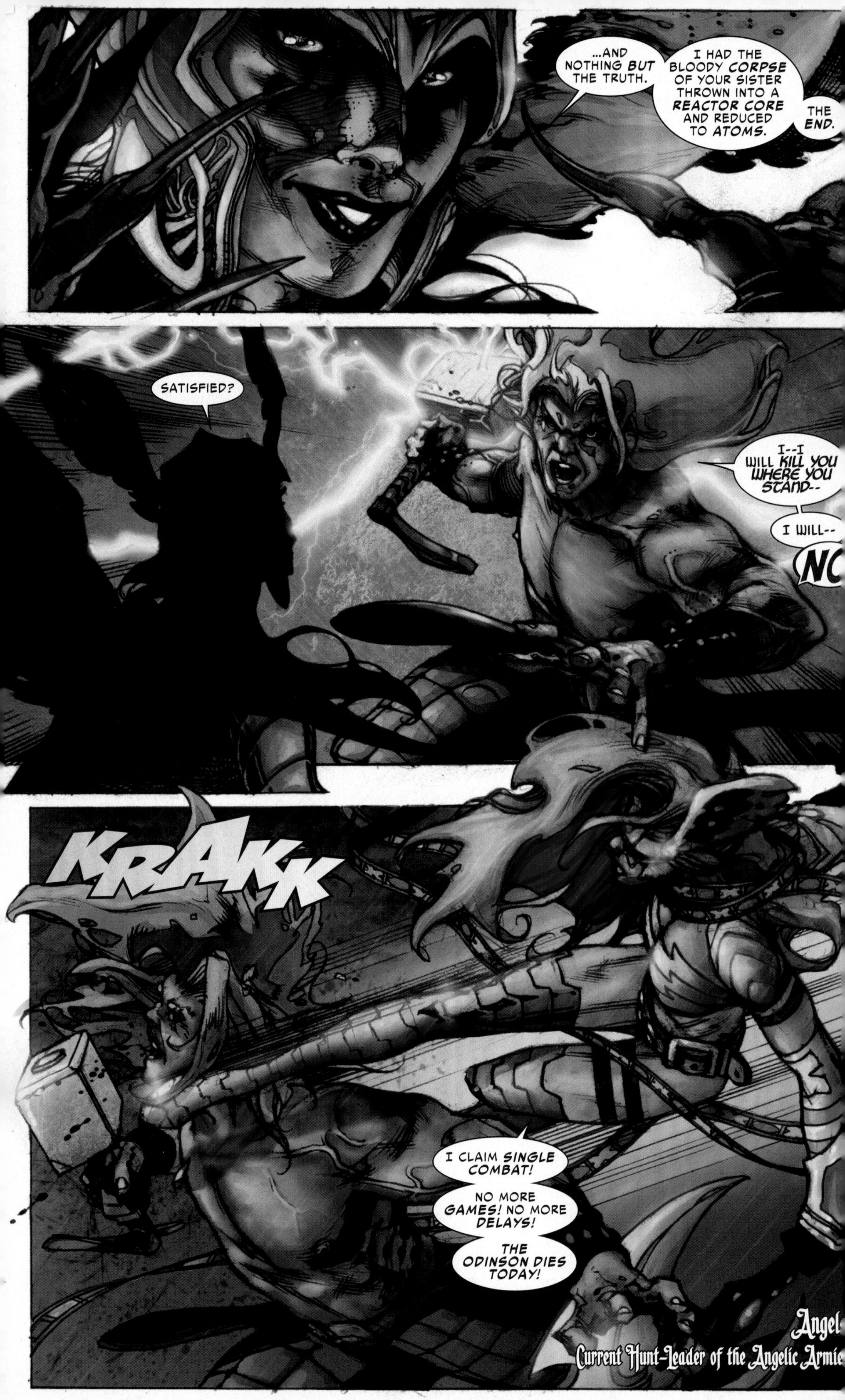

...AND NOTHING BUT THE TRUTH.
I HAD THE BLOODY CORPSE OF YOUR SISTER THROWN INTO A REACTOR CORE AND REDUCED TO ATOMS.
THE END.
SATISFIED?
I--I WILL KILL YOU WHERE YOU STAND--
I WILL--
NO
KRAKK
I CLAIM SINGLE COMBAT!
NO MORE GAMES! NO MORE DELAYS!
THE ODINSON DIES TODAY!
Angel
Current Hunt-Leader of the Angelic Armie

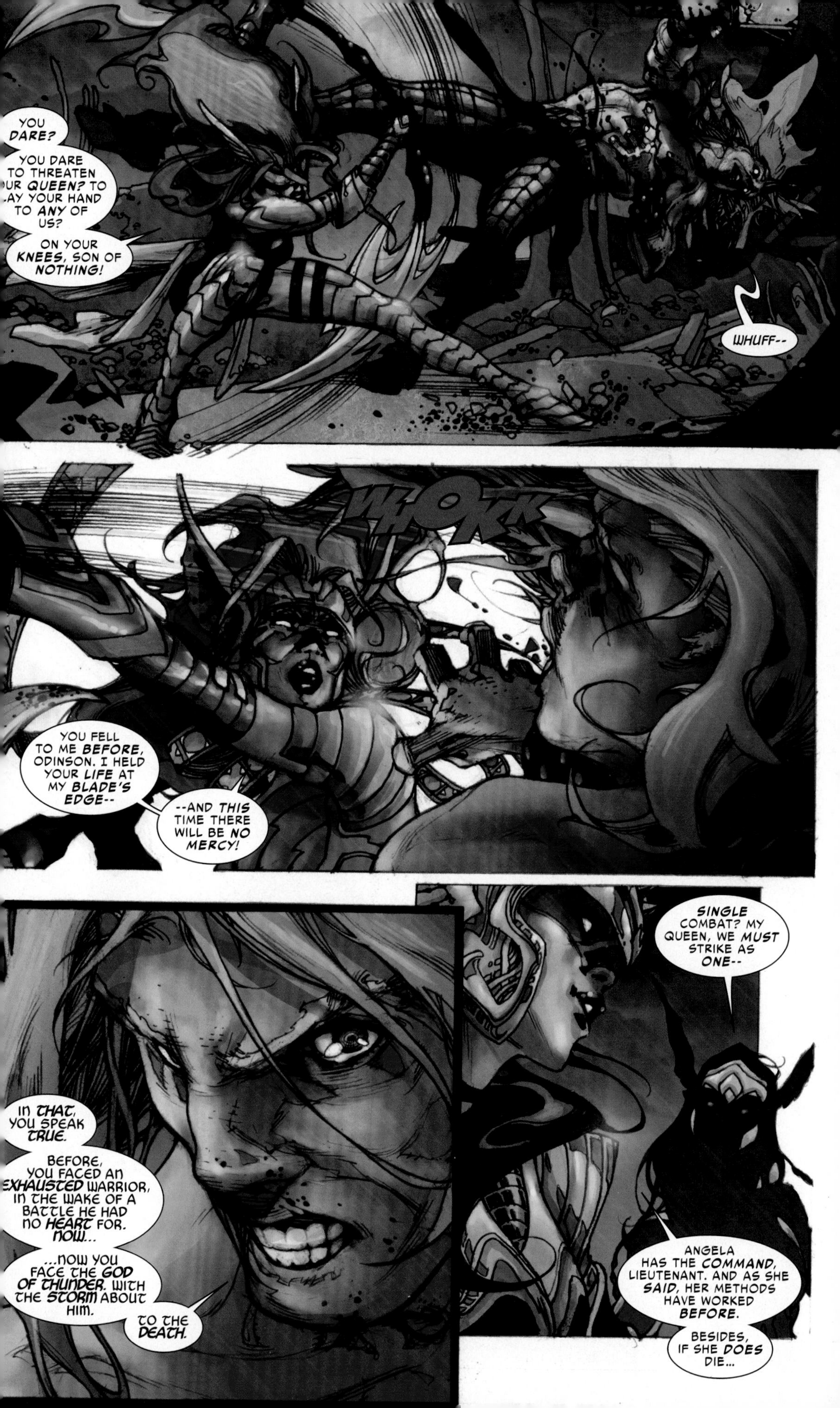
YOU DARE?
YOU DARE TO THREATEN OUR QUEEN? TO LAY YOUR HAND TO ANY OF US?
ON YOUR KNEES, SON OF NOTHING!
WHUFF--
WHOK
YOU FELL TO ME BEFORE, ODINSON. I HELD YOUR LIFE AT MY BLADE'S EDGE--
--AND THIS TIME THERE WILL BE NO MERCY!
IN THAT, YOU SPEAK TRUE.
BEFORE, YOU FACED AN EXHAUSTED WARRIOR, IN THE WAKE OF A BATTLE HE HAD NO HEART FOR. NOW...
...NOW YOU FACE THE GOD OF THUNDER. WITH THE STORM ABOUT HIM.
TO THE DEATH.
SINGLE COMBAT? MY QUEEN, WE MUST STRIKE AS ONE--
ANGELA HAS THE COMMAND, LIEUTENANT. AND AS SHE SAID, HER METHODS HAVE WORKED BEFORE.
BESIDES, IF SHE DOES DIE...

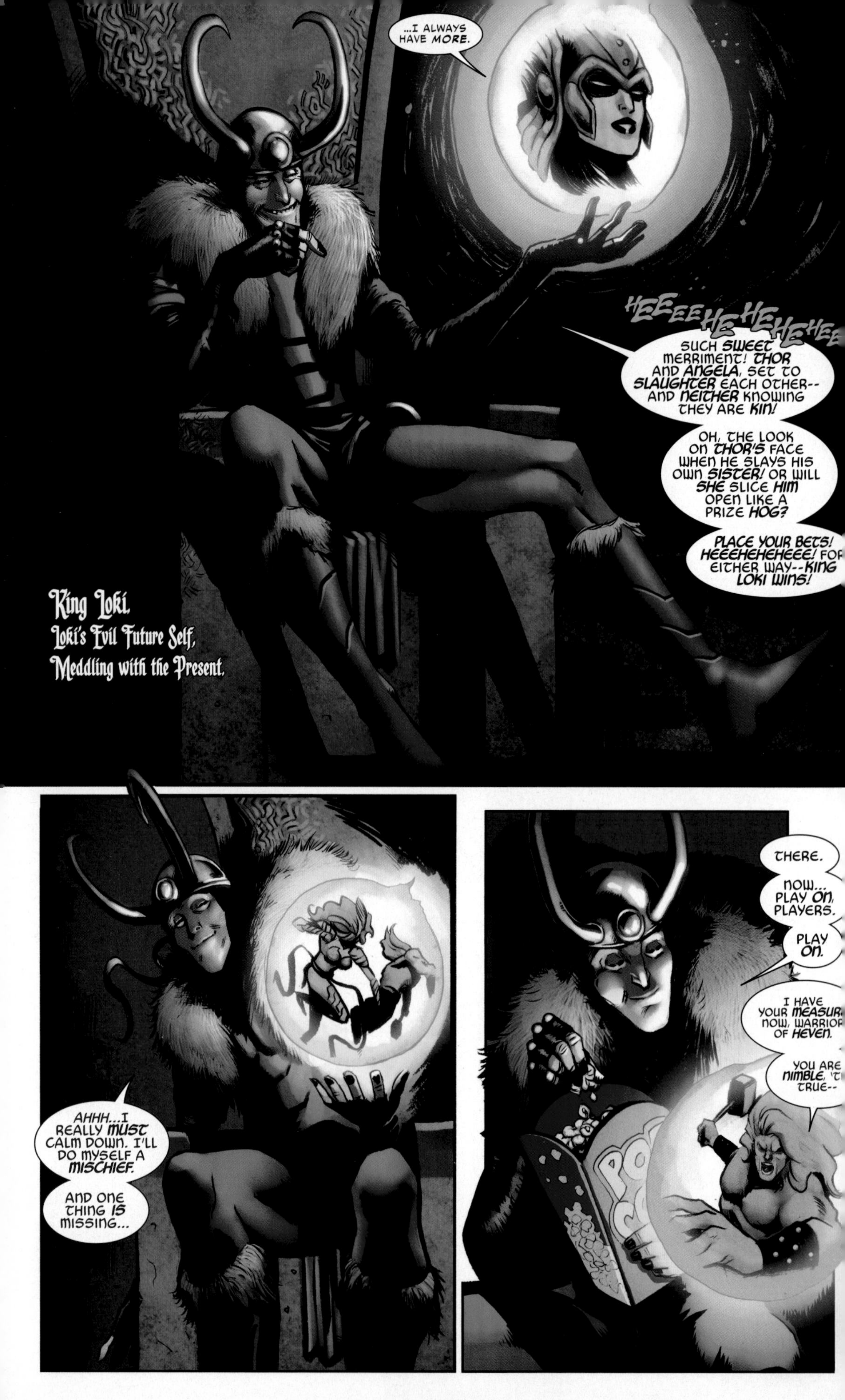
...I ALWAYS HAVE MORE.
HEEEEEHEHEHEHEE
SUCH SWEET MERRIMENT! THOR AND ANGELA, SET TO SLAUGHTER EACH OTHER-- AND NEITHER KNOWING THEY ARE KIN!
OH, THE LOOK ON THOR'S FACE WHEN HE SLAYS HIS OWN SISTER! OR WILL SHE SLICE HIM OPEN LIKE A PRIZE HOG?
PLACE YOUR BETS! HEEEHEHEHEEE! FOR EITHER WAY--KING LOKI WINS!
King Loki,
Loki's Evil Future Self,
Meddling with the Present.
AHHH...I REALLY MUST CALM DOWN. I'LL DO MYSELF A MISCHIEF.
AND ONE THING IS MISSING...
THERE.
NOW... PLAY ON, PLAYERS.
PLAY ON.
I HAVE YOUR MEASURE NOW, WARRIOR OF HEVEN.
YOU ARE NIMBLE, 'TIS TRUE--

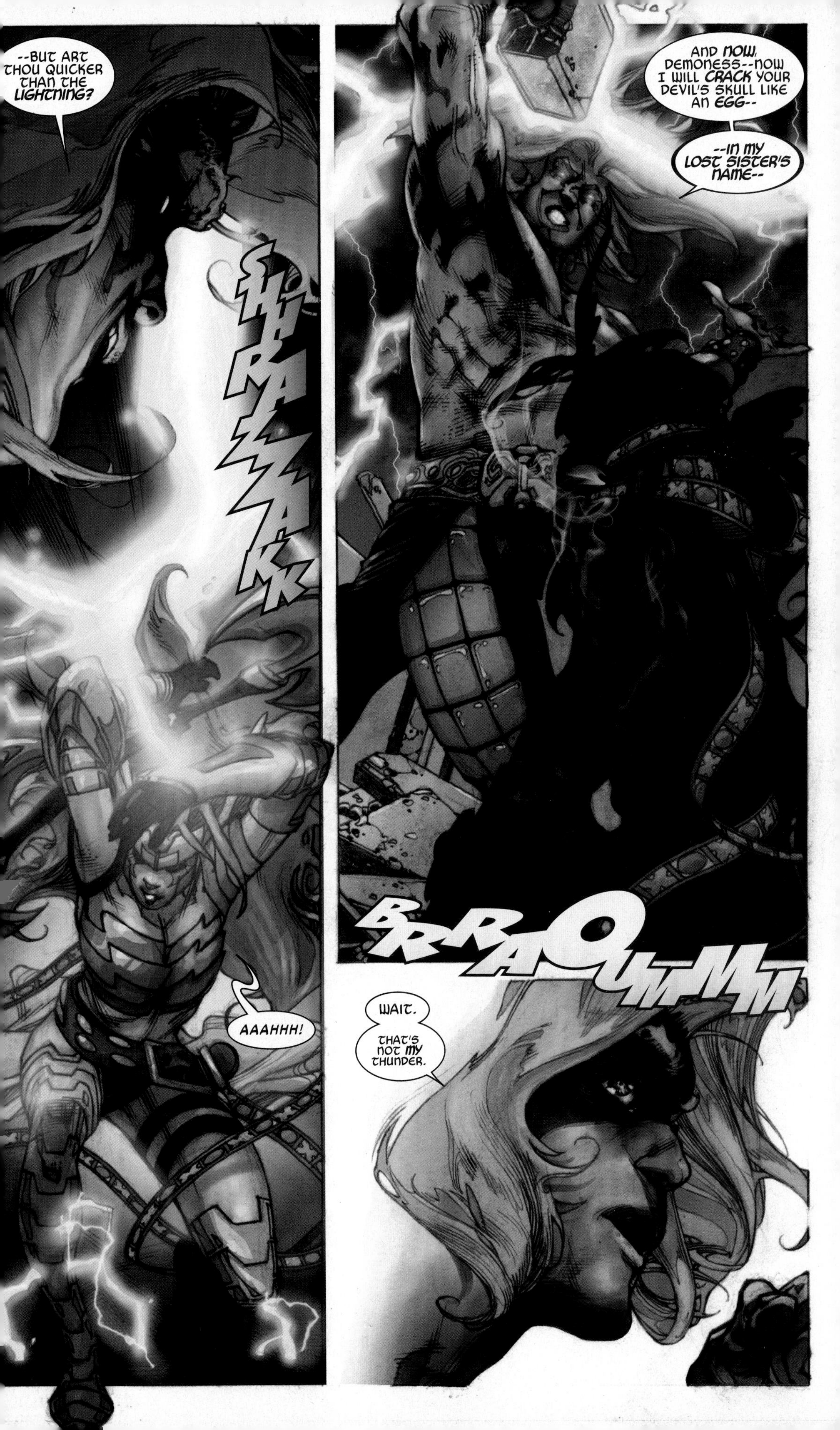

--BUT ART THOU QUICKER THAN THE LIGHTNING?
SHHRAKKZZAKK
AAAHHH!
AND NOW, DEMONESS--NOW I WILL CRACK YOUR DEVIL'S SKULL LIKE AN EGG--
--IN MY LOST SISTER'S NAME--
BRRRAOUMMMM
WAIT.
THAT'S NOT MY THUNDER.

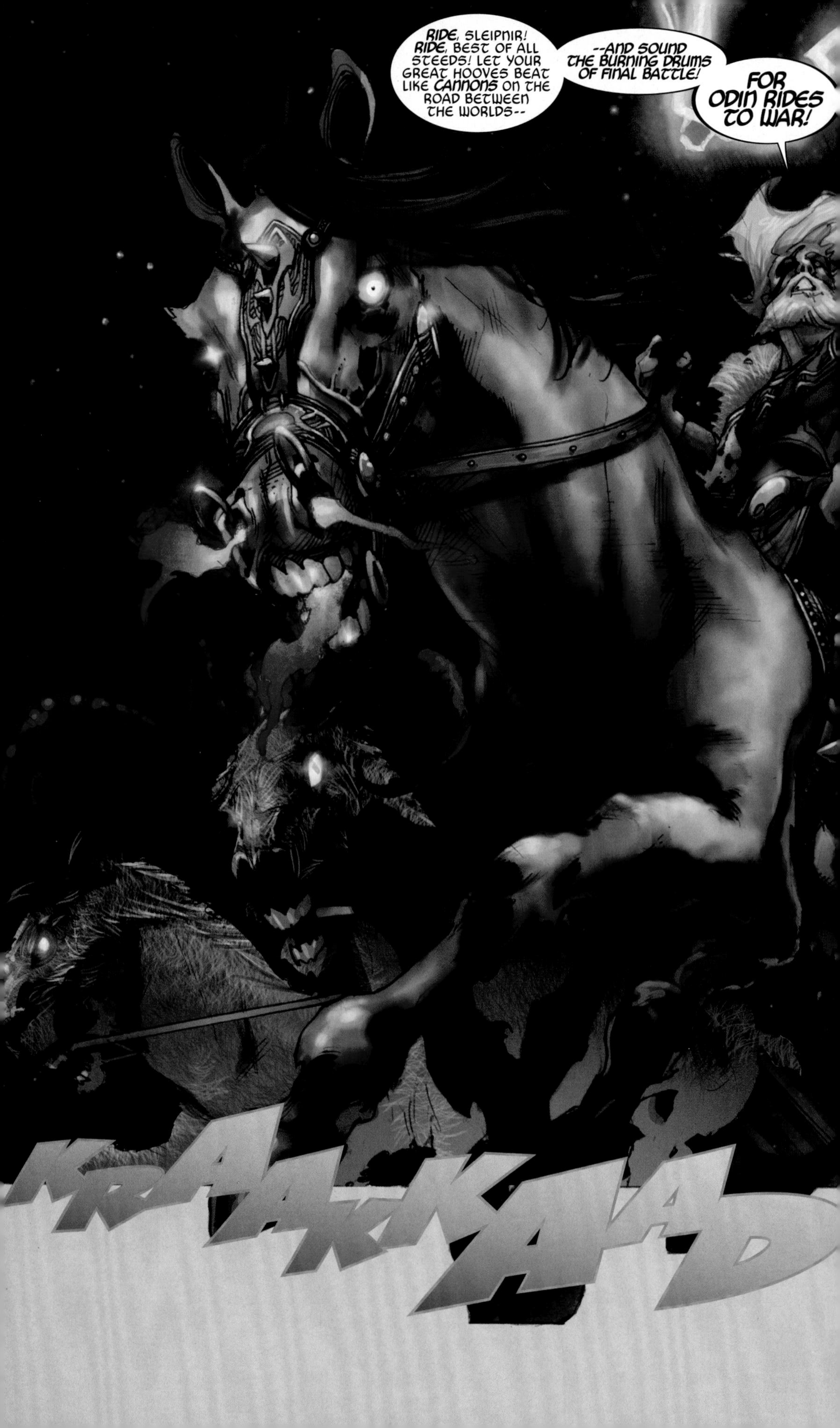
RIDE, SLEIPNIR! RIDE, BEST OF ALL STEEDS! LET YOUR GREAT HOOVES BEAT LIKE CANNONS ON THE ROAD BETWEEN THE WORLDS--
--AND SOUND THE BURNING DRUMS OF FINAL BATTLE!
FOR ODIN RIDES TO WAR!
KRAAKKAAD

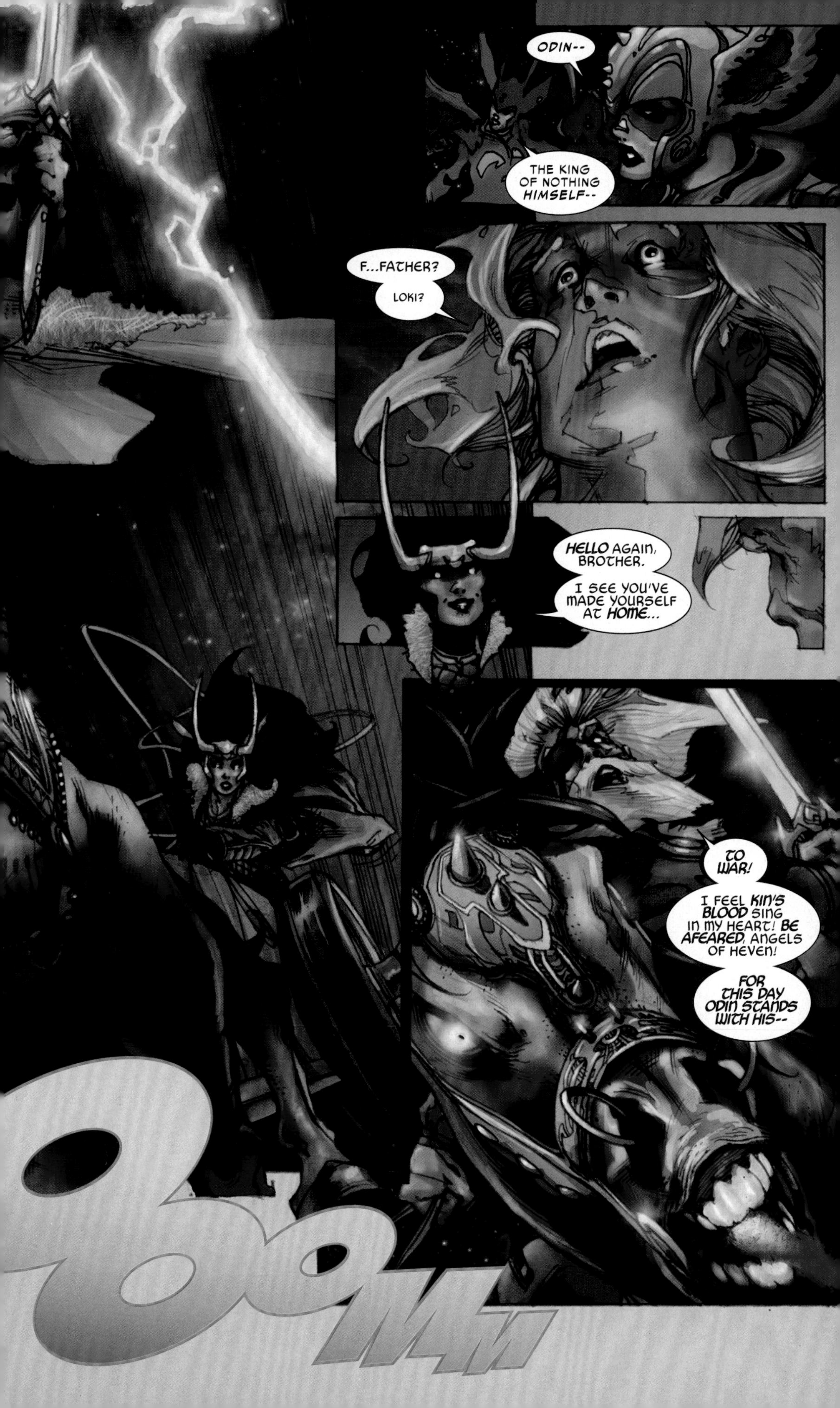
ODIN--
THE KING OF NOTHING HIMSELF--
F...FATHER?
LOKI?
HELLO AGAIN, BROTHER.
I SEE YOU'VE MADE YOURSELF AT HOME...
TO WAR!
I FEEL KIN'S BLOOD SING IN MY HEART! BE AFEARED, ANGELS OF HEVEN!
FOR THIS DAY ODIN STANDS WITH HIS--

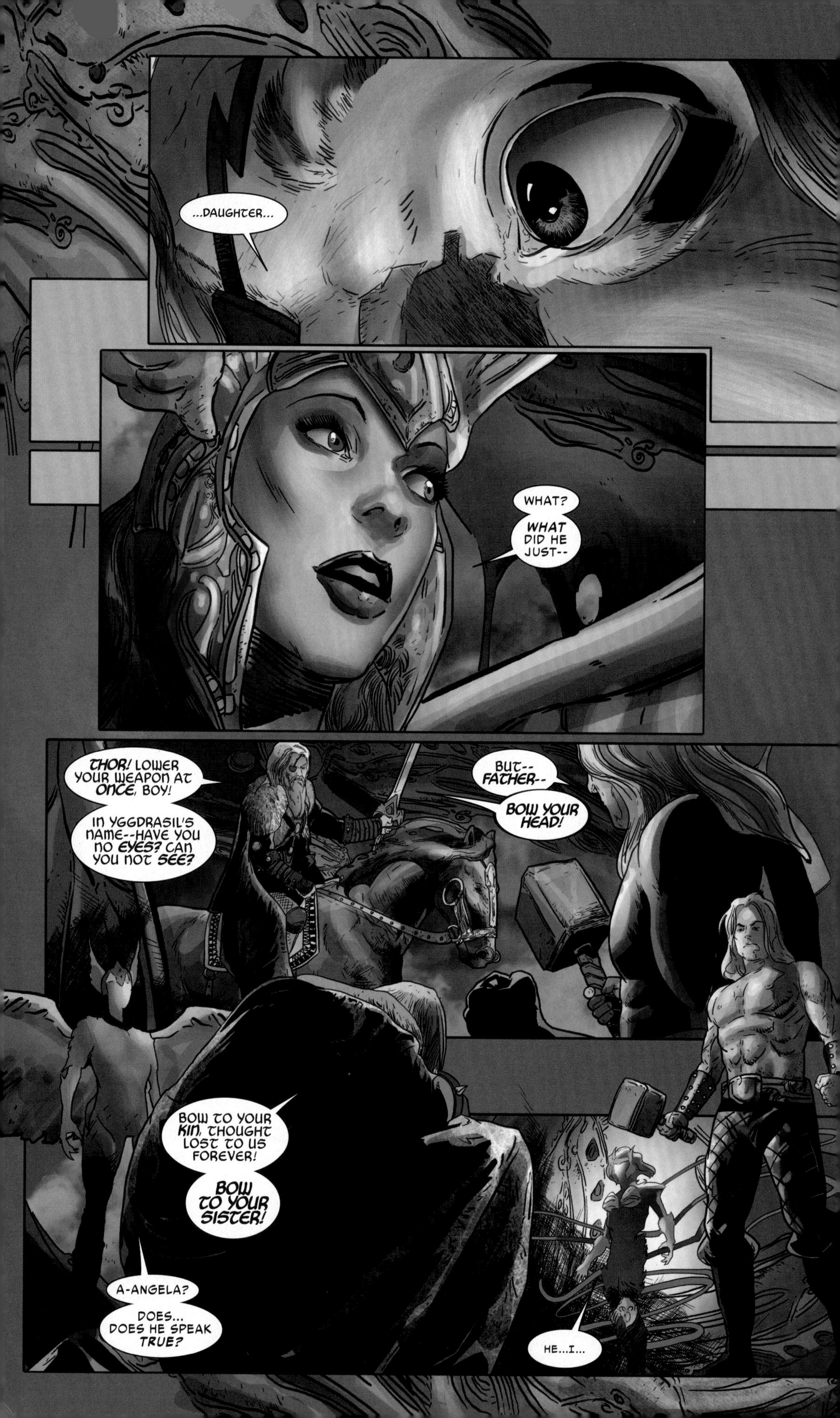
...DAUGHTER...
WHAT? WHAT DID HE JUST--
THOR! LOWER YOUR WEAPON AT ONCE, BOY!
IN YGGDRASIL'S NAME--HAVE YOU NO EYES? CAN YOU NOT SEE?
BUT-- FATHER--
BOW YOUR HEAD!
BOW TO YOUR KIN, THOUGHT LOST TO US FOREVER!
BOW TO YOUR SISTER!
A-ANGELA? DOES... DOES HE SPEAK TRUE?
HE...I...

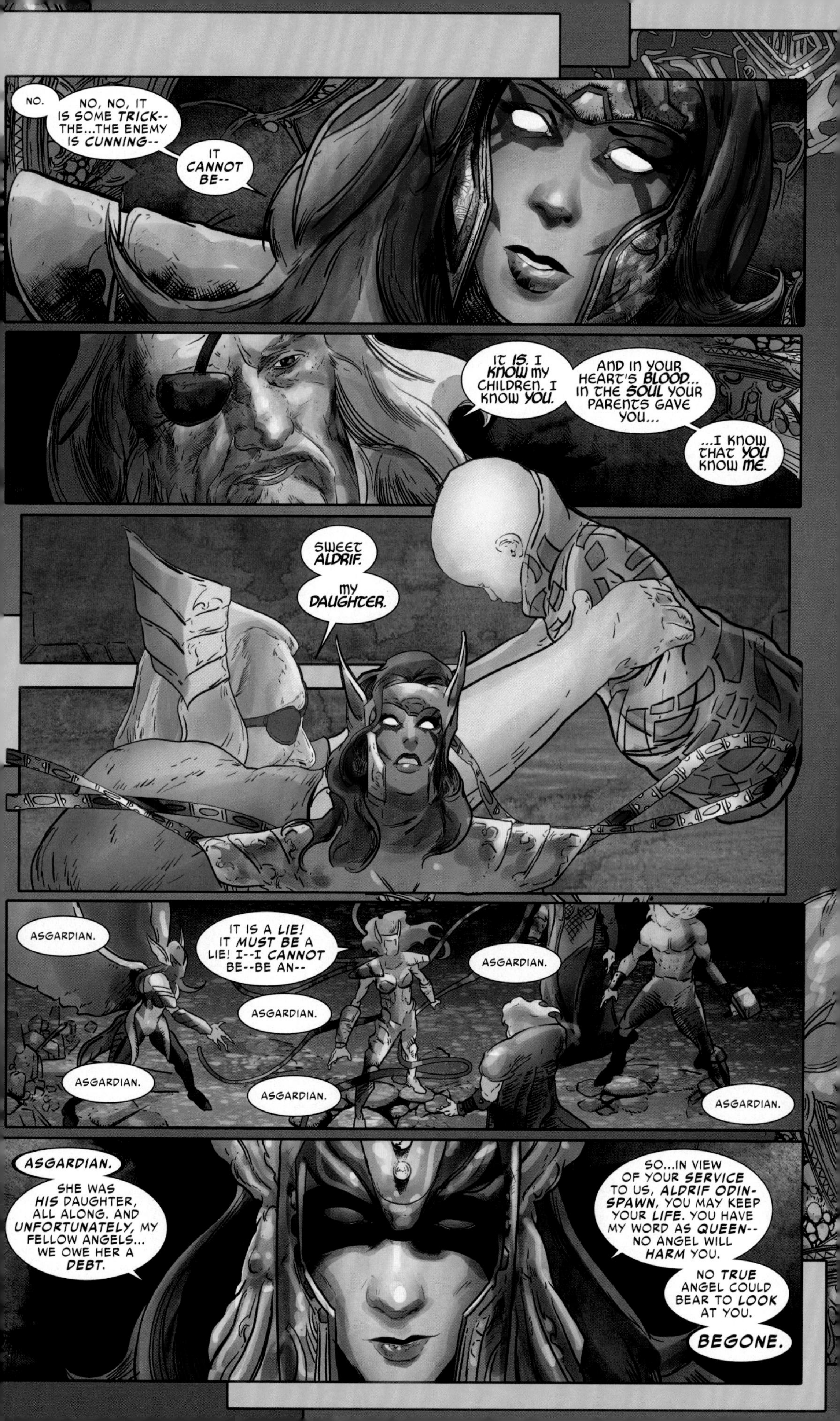

NO.
NO, NO, IT IS SOME TRICK-- THE...THE ENEMY IS CUNNING--
IT CANNOT BE--
IT IS. I KNOW MY CHILDREN. I KNOW YOU.
AND IN YOUR HEART'S BLOOD... IN THE SOUL YOUR PARENTS GAVE YOU...
...I KNOW THAT YOU KNOW ME.
SWEET ALDRIF.
MY DAUGHTER.
ASGARDIAN.
IT IS A LIE! IT MUST BE A LIE! I--I CANNOT BE--BE AN--
ASGARDIAN.
ASGARDIAN.
ASGARDIAN.
ASGARDIAN.
ASGARDIAN.
ASGARDIAN.
SHE WAS HIS DAUGHTER, ALL ALONG. AND UNFORTUNATELY, MY FELLOW ANGELS... WE OWE HER A DEBT.
SO...IN VIEW OF YOUR SERVICE TO US, ALDRIF ODINSPAWN, YOU MAY KEEP YOUR LIFE. YOU HAVE MY WORD AS QUEEN-- NO ANGEL WILL HARM YOU.
NO TRUE ANGEL COULD BEAR TO LOOK AT YOU.
BEGONE.

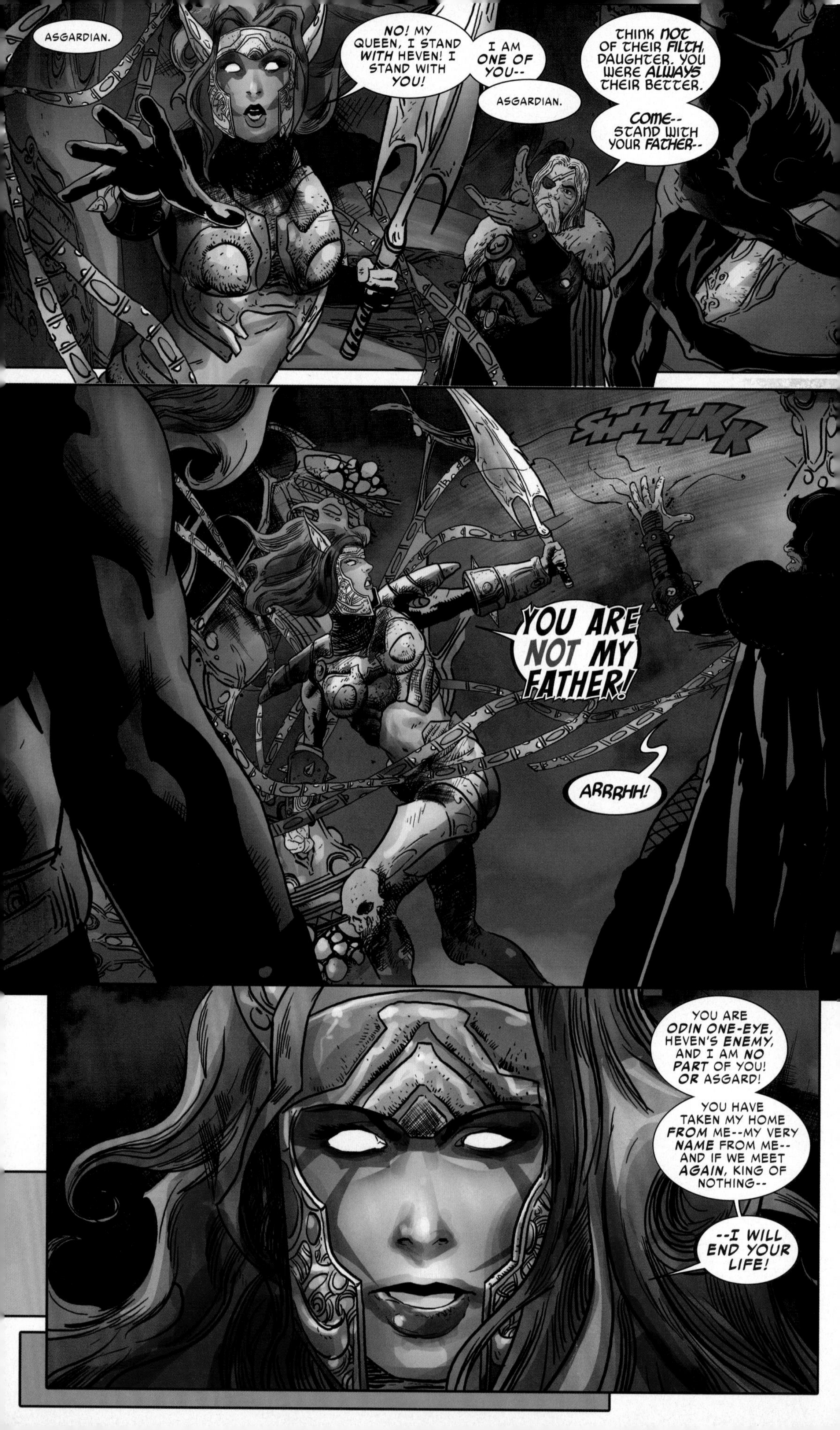
ASGARDIAN.
NO! MY QUEEN, I STAND WITH HEVEN! I STAND WITH YOU!
I AM ONE OF YOU--
ASGARDIAN.
THINK NOT OF THEIR FILTH, DAUGHTER. YOU WERE ALWAYS THEIR BETTER.
COME-- STAND WITH YOUR FATHER--
SHHLIKK
YOU ARE NOT MY FATHER!
ARRRHH!
YOU ARE ODIN ONE-EYE, HEVEN'S ENEMY, AND I AM NO PART OF YOU! OR ASGARD!
YOU HAVE TAKEN MY HOME FROM ME--MY VERY NAME FROM ME--AND IF WE MEET AGAIN, KING OF NOTHING--
--I WILL END YOUR LIFE!

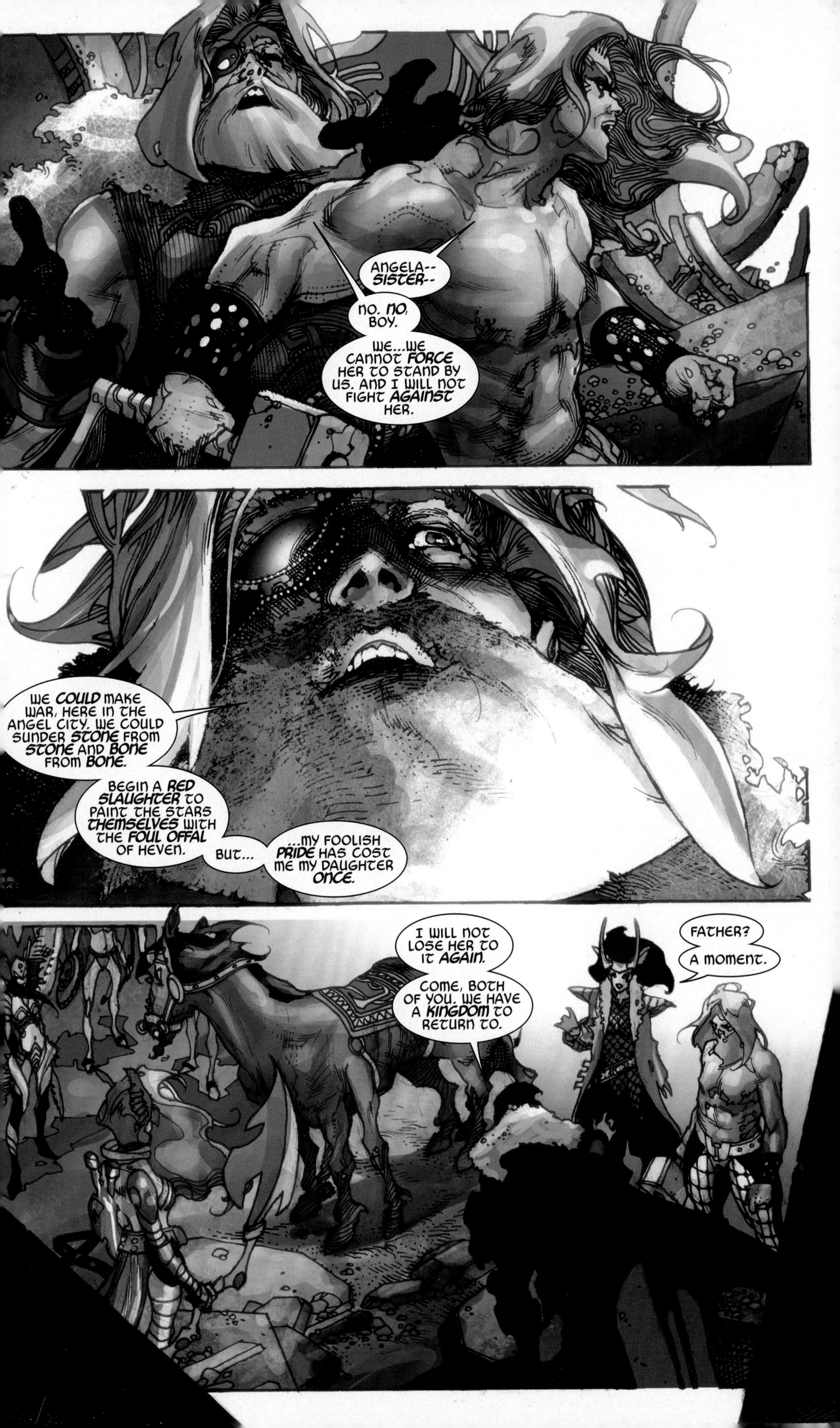
ANGELA--
SISTER--
NO. NO, BOY.
WE...WE CANNOT FORCE HER TO STAND BY US. AND I WILL NOT FIGHT AGAINST HER.
WE COULD MAKE WAR, HERE IN THE ANGEL CITY. WE COULD SUNDER STONE FROM STONE AND BONE FROM BONE.
BEGIN A RED SLAUGHTER TO PAINT THE STARS THEMSELVES WITH THE FOUL OFFAL OF HEVEN.
BUT...
...MY FOOLISH PRIDE HAS COST ME MY DAUGHTER ONCE.
I WILL NOT LOSE HER TO IT AGAIN.
COME, BOTH OF YOU. WE HAVE A KINGDOM TO RETURN TO.
FATHER?
A MOMENT.

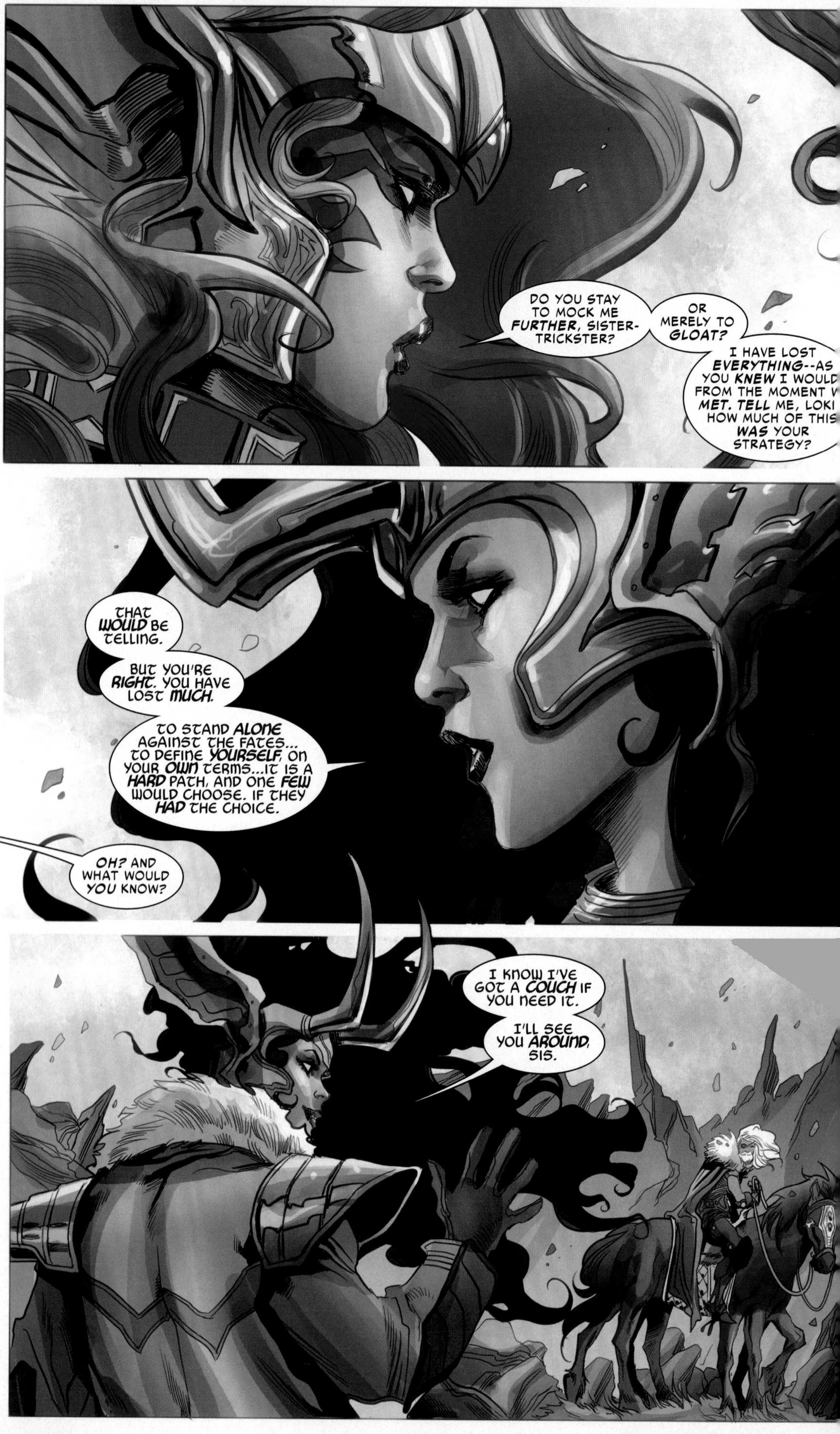
DO YOU STAY TO MOCK ME FURTHER, SISTER-TRICKSTER?
OR MERELY TO GLOAT?
I HAVE LOST EVERYTHING--AS YOU KNEW I WOULD FROM THE MOMENT W MET. TELL ME, LOKI HOW MUCH OF THIS WAS YOUR STRATEGY?
THAT WOULD BE TELLING.
BUT YOU'RE RIGHT. YOU HAVE LOST MUCH.
TO STAND ALONE AGAINST THE FATES... TO DEFINE YOURSELF, ON YOUR OWN TERMS...IT IS A HARD PATH, AND ONE FEW WOULD CHOOSE. IF THEY HAD THE CHOICE.
OH? AND WHAT WOULD YOU KNOW?
I KNOW I'VE GOT A COUCH IF YOU NEED IT.
I'LL SEE YOU AROUND, SIS.

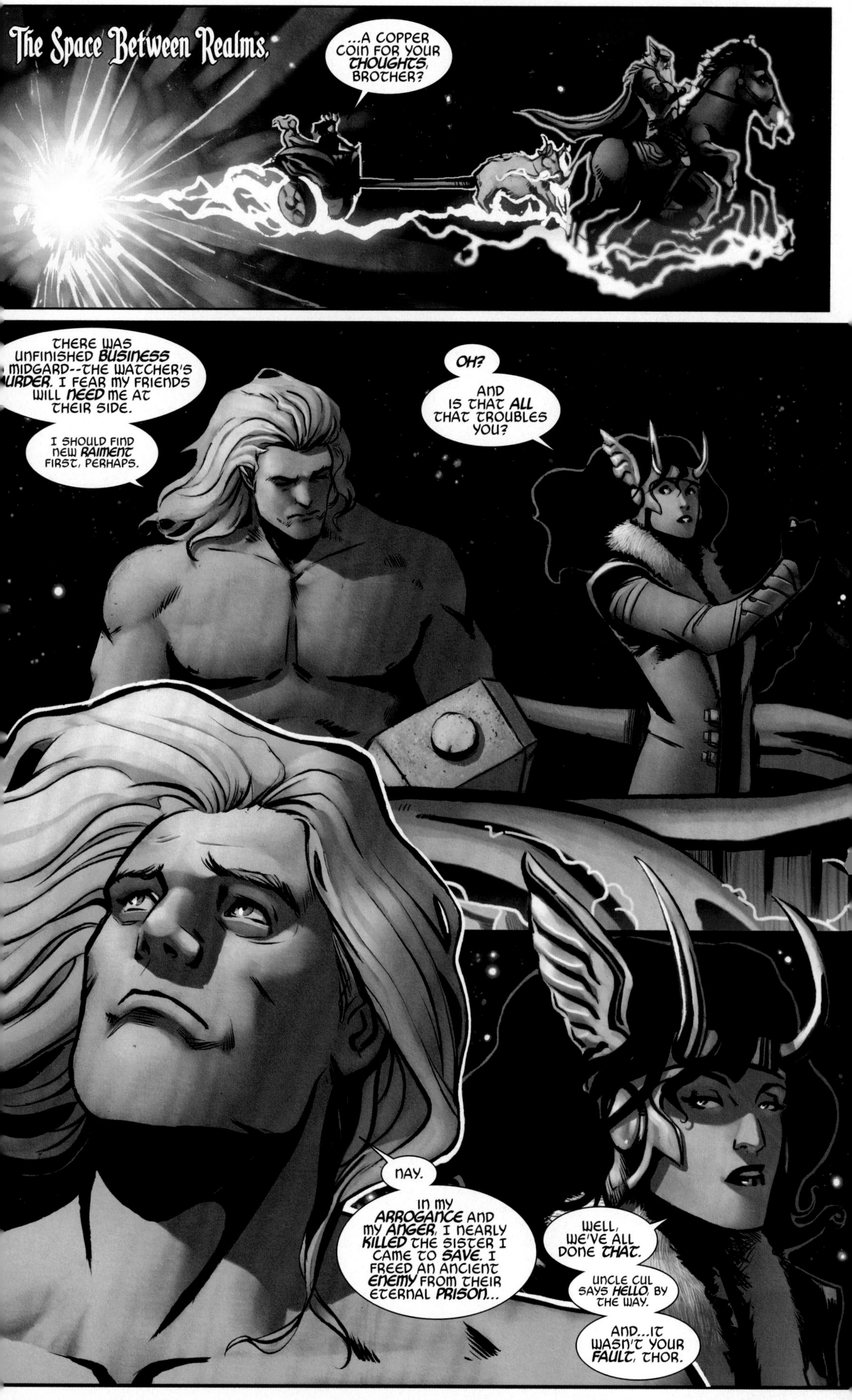
The Space Between Realms.
...A COPPER COIN FOR YOUR THOUGHTS, BROTHER?
THERE WAS UNFINISHED BUSINESS MIDGARD--THE WATCHER'S URDER. I FEAR MY FRIENDS WILL NEED ME AT THEIR SIDE.
I SHOULD FIND NEW RAIMENT FIRST, PERHAPS.
OH?
AND IS THAT ALL THAT TROUBLES YOU?
NAY.
IN MY ARROGANCE AND MY ANGER, I NEARLY KILLED THE SISTER I CAME TO SAVE. I FREED AN ANCIENT ENEMY FROM THEIR ETERNAL PRISON...
WELL, WE'VE ALL DONE THAT.
UNCLE CUL SAYS HELLO, BY THE WAY.
AND...IT WASN'T YOUR FAULT, THOR.

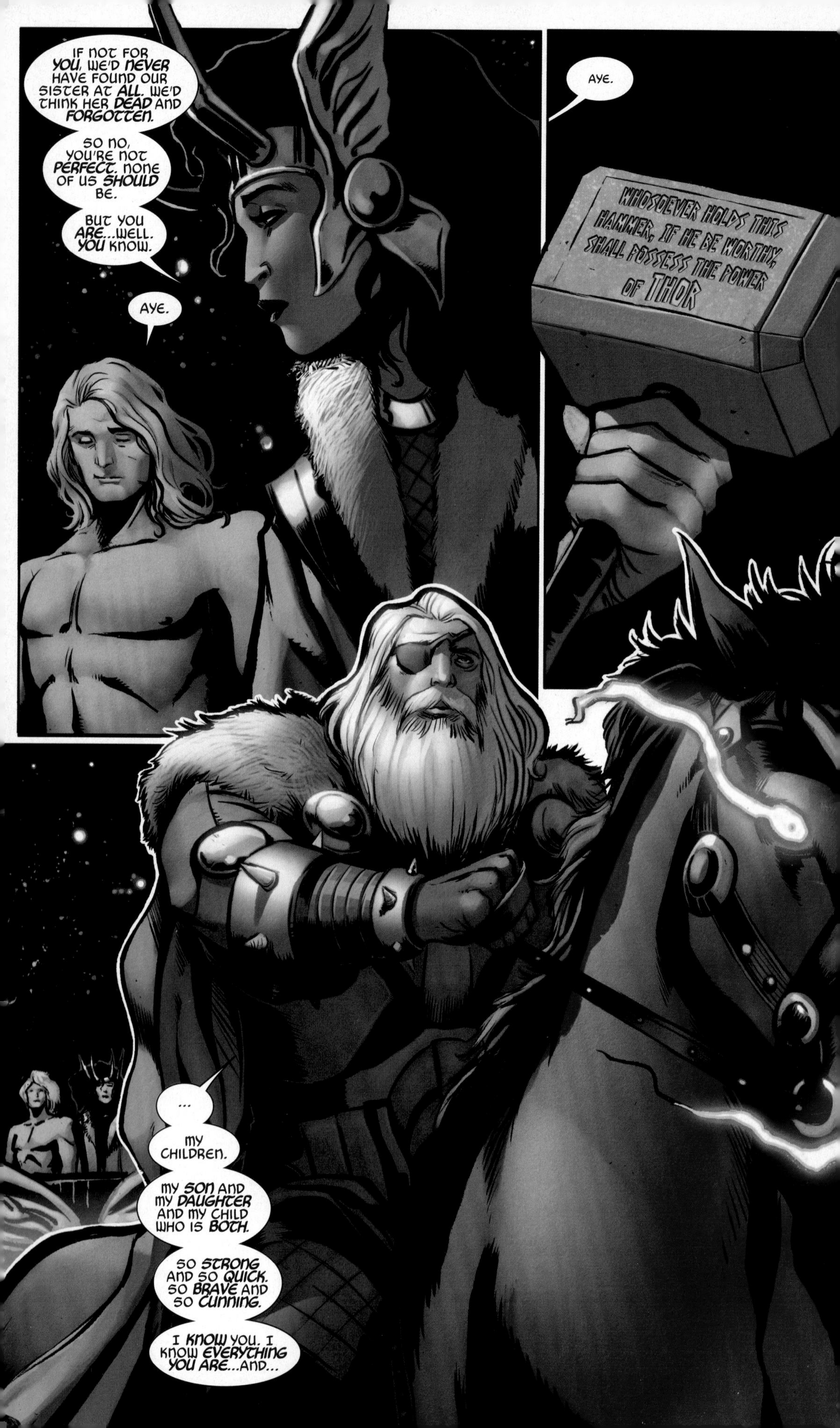
IF NOT FOR YOU, WE'D NEVER HAVE FOUND OUR SISTER AT ALL. WE'D THINK HER DEAD AND FORGOTTEN.
SO NO, YOU'RE NOT PERFECT. NONE OF US SHOULD BE.
BUT YOU ARE...WELL. YOU KNOW.
AYE.
AYE.
WHOSOEVER HOLDS THIS HAMMER, IF HE BE WORTHY, SHALL POSSESS THE POWER OF THOR
...
MY CHILDREN.
MY SON AND MY DAUGHTER AND MY CHILD WHO IS BOTH.
SO STRONG AND SO QUICK. SO BRAVE AND SO CUNNING.
I KNOW YOU. I KNOW EVERYTHING YOU ARE...AND...

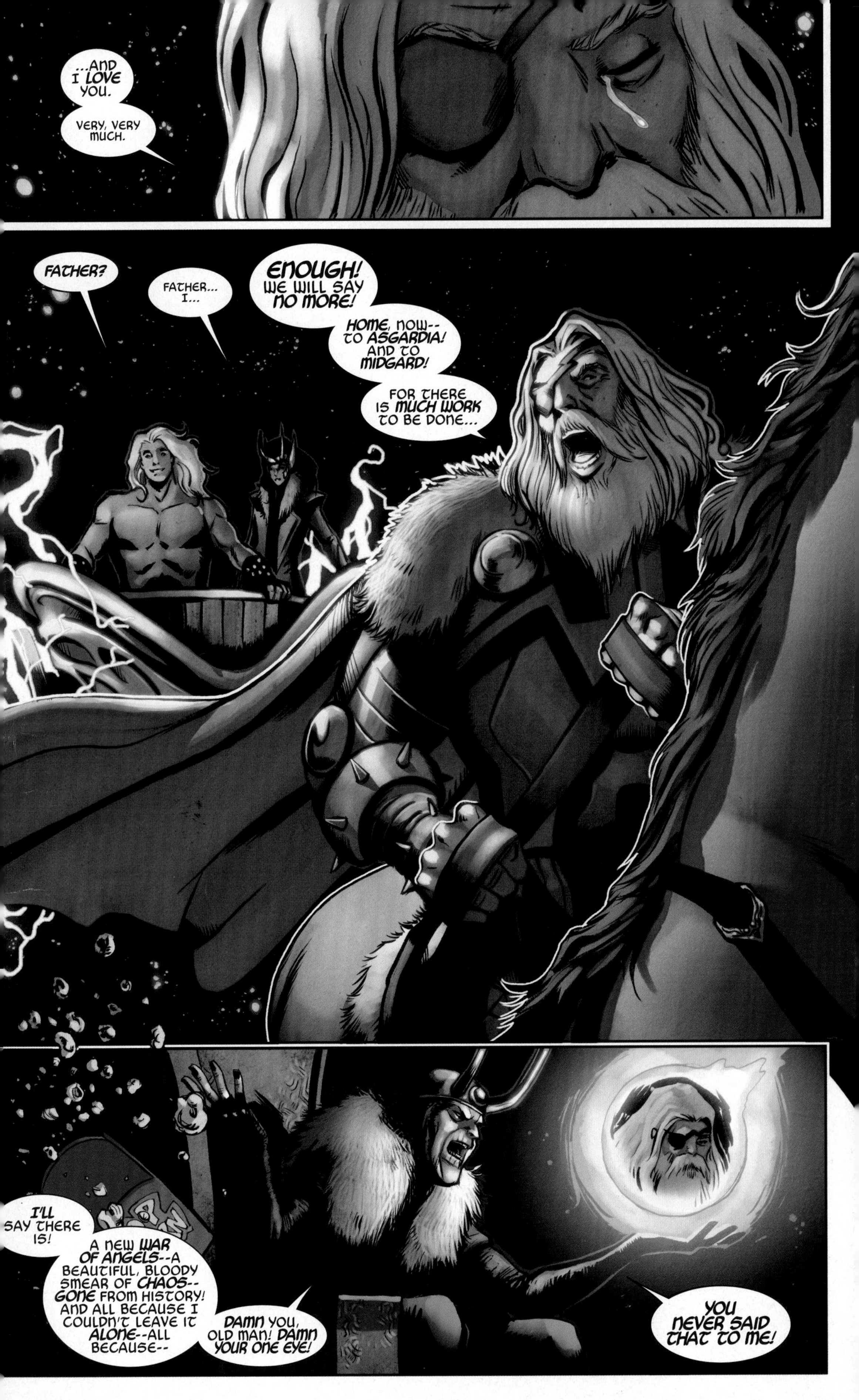
...AND I LOVE YOU.
VERY, VERY MUCH.
FATHER?
FATHER... I...
ENOUGH! WE WILL SAY NO MORE!
HOME, NOW-- TO ASGARDIA! AND TO MIDGARD!
FOR THERE IS MUCH WORK TO BE DONE...
I'LL SAY THERE IS!
A NEW WAR OF ANGELS--A BEAUTIFUL, BLOODY SMEAR OF CHAOS-- GONE FROM HISTORY! AND ALL BECAUSE I COULDN'T LEAVE IT ALONE--ALL BECAUSE--
DAMN YOU, OLD MAN! DAMN YOUR ONE EYE!
YOU NEVER SAID THAT TO ME!

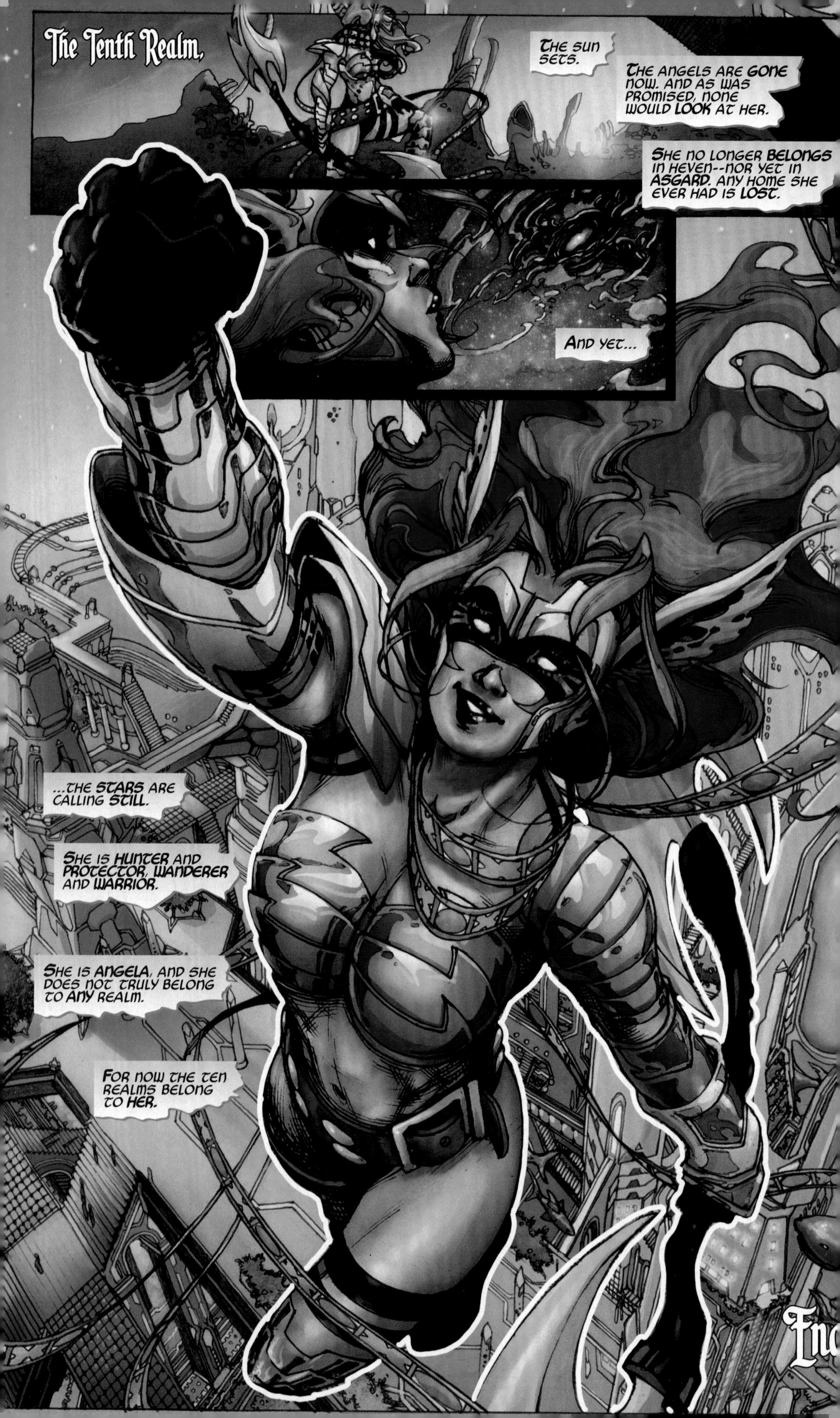
The Tenth Realm,
The sun sets.
The angels are GONE now. And as was promised, none would LOOK at her.
She no longer BELONGS in Heven--nor yet in ASGARD. Any home she ever had is LOST.
And yet...
...the STARS are calling STILL.
She is HUNTER and PROTECTOR, WANDERER and WARRIOR.
She is ANGELA, and she does not truly belong to ANY realm.
For now the ten realms belong to HER.

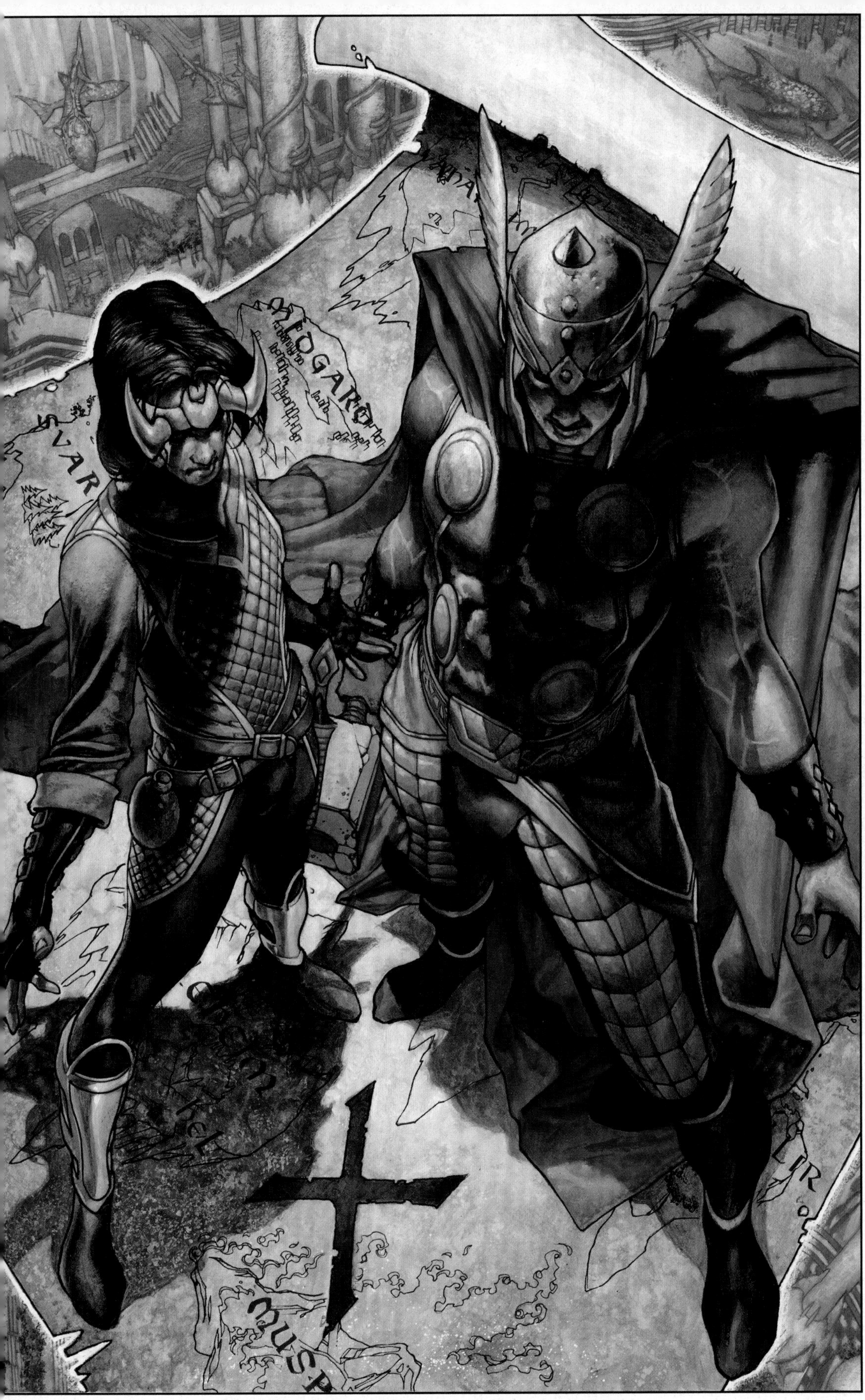

ORIGINAL SIN: THOR & LOKI #1 VARIANT
BY SIMONE BIANCHI

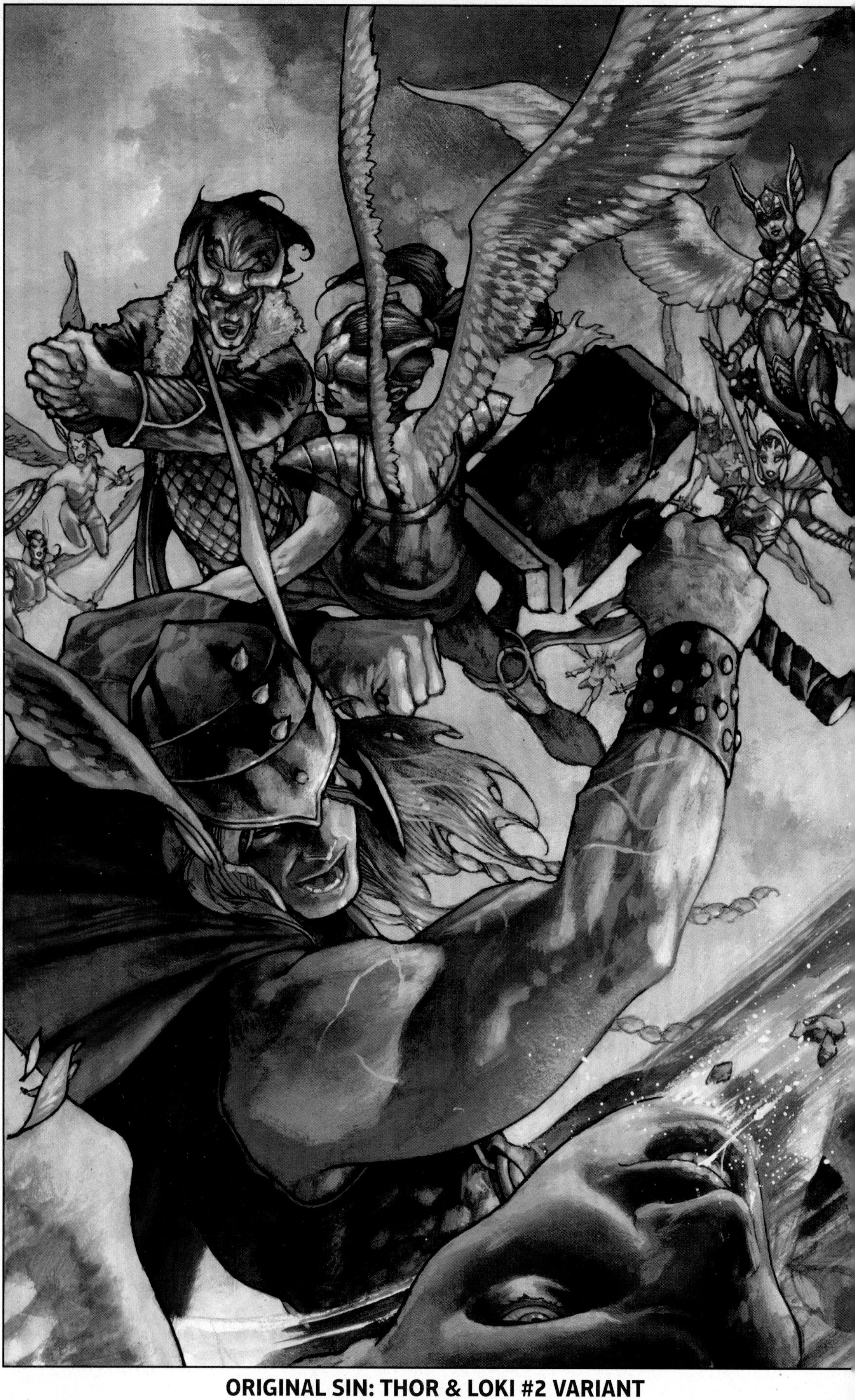

ORIGINAL SIN: THOR & LOKI #2 VARIANT
BY SIMONE BIANCHI